# ARISTOCRATIC EXPERIENCE
# AND THE ORIGINS OF
# MODERN CULTURE

# ARISTOCRATIC EXPERIENCE AND THE ORIGINS OF MODERN CULTURE

## FRANCE, 1570–1715

Jonathan Dewald

University of California Press
*Berkeley · Los Angeles · Oxford*

University of California Press
Berkeley and Los Angeles, California

University of California Press, Ltd.
Oxford, England

© 1993 by
The Regents of the University of California

**Library of Congress Cataloging-in-Publication Data**

Dewald, Jonathan.
    Aristocratic experience and the origins of modern culture:
France, 1570–1715 / Jonathan Dewald.
        p.      cm.
    "A Centennial book."
    Includes bibliographical references and index.
    ISBN 0-520-07837-3
    1. France—Civilization—17th and 18th centuries.
2. Nobility—France—Intellectual life.   3. Aristocracy
(Social class) in literature.   4. Social evolution.   I. Title.
DC121.7.D48      1993
944'.03—dc20                                           92-6572
                                                           CIP

Printed in the United States of America
9  8  7  6  5  4  3  2  1

The paper used in this publication meets the minimum
requirements of American National Standard for Information
Sciences—Permanence of Paper for Printed Library Materials,
ANSI Z39.48-1984. ∞

*For Liana*

# Contents

# Preface

This study began from an essentially bibliographical curiosity. In the late 1970s I became interested in the mass of memoirs that the French nobility produced during the seventeenth century. I had turned to these accounts in the course of other researches, hoping to find in them descriptions of nobles' private experiences and emotions. Like other readers, I at first found the memorialists vexingly reticent about their inner lives. Yet I remained impressed at the flowering of this literature within an aristocratic milieu, and I became increasingly aware of the personal elements that it did contain. These texts seemed an important effort by both men and women (important partly because it involved both men and women) to see their lives as in some sense personal creations, full of surprising turns, inexplicable in terms of mere origins. Selfhood in the seventeenth century had apparently come to require narration and reflection, and there apparently existed an audience as well as authors for such stories; contemporaries avidly read and discussed the memorialists' self-depictions.

I was thus drawn to exploring the history of individuality, to asking why both authors and audiences should have been so interested in viewing selfhood as a construct rather than a given. Exploring this view of the self led to further questions, for it suggested fundamental contradictions within the cultural order of the seventeenth century. After all, an essential principle of aristocratic society is assurance about identity, to which both biological inheritance and carefully contrived upbringing are thought to contribute. Certainly French nobles often spoke in these terms, claiming that no bourgeois could acquire the traits that birth and breeding gave all nobles. Yet their autobiographical practice suggested other ideas, and other practices too suggested contradictory worldviews. Political ideas proved especially unsettled, because of the mix of admiration and dislike that the seventeenth-century state evoked from the nobility, its most privileged subjects. But I was also impressed by the intensity of other contradictions, in attitudes toward money, Christian morality, social change, even writing itself. About all of these topics the nobles expressed ideas that fitted poorly with aristocratic ideological schemas and with the belief that tradition could govern current life.

Here, then, are the twin themes in what follows. Seventeenth-century nobles became preoccupied with the nature of selfhood, this book argues, and they came at the same time to doubt many of the moral underpinnings of their society. They came, in other words, to see the isolated self as real, important, and complicated, and they correspondingly doubted the value, even the reality, of the social conventions that surrounded it. This combination of sensibilities seems to me distinctively modern, at least in the limited sense that we today imply by speaking of ourselves as post-modern; and I intend this book to contribute to our understanding of the circumstances that brought this modernity into being. I do not claim that these were the only groups and circumstances that brought about modern culture thus understood. But I believe that relations between traditional and modern cultures were more complex than historians have usually thought, and that we need to explore these relations if we are to understand modernity itself. For this reason the development of modern values within so tradition-minded a group as the French nobility seems to me to deserve particular attention.

Numerous institutions and individuals have helped me in this project. Fellowships from the University of California, Irvine, and the Guggenheim Foundation allowed for periods of research and writing; the Stanford Humanities Center and the University of Rochester provided stimulating temporary academic homes. For many years I benefited from the intellectual excitement and generosity of the department of history of the University of California, Irvine, and it is a pleasure to acknowledge its influence on this book. Lloyd Moote, Orest Ranum, Charles Stinger, and Timothy Tackett read the entire manuscript and offered suggestions and support. Liana Vardi also read the manuscript, and the project probably could not have been completed without her encouragement, sustained over several years. Groups of scholars at Irvine; the University of California, Berkeley; the University of California, San Diego; Emory University; Syracuse University; Tulane University; Boston University; SUNY at Buffalo; and Brown University considered individual chapters. I have profited both from their specific advice and from the encouragement they offered.

# Introduction

This book explores ways in which men and women of the French nobility thought about their world and themselves during the later sixteenth and seventeenth centuries. It asks how nobles responded to a series of recurrent problems in their lives: problems of personal worth, ambition, and the unfolding of an individual's career; problems of money, friendship, sexuality, and civic order; problems of time and communication. Each of these is a distinct topic, which I initially selected because of its frequency in aristocratic correspondence and literature of the period. But these topics can also be understood as aspects of a single larger problem. Each represents one form of connection between the individual and her or his society. What follows, then, is an extended essay on how aristocratic men and women understood their bonds to the society around them at a decisive moment in the evolution of early modern society.

To ask such questions about the nobility, of course, is to consider only a small group within French society, perhaps 1 percent of its total population. Because much of what follows rests on literary sources, the group considered here is in fact still more restricted. It includes mainly the wealthiest and most articulate nobles, those most closely attached to Paris and the royal court, those most intent on giving written form to their experiences and concerns.

This limited group nonetheless deserves close study, partly because, like any ruling class, the high French aristocracy exercised an influence on the rest of society out of proportion to its numbers, and partly because the group's culture seems to me still poorly understood, despite a recent revival of historians' interest in the nobility. More important than these considerations, however, the nobility embody in acute form a problem that many participants in early modern culture shared. The French nobles illustrate the emergence of an essentially modern culture, one still familiar to us, within a deeply traditional social order. For sixteenth- and seventeenth-century nobles, that traditional order rested on ideas about inheritance and familial continuity. Property and political rights descended from the past, and so too did personal qualities, a dual inheritance from the individual family and the larger aristocratic order. Most nobles simply assumed these values, and their use in ideological debate persisted into the eighteenth century. Such persistence is not surprising, for these ideas implied a powerful coherence between the realm of nature and that of the social order. Nobles could view their behavior and their political powers as reflections of the world's natural order; they could view individual qualities and choices as reflections of the family's qualities and needs. To see links between the biological and the social inspired intellectual and moral assurance.[1]

Yet the French nobles (as we shall see in more detail below) also participated enthusiastically in many of the most innovative currents in early modern culture. They followed and helped to shape cultural movements toward individualism, skepticism about established social arrangements, and belief in the primacy of change in human affairs. They adopted modes of thought and languages that had first developed in the city-states of Renaissance Italy, and in many ways these contradicted long-standing assumptions about how nature and the moral order intersected. This tension emerges even in the nobles' most public forms of self-expression, those ideological defenses of the aristocracy that have mainly interested historians. Tension was still more evident when the nobles spoke privately, in memoirs, letters, fiction. In these explorations of daily experience the nobles expressed assumptions and fears that had little to do with the confident ideology of dynastic continuity; rather, they used language that emphasized particularity and the problematic relationship of individual to polity. Describing this language and understanding how it could coexist with an

1. See Roberto Mungabeira Unger, *Law in Modern Society: Toward a Criticism of Social Theory* (New York, 1976), esp. 38. For an emphatic description of the role of *race* in sixteenth-century thought, see Arlette Jouanna, *Ordre social: Mythes et hiérarchies dans la France du XVIe siècle* (Paris, 1977). Throughout this study I use the term "society of orders" to describe this idealized vision of a society organized according to birth and sharply delineated social roles; for a discussion of the term, its sources, and its limitations, see Armand Arriaza, "Mousnier and Barber: The Theoretical Underpinning of the 'Society of Orders' in Early Modern Europe," *Past and Present* 89 (November 1980): 39–57. As will become clear below, this concept seems to me misleading as a description of much early modern behavior and feeling; it is helpful, however, in describing an important group of early modern ideals.

aristocratic ideology are the central tasks of this essay. This is an effort to understand how an individualistic, skeptical, and in many ways anxious culture emerged within a "society of orders."[2]

Alexis de Tocqueville analyzed the cultural implications of an aristocratic social order as follows: "Take the case of an aristocratic people interested in literature," he wrote, as he thought about the democratic culture he had encountered in the United States: "When a small, unchanging group of men are concerned at the same time with the same subject, they easily get together and agree on certain guiding principles to direct their efforts. If it is literature with which they are concerned, strict canons will soon prescribe rules that may not be broken. If these men occupy a hereditary position in their country they will naturally be inclined not only to invent rules for themselves but to follow those laid down by their ancestors. Their code will be both strict and traditional. . . . Such men, beginning and ending their lives in comfortable circumstances, naturally conceive a taste for choice pleasures, full of refinement and delicacy. Moreover, the long and peaceful enjoyment of so much wealth will have induced a certain softness of thought and feeling, and even in their enjoyments they will avoid anything too unexpected or too lively. They would rather be amused than deeply moved; they want to be interested but not carried away."[3]

Tocqueville saw classicism and class fitting neatly together. Because of the assured social position that members of the nobility enjoyed, few basic issues found a place in their writings; because the very principle of aristocracy was adherence to tradition, their writings followed inherited models and were judged in terms of elegance rather than originality. Regularity and assurance in both writing and behavior were primary values, values that arose naturally from experience of society itself.

Such ideas continue to shape historians' understanding of aristocratic culture during the Old Regime, with the difference that what Tocqueville attributed to the social system as a whole, more recent

2. Cf. William Bouwsma, "Anxiety and the Formation of Early Modern Culture," in William Bouwsma, *A Visible Past: Essays in European Cultural History* (Berkeley, 1990).

3. *Democracy in America*, trans. George Lawrence, ed. J.-P. Mayer (New York, 1969), 472.

scholars have tended to attribute to divergent class experiences. In its broadest terms, thus, the contrast between aristocratic and bourgeois cultures appears in Ian Watt's argument that the modern novel is an essentially bourgeois creation, fundamentally cut off from earlier, aristocratic narrative forms.[4] From a narrower focus on the Old Regime, historians have likewise tied culture to class. They have interpreted hierarchical thought as the ideological stance of the older nobility, the warrior nobility of birth, and they have situated more liberal impulses in specifically urban social groups: the lawyers and judges who made up the world of the *robe*, and, more broadly, the bourgeoisie. Having reviewed "the intellectual leaders" of the seventeenth century, for instance, Erich Auerbach concludes that "we may disregard the handful of nobles. The vast majority of the others were descended from the various categories of *robe*."[5] Erica Harth writes that "[t]he cultural history of seventeenth-century France is one of progressive obsolescence: the progressive forces of a forming bourgeoisie undermined an increasingly outworn representational mold," and that "[t]he bourgeois challenge to authority and tradition" propelled what was most novel in seventeenth-century culture.[6] From very different theoretical suppositions, William Bouwsma has interpreted cultural innovation in terms of the specific professional demands of legal practice and in terms of the uncertainties of urban life.[7] Stephen Greenblatt has offered a similar view of sixteenth-century England. Interest there in "the construction of identity," he argues, arose among writers who "all embody, in one form or another, a profound mobility," who "are all displaced in significant ways from a stable, inherited social world."[8]

Conversely, for Emmanuel Le Roy Ladurie, "[t]he hierarchical principle in various forms . . . informs not only the ranks of the Court, but the various analyses that intelligent contemporaries give of its dis-

4. *The Rise of the Novel: Studies in Defoe, Richardson and Fielding* (Berkeley, 1962), esp. 58–59, 94–95. See also Tony Tanner, *Adultery in the Novel: Contract and Transgression* (Baltimore, 1979), for a view of *Elective Affinities* as a bourgeois novel, when its characters are retired courtiers and soldiers.

5. " 'La Cour et la Ville,' " repr. in Erich Auerbach, *Scenes from the Drama of European Literature* (Minneapolis, 1984), 168, 171.

6. *Ideology and Culture in Seventeenth-Century France* (Ithaca, 1983), 18, 20.

7. "Lawyers and Early Modern Culture," in *A Usable Past*; "Anxiety and the Formation of Early Modern Culture."

8. *Renaissance Self-Fashioning, from More to Shakespeare* (Chicago, 1980), 7, 8.

sensions. The Court forms *chronologically* the last phase of the society of ranks, before the wave of egalitarianism that will begin in the age of Enlightenment. With Saint-Simon, Madame, and a few others, the Court arrives at a clear awareness or at least a perfect expression of its ideology, focussed on the limited space of a great palace."[9] In this view, seventeenth-century aristocratic writers offered an elaborate but still recognizable version of ideas that had dominated Western thought over the previous millennium. Paul Bénichou's brilliant analysis of the seventeenth-century *moralistes* assigns them a very different historical place but rests on similar assumptions about the progress of ideas. For Bénichou, a new realism in the seventeenth century allowed writers to incorporate a steadily more complete, richer view of human life into their writings.[10]

Like Tocqueville, these historians seek to connect specific cultural expressions both to experience and to the ideology of inheritance that undergirded the aristocracy's existence during the Old Regime. Several immediate difficulties, however, deserve attention. First, such an interpretation as Le Roy Ladurie's requires that we detach the eighteenth century from its seventeenth-century antecedents and that we see a "wave of egalitarianism"—coming apparently from outside the existing cultural system—only in the Enlightenment. Such a view seems systematically to undervalue intellectual innovation in the seventeenth century, for instance by attaching Madame de Lafayette's *Princesse de Clèves* to the merely ideological defense of social hierarchy. That view seems also to do violence to our intuitive sense of connectedness to the best-known seventeenth-century aristocratic writers, our sense of a shared sensibility with Madame de Lafayette, La Rochefoucauld, and Retz, to say nothing of Pascal. Le Roy Ladurie's view seems also to violate the more technical awareness developed by historians of philosophy, that the seventeenth century's assumptions about human understanding continued to dominate philosophy well into the twentieth century. At the core of much seventeenth-century writing, as Suzanne Langer and others have shown, stood a conviction of the individual's separation from the world around her/him;

9. "Auprès du roi, la cour," *Annales ESC* 38, 1 (January-February 1983): 21–41 (emphasis in original).

10. *Morales du grand siècle* (Paris, 1948), passim; see, for instance, Bénichou's view that the seventeenth century represented an achievement of naturalism, an end to "*le dégoût de l'homme pour sa nature*" (372).

this individualism had obvious affinities with the assumptions of liberal political culture.[11]

Second, the association of intellectual leadership with social mobility encounters empirical problems. For instance, seventeenth-century interest in what Greenblatt calls "the construction of identity" might more reasonably be attributed to aristocratic autobiographers and novelists than to lawyers or bourgeois. At the least we need to account for the very large number of written self-depictions by members of the seventeenth-century French aristocracy. Clearly there were pressures within settled, aristocratic society that led to self-exploration and self-depiction—and that led to unsettling depictions of what the self was like. Further, all of these sociological interpretations of cultural differences fit awkwardly with our growing knowledge of how upper-class society actually functioned in the sixteenth and seventeenth centuries. Implying as they do sharp separation between the situations of different classes, these interpretations leave little room for evidence showing the permeability of these social boundaries and the importance of interchange between robe and sword.[12]

But even if sociological interpretation could give us an adequate view of the processes of literary creation, there would remain the problem of audience, the fact that ideas were not only produced but were followed and enthusiastically supported by a wide range of social groups. Rousseau suggested the complex relations that might prevail between plebeian author and aristocratic audience when he described the reception of his *Nouvelle Héloïse*. The novel, he wrote, "requires a delicacy of understanding that can only be acquired in the school of the world to detect the niceties of feeling, if I may so describe them, with which [the novel] is full. I am not afraid to compare the Fourth Part with the *Princesse de Clèves* (Mme de Lafayette's novel), and I assert that if these two works had only been read in the provinces their full value would never have been known. It is not surprising

11. Suzanne Langer defined the seventeenth century's intellectual stance in terms of "a mighty and revolutionary generative idea: the dichotomy of all reality into *inner experience* and *outer world*, subject and object, private reality and public truth" (*Philosophy in a New Key: A Study in the Symbolism of Reason, Rite, and Art* [Cambridge, Mass., 1942], 12). Langer's formulation presents seventeenth-century thought in terms of a deeply felt, thorough individualism.

12. See Jonathan Dewald, *The Formation of a Provincial Nobility: The Magistrates of the Parlement of Rouen, 1499–1610* (Princeton, 1980); Ellery Schalk, *From Valor to Pedigree: Ideas of Nobility in France in the Sixteenth and Seventeenth Centuries* (Princeton, 1986), 159–62, 210–11.

that the book's greatest success was at Court."[13] Despite his own background, Rousseau set both the novel's appeal and the literary tradition from which it arose within a context of aristocratic experiences. He saw his sensibility as in some measure inherited from that of the aristocratic seventeenth-century novelist, and he saw few tensions between aristocratic social position and appreciation of his outlook; for him there was a natural progression from the seventeenth to the eighteenth century, rather than a sharp break between them.

Many of these interpretive problems reflect, I believe, the fact that social interpretation of early modern culture has tended to treat aristocratic culture as essentially ideological, that is, as a univocal expression and justification of the group's experiences, situations, and interests. Such an approach has obvious value but important limitations: it implies a fundamental unity in culture, and thus shields from our view its points of uncertainty or contradiction; it often implies a functionalist view of how ideas and values form, and this seems inadequate to the complexities both of the ideas themselves and of the processes by which they developed; above all, an ideological approach to aristocratic culture treats culture as only a reflection of deeper realities, a secondary level of reality, a superstructure. To treat culture as a utilitarian mechanism by which interests are justified or concealed allows little room for the causal force of culture itself.[14]

In contrast, cultural tensions and contradictions play a central role in the account that follows. Nobles (this book argues) found their lives being shaped by a series of forces whose weight increased as the seventeenth century advanced. Lineage gained increasing importance in public life, as social status became more clearly a matter of birth and as venal office-holding created castes within the military and the civil service; in consequence, families increasingly organized themselves along dynastic lines, celebrating paternal authority and subordinating individual desires to dynastic needs. Standards of personal behavior rose, a process encouraged both by a reinvigorated Catholicism and by courtly libertinism; each demanded that men and women more tightly control their impulses and fit their behavior to elaborate standards.

---

13. In *The Confessions*, trans. J. M. Cohen (London, 1953), 504–5.

14. For criticism of "the idea that human cultures are formulated out of practical activity and, behind that, utilitarian interest," see Marshall Sahlins, *Culture and Practical Reason* (Chicago, 1976).

Above all, the state heightened its demands. The state too required conformity, the rigid subordination of individual impulse to collective orderings. The state also intervened throughout society, making clear that property, local law, and distinctions of birth might all be undercut by the complex play of political influences. Though at points I will discuss these processes in some detail, for the most part they remain in the background of this study, not because I think them unimportant, but because they have been so clearly established by recent scholarship.

Rather, I am mainly concerned here with individuals' responses to these pressures. One response, of course, was celebration. Seventeenth-century nobles produced elaborate defenses of their order's superiority to the rest of society and emphasized the value of noble birth. Despite moments of hesitation and resistance, ultimately they celebrated the monarchy as well, both in the person of Louis XIV and in a larger vision of their society. In this vision, kingship and nobility allied in a single social order, founded on bloodlines, ancient rights, and traditional expectations. The increasing weight of patriarchal authority might lead to elaborate expressions of patriarchal ideology.

But it also led to other, contradictory responses, for important aspects of aristocratic life directly undercut respect for tradition and inheritance. Enthusiasm for courtly manners involved a startlingly explicit rejection of the past as a guide; and this rejection recurred in other domains, as nobles stressed the superiority of their own culture to that of the past. Similarly, the conditions of seventeenth-century warfare required sophisticated political and numerical calculations and encouraged familiarity with classical writers, who acquired renewed relevance in an age dominated by carefully organized masses of infantry. Seventeenth-century political careers demanded similar thought and focused attention on individual ambition rather than dynastic continuity as a key to understanding social arrangements. By selling high positions and by intervening so often in matters of property, the state itself disrupted belief in a stable social order and forced nobles to think carefully about money; in such circumstances, nobles came to view their society as in some sense an artificial creation rather than an organic hierarchy. In these and a variety of other specific ways, seventeenth-century conditions undermined patriarchal ideas and forced nobles into more individualistic modes of thought.

But I also argue here for a more fundamental contradiction within patriarchal thought and feeling. The seventeenth century's demands for personal subordination produced inner rebellions as well as celebration. Hence one of the central paradoxes of the age: as family, state, and ethical ideals increasingly demanded renunciation of individual desires, men and women became increasingly absorbed in understanding themselves as individuals, and indeed in understanding personal desire itself. They explored their inner lives in autobiographies[15] and novels, and they presented their lives in terms of personal achievement. They became increasingly preoccupied with emotion, which attached them to friends and lovers—in other words, to chosen objects of affection. Such deepening concern with the personal offered one response to the oppressiveness of seventeenth-century expectations.

Exploration of other kinds of social arrangement provided another such response. Thus nobles played surprisingly readily with social forms in which anonymity disguised distinctions of birth—in which nobility itself vanished. The rejection was explicit in the case of the Académie Française, which admitted men without reference to rank. It was implicit in such events as the masked ball, the gambling party, and the decision (taken with growing frequency in the seventeenth century) to write or appear in published literary works, works that exposed author and subject to the judgment of any book-buyer. All of these choices presented momentary, experimental departures from aristocratic society itself. Like the exploration of the personal, they expressed nobles' ambivalence about their social order. Nobles fully accepted the ordering that dynastic ideology proposed and that accorded them such a privileged place. But they also felt acutely the weight of that order.

This book argues, then, for seeing a complex relationship between modern cultural forms and the cultural assumptions of the seventeenth-

---

15. This study thus dissents from the position, taken by Philippe Le Jeune and followed by Madeleine Foisil, that seventeenth-century memoirs should be sharply differentiated from the autobiographical literature that followed Rousseau (Le Jeune, *L'autobiographie en France* [Paris, 1973], and Foisil, "The Literature of Intimacy," in Roger Chartier, ed., *A History of Private Life*, vol. 3, trans. Arthur Goldhammer [Cambridge, Mass., 1989], 327–61, esp. 329). Though aristocratic memoirs often stay at the surface of events, they display a view of the self as contingent in its history, undergoing processes of creation over time.

century nobles: for seeing the connectedness of individualistic, liberal assumptions and the apparently more ancient, atavistic warrior culture that liberalism ultimately overthrew. In this respect my argument fits among those recent studies of the French nobility that have emphasized the order's modernity, its involvement in the processes of change within early modern French society. These studies have argued persuasively for the nobility's economic vitality during the Old Regime, and reevaluation of the order's political role is now well along. Nobles' political choices can no longer be treated as simply a matter of reaction or the pursuit of pure self-interest; Richelieu and the other architects of absolutism no longer seem so clearly superior to their opponents, or even so different from them.

I intend, however, that this study point in a rather different direction. Much in recent writing on the nobility, I believe, unduly simplifies the cultural tensions the nobles experienced in the sixteenth and seventeenth centuries. Scholarship has long tended to place the nobles on one side or the other of a series of dichotomies, opposing tradition with economic rationality, oral culture with written, dynasticism with individualism. Recent scholarship in several domains has changed the nobles' place in this pattern of oppositions but has continued situating the nobles somewhere within the polarity between tradition and modernity. I hope to show here the inadequacy of this model of culture. Many French nobles combined qualities that we might suppose incompatible; often, as I hope will become apparent, apparently contradictory ideas were in fact closely linked. Nobles explored alternatives to patriarchal ideology not because it was weakening in the seventeenth century but because its hold over them was so very strong.

Some choices of method run through this study and may require defense at the outset. First, because this book seeks to explicate the cultural tools that nobles had available for understanding their lives, I have quoted from them extensively; their language of self-perception is a central problem here, and it needs to be heard at length. Second, I have sought throughout to combine literary and archival sources. I make no claim that the literary sources I have used accurately mirrored daily life, though I believe that they often do show us what contemporaries believed to be the possible and the plausible in daily life. Nor do I claim that the archival sources used here present a typical picture of the seventeenth-century aristocracy. Rather than accuracy or typicality, the combination of literary and archival sources offers an understanding of norms and expectations. These sources can help us to understand what seventeenth-century nobles expected to see when they looked at their world and how they expected to deal with it. To some extent, the combination of archival and literary sources can also clarify the interplay between cultural norms and daily practice.

Because of this concern to trace cultural norms, I have drawn my examples widely, from a loosely defined group that includes great aristocrats, high magistrates, parvenus like the financier Gourville, and even such marginals as the classical dramatists and such bourgeois observers as Tallemant des Réaux—in short, from all the groups that made up Parisian high society. Such a choice pays relatively little attention to the real differences that divided these groups, though such differences will have a central place in the discussion of some issues. Yet however complex their interaction, the groups constituting seventeenth-century high society knew one another well and shared many values. This was a small world. It mingled occasionally, as at Ninon de L'Enclos's late-seventeenth-century salon; when Elisabeth de La Trémoille died in 1640, the family received and copied into a single book condolences from a cross-section of this world, nobles of robe and sword, Protestants and Catholics, professional writers, friends and opponents of Richelieu. Secrets from the high aristocracy spread quickly, so that even bourgeois like Tallemant knew intimate details about nobles' lives. Professional writers spoke to an aristocratic audience, and typically the process of composition involved comments and contributions from that audience.[16]

Finally, this study gives relatively little attention to change over the seventeenth century and emphasizes instead the coherence of aristocratic culture between the late sixteenth century and the early eighteenth. Important changes both in the nobles' own situation and in the society around them certainly took place during these years. Royal government became stronger and less tolerant of dissent; nobles relinquished duelling, armed rebellion, and many other forms of public and private violence; landed incomes first boomed, then declined after about 1660. Most important for this study, the weight of dynastic belief and practice grew, both within families' private arrangements and

16. For a strong statement of the view that Parisian upper-class society was essentially homogeneous during the seventeenth century, see Françoise Bayard, *Le monde des financiers au XVIIe siècle* (Paris, 1988), 421–49.

within the state as a whole. However, discussions of early modern culture seem to me typically to have overstated these changes and to have overstated the novelty of cultural responses to them. Historians of literature in particular, I believe, have given excessive weight to nobles' discouragement in the face of Louis XIV's absolutism.[17] Discouragement there certainly was, but recent studies have emphasized the benefits that nobles drew from absolutism and the order's fundamental prosperity throughout the seventeenth century. As important (so I argue here), such discouragement as nobles felt expressed itself within well-worn cultural traditions, which had made failure and exile predictable elements in an aristocratic career. These themes dominated aristocratic language long before Versailles became the focus of national life. Rather than see a decisive turning point in the mid-seventeenth century, I would prefer to see early modern aristocratic culture as a single set of traditions, a repertoire of perceptions and responses. Like any such set of traditions, that of the French nobles evolved, and from the outset it contained numerous unresolved tensions and points of uncertainty; changing circumstances brought some of these to the fore at specific moments, converting implicit and untroubling contradictions into serious moral problems. Despite changes and uncertainties, however, nobles drew much of their thought from a stable set of ideas.

I have not attempted here to explore the fate of these cultural traditions in the eighteenth century. This essay does, however, suggest ways of viewing the transition from the seventeenth century to the Enlightenment. In certain respects, this transition represented a triumph of values that had little place in seventeenth-century aristocratic thinking. Seventeenth-century writers treated estate management, for instance, as morally neutral or even negative, distractions from the engagements of citizenship; the eighteenth century made economic life an aspect of citizenship. In other ways, however, the eighteenth century appears to represent not so much revision of seventeenth-century values as choice among them. Seventeenth-century aristocratic culture, so runs a central argument of this essay, placed contradictory demands on its participants, between, for instance, ideals of inheritance and of individual ambition. By the early eighteenth century, the

17. For a recent example, see Elizabeth Goldsmith, *Exclusive Conversations: The Art of Interaction in Seventeenth-Century France* (Philadelphia, 1988).

weight of these contradictions had for many nobles become intolerable. The more egalitarian ideologies of the eighteenth century, it may be suggested, offered resolution of contradictions that had become burdensome beyond endurance. From this vantage point, Louis XIV's rise to power seems less a turning point than does his death.

# I

# Ambition and the Polity

French noblemen talked steadily more about lineage and descent after 1570 or so. Noble blood acquired greater importance in these years, increasingly obscuring other plausible justifications of privilege. The monarchy contributed to this enhanced evaluation, by inspecting genealogies more carefully and penalizing those who lacked proper ancestry. Concepts of lineage (*race* in the language of the seventeenth century) performed comforting ideological functions. They provided ways for individuals to understand their situations and for the aristocracy as a whole to understand its relationship to the rest of society. Few in the seventeenth-century nobility would have questioned this complex of ideas; most simply took them for granted.[1]

I argue here, however, that another, in some ways contradictory, set of ideas ultimately had greater importance in defining the French nobility's sense of itself. In describing their lives, nobles spoke less of lineage and ancestry than of personal ambition. They presented themselves as individuals creating their own social positions, rather than as family members growing into positions. A first task of this chapter, then, is to make clear the pervasiveness and intensity of this language of ambition within aristocratic self-depictions. A larger task is to explore what this language meant for nobles' understanding of themselves and of the polity to which they belonged. Within the setting of seventeenth-century polite society, ambition had specific qualities. It was closely associated with youth, as classical psychological theory taught and as experience in the army and at court confirmed; thus preoccupation with ambition encouraged an awareness of change and impermanence. To focus on the individual's drive for success meant as well to reflect on causes of failure, and this preoccupation led to

1. For somewhat different interpretations of this process, see Arlette Jouanna, *Ordre social: Mythes et hiérarchies dans la France du XVIe siècle* (Paris, 1977), and Ellery Schalk, *From Valor to Pedigree: Ideas of Nobility in France in the Sixteenth and Seventeenth Centuries* (Princeton, 1986).

reflections on the role of chance in human affairs and on the complexity of political events.

Above all, in the seventeenth century ambition had meaning only within the realm of public life, and thus preoccupation with ambition led to thought about the nature of that public life itself. Nobles typically defined retreat from public life—retreat to a country home—as a mark of incapacity, as morally shameful. Yet moral doubts pervaded the language they used to define public life. To view political society as a collection of competing ambitions, of course, implied the frequency of enmities and deceptions within it. But, as important, nobles explained their political attachments in terms of emotion rather than reason, and they felt acutely the dependencies and loss of control that these attachments often produced. They commonly described the larger polity as a form of theater, a system of illusions meant to manipulate subjects' emotions. Seventeenth-century aristocratic culture, this chapter argues, offered problematic visions both of the self and of the public world within which it moved. The self and its roles had in some measure to be artificial creations, the unstable products of effort and achievement; but the polity itself was likewise an artifact.

Ambition emerged early as a central theme in the memoirs that the French aristocracy produced. The Catholic military hero Blaise de Monluc, whose *Commentaries* are among the earliest examples of this autobiographical literature, placed ambition and social advancement among the guiding themes of his life: "I have seen [some] succeed who carried a pike for 6 francs wages, because they performed such warlike acts and were found to be so capable that, though they were sons of poor farmers, they advanced farther than many nobles, through their bravery and virtue. . . . Even though I am a gentleman, I too have nonetheless succeeded [*parvenu*] step by step, like the poorest soldier in the kingdom." Monluc presented these observations as a basis for broader moral commentary. Successful soldiers who have served the king honorably, he wrote, "when they return to their homeland [*leur patrie*] . . . are honored by men of all ranks, not for their birth [*le lieu d'où ils sortent*], nor for their wealth, but for their merit."[2] To make the point clearer still, Monluc overstated the obscurity of his own be-

2. Blaise de Monluc, *Commentaires, 1521–1576*, ed. Paul Courteault (Paris, Pléiade, 1964), 22–23, 27.

ginnings, presenting himself as a "poor younger son" rather than the well-supported oldest son that in fact he was. Monluc believed his life story to be of general interest because it illustrated what impoverished provincials could achieve through loyal military service.

Later memorialists imitated and broadened these themes. The sieur de Pontis, a Jansenist soldier born in 1584, described his frustration in the provincial home of his older brother, who had inherited the family's property. At the age of sixteen, de Pontis wrote, "I resolved to leave for Paris, and to work by myself to advance as I could in the world." He explained his hopes more fully to the provincial governor, the duc de Lesdiguières, whose help he sought soon after leaving home: what he wanted, he told Lesdiguières, "was to learn to become an *honnête homme*," a term that suggested both personal qualities of grace, ability, and self-control, and a respected position in the wider world.[3]

De Pontis thus suggested a broader understanding than Monluc's of what ambition might entail; he linked his hopes of external success to an inner transformation. Lesdiguières sympathized with these impulses, for (so a later writer reported) he himself "loved to recall his humble beginnings [*sa première fortune*], and one sees today a strong mark of this, in that, having constructed a superb palace at Lesdiguières, he took pleasure in leaving intact, right next to it, the small house where he had been born and where his father had lived."[4] The contrast between humble beginnings and eventual triumph here received permanent and public representation. Conversely, Henri de Campion (another soldier, writing in the 1650s) stressed the emotional intensity of ambition and the pain brought by eventual failure: "Ambition and the desire to acquire a reputation left me no rest," he wrote, "and were my strongest passion from my tenderest youth." He described himself as "only a poor cadet who is seeking to make his fortune." Only failure—"*ma mauvaise fortune . . . mon peu d'avancement*"—eventually cured him of his passion.[5]

3. Sieur de Pontis, *Mémoires*, in M. Petitot, ed., *Collection des mémoires relatifs à l'histoire de France*, 31–32 (Paris, 1824), 31: 213–14. On the problem of de Pontis as an historical source, see Emile Bourgeois and Louis André, *Les sources de l'histoire de France, XVIIe siècle (1610–1715)*. Volume 2: *Mémoires et lettres* (Paris, 1913), 17–18.

4. Gédéon Tallement des Réaux, *Historiettes*, ed. Antoine Adam, 2 vols. (Paris, Pléiade, 1960–61), 1: 52.

5. *Mémoires*, ed. Marc Fumaroli (Paris, 1967), 43, 47, 44. For an excellent discussion of Campion's career, ambitions, and values, see Yves Castan, "Politics and Private

Monluc, de Pontis, Lesdiguières, and Campion all set the theme of ambition within a context of familial poverty which required that they make their fortunes on their own. But rich nobles as well shared this rhetoric of ambition; it was part of a larger pattern of expectations that had little to do with economic standing. Bussy-Rabutin, who was born to a prosperous and well-connected family, began his memoirs with the lines: "When I came into the world, my first and strongest inclination was to become an *honnête homme* and to succeed to the great honors of warfare."[6] Like de Pontis, he stressed the connectedness of inner and outer change, between his education as an *honnête homme* and his hopes for success as a captain. Despite his wealth, though, Bussy also shared Campion's bitterness at failure; his distress at the eventual thwarting of his ambitions, he explained, produced severe physical illness.[7] Late in life, after his pious retirement to Port Royal, de Pontis himself emphasized the appropriateness of ambition to wealthy as well as poor noblemen. Having been asked for educational advice by the tutor of two wealthy young nobles, he urged, "Above all, take care never to try to strangle their passions by your sole authority, or by excessive correction . . . for some are not criminal and are suited to the condition of a great noble [*un grand*], for instance, ambition."[8] De Pontis's piety and retreat from active life had not changed his view of the propriety of ambition. He described it as a natural passion, and one that needed only proper guidance, not outright repression; ambition formed part of an ethical system.

Even princes subscribed to these values, using language that emphasized the ambitions they shared with ordinary gentlemen like Monluc and de Pontis. Marguerite de Valois recalled her brother, the future king Henri III, telling her, "You see the fine and great offices to which God has called me, and to which the queen our mother has elevated me"; he asked that Marguerite help maintain him in the "*fortune où je suis*."[9] For an heir to the throne to use such a rhetoric of social mobility suggests the force that these ideals had, and they retained their power through the seventeenth century. The future Grand

Life," in Roger Chartier, ed., *A History of Private Life*, vol. 3, trans. Arthur Goldhammer (Cambridge, Mass., 1989), 21–37.

6. Roger de Bussy-Rabutin, *Mémoires*, ed. Ludovic Lalanne, 2 vols. (Paris, 1857; repr. Westmead, 1972), 1: 3.

7. Ibid., 2: 75.

8. De Pontis, *Mémoires*, 32: 489.

9. Marguerite de Valois, *Mémoires et lettres*, ed. F. Guessard (Paris, 1842), 13.

Condé described the "holy ambition" his father's achievements had inspired in him.[10] Conversely, Saint-Simon described the bitterness of the prince de Conti, another prince of the blood and one of the richest men in France, "driven to despair at not being able to attain the slightest thing," and then dying just as the return of the king's favor seemed to promise what Saint-Simon called "the opening of a brilliant career." Like Bussy-Rabutin, Saint-Simon believed failure to be so distressing that it brought physical illness; Conti fell ill, Saint-Simon claimed, partly because of his disappointed hopes.[11]

That ambition and achievement dominated the concerns even of those who already occupied the highest positions in French society was suggested also by the wave of mid-seventeenth-century publications describing *The Art of Pleasing at Court* and *The Road to Fortune and the Favors of the Court*. In these books, reported the literary commentator Charles Sorel, "one can see the means of advancing in all conditions, and especially in that of courtier."[12] Such books implied both symbolic and practical associations between the world of the high nobility and social advancement. Apparently enough outsiders, poor provincials like Monluc and de Pontis, hoped to make their way at court that printed guides could find a market. Oral communications and personal relations no longer sufficed to instruct such hopefuls, however slight might be their real chances of success when armed only with such printed aids. But the symbolic significance of such books is still greater. Success at court, among the high nobility, had become a model, as Sorel indicated, for "advancing in all conditions."

Ambition, then, was a pervasive theme in seventeenth-century aristocratic discussions—a theme that deserves emphasis, in view of some historians' assumption that "the drive to succeed [was] foreign to a nobility sufficiently distinguished by its old titles."[13] Nobles expected, not simply to grow into their social roles, but to create them as they advanced in life; and they presented their ambitions in terms of social norms rather than as sordid reality that might contrast with higher

10. M. le duc d'Aumale, *Histoire des princes de Condé pendant les XVIe et XVIIe siècles,* 6 vols. (Paris, 1885), 3: 332.

11. Louis de Rouvroy, duc de Saint-Simon, *Mémoires,* ed. Gonzague Truc, 8 vols. (Paris, Pléiade, 1953–61), 3: 56, 57.

12. Charles Sorel, *La bibliothèque françoise,* 2d ed. (Paris, 1667; repr. Geneva, 1970), 69.

13. Adeline Daumard, quoted in Robert A. Nye, "Honor, Impotence, and Male Sexuality in Nineteenth-Century French Medicine," *French Historical Studies* 16, 1 (Spring 1989), 51. The quotation apparently refers specifically to the nineteenth century, but its assumptions about the origins of ambition are what need attention here.

ideals. They described ambition as a passion, an urge that was normal and almost beyond the individual's control. Like other passions, ambition could be dangerous, and it required proper direction, but its complete eradication posed still greater dangers. Ambition was part of what made a good man. It is suggestive of the centrality of ideas about ambition in seventeenth-century French culture that *carrière* seems to have acquired its modern meaning, as the individual's pursuit of success, before 1630; comparable use of the English "career" first appeared in 1803.[14] French writers, it seems, early needed words for describing the kinds of lives that Monluc and the others had created for themselves. They were not thinking only about the achievement of glory and preeminence. Rather, they sought to define how the interplay of inner drive and external events had produced the life story that was now before the reader.

French nobles not only placed ambition at the center of their lives; they offered an extended critique of a plausible alternative social model, that of the country gentleman and the country house as a center of virtue, a counterweight to the corruptions of city and court. Nobles described lives that centered on the private country home as the result of political failure, physical decay, or indifference to honor. "Follow the example," Monluc urged, a century before Louis XIV's efforts to draw nobles to the court, "of those who, having been loyal in the positions they have held, hold their heads high before everyone . . . , and not of those who, because of their vices, hang their heads in their houses, or their children for them."[15] For Monluc the country house was the retreat of vice, rather than a center of virtue. For his younger contemporary Jean de Mergey, retreat to the country represented, rather, old age and incapacity. He described a relative and benefactor "having become paralytic and impotent in all his members, and for this reason no longer able to reside at court, and having retired to his home," where he found pleasure in extensive rebuilding.[16]

The next century brought further development of these images. La Rochefoucauld explained attachment to country houses in terms of

14. Paul Imbs, ed., *Trésor de la langue française*, 11 vols. (in progress) (Paris, 1971– ), s.v. *carrière*, lists the first such meaning as coming before 1630; *Oxford English Dictionary*, s.v. "career," lists the first such English meaning as coming in 1803. I owe this point to Professor Joyce Appleby.

15. Monluc, *Commentaires*, 28–29.

16. Jean de Mergey, *Mémoires*, in Michaud and Poujolat, eds., *Nouvelle collection des mémoires relatifs à l'histoire de France . . .* , 9 (Paris, 1857), 559.

the psychological decay that old age brought: the old, he believed, had lost interest in society and instead invested their emotions in houses and other inanimate objects.[17] His fellow frondeur Pierre Lenet embellished this critique by defining the country gentleman in terms of ignorance and conceit. Just after the Fronde, he wrote of "those gentlemen hiding out in their houses, who hold themselves up as the arbiters of their province." In his youth he had mocked these gentlemen in a satirical poem: they were, he wrote, "attached to their homes beyond all reason" because of the tranquillity of country life, its modest scale of expenses (which "extends your revenue further than it would ever have gone"), and the pleasure of being talked of in the village "conjointly with the king."[18]

Such associations of the rural household with vice, ignorance, conceit, failure, and personal decrepitude are especially striking because French nobles had available to them an alternative set of symbols. Since the late sixteenth century and Ben Jonson's "To Penshurst," English writers had viewed the country house as a site of virtue and a physical manifestation of the continuity between public and private life. The country house displayed the family's continuity over the generations and its ongoing political role, a role that was only strengthened by its associations with country life. This was how Marvell used the Fairfaxes' Appleton House. He traced the association between house and family from before the Reformation, showed the house as the appropriate background to its owners' public role, and stressed throughout the theme of order: "[A]ll things are composed here / Like Nature, orderly and near."[19] French nobles (as we will see in a later chapter) took houses very seriously, often pouring enormous sums of money into them. But no country ideology seems to have ensued. In effect, aristocratic culture had closed off this alternative to the rhetoric of ambition. Nobles had to make their way within a public sphere.

The language of ambition had specific social contours; it characterized the military nobility, the nobility of the sword. French nobles during the sixteenth and seventeenth centuries displayed an acute

17. François de La Rochefoucauld, *Maximes et réflexions diverses*, ed. Jacques Truchet (Paris, 1977), 137 ("De la retraite").

18. Pierre Lenet, *Mémoires*, in M. Petitot and J. N. Monmerqué, eds., *Collection des mémoires relatifs à l'histoire de France*, 53 (Paris, 1826), 249–50, 4–5.

19. "Upon Appleton House," lines 25–26.

awareness that new families had entered their order and that the expansion of the state had produced an entirely new form of nobility, a university-trained nobility of administrators and judges. This consciousness of innovation might lead to disdainful condemnations of the new nobility as "bourgeois" and to glorifications of ancient lineages. But relations between military and judicial nobilities, between robe and sword, were more complex than such dismissals might suggest. For contemporaries also knew that familial relations between robe and sword were often close, and they spoke readily of a young man's choice between robe and sword as a choice between professions and cultural milieux. "I do not yet know," wrote the mid-seventeenth-century comte de Souvigny to his sons, after his own successful military career, "what it will please God to dispose with regard to the profession for which he has destined you in the world, whether to his holy service in the church, to that of the king in his armies and at court, or to wear the robe at the bar."[20] For Souvigny, as for many others, robe and sword did not represent differences of birth. Magistrates and soldiers came from similar backgrounds.

But they did not for that reason share a common outlook, and divergent views of ambition constituted a fundamental difference between them. The poet Malherbe, a courtier and notoriously sensitive about his noble status, in 1627 advised his son to begin a career as a royal magistrate. The choice itself testified to fluidity of movement between magistracy and military nobility, though Malherbe acknowledged the prejudices that continued to surround such choices. But Malherbe added to his advice reflections about the differences between the two kinds of careers: "It is true that a military career raises one to eminence. But the climb is so arduous that to succeed in it fortune, against her habit, must give extraordinary assistance to ability. It is not thus for offices in the Parlement. There all the difficulty is in beginning. Once one has started on the path, one can say that he has accomplished the main part of the journey. These are not positions that will carry a man to the clouds; but they place him high enough to see many others beneath him."[21]

20. Comte de Souvigny, *Mémoires*, ed. Ludovic de Contenson, 3 vols. (Paris, 1906–09), 3:62.

21. Quoted by Henning Scheffers, *Höfische Konvention und die Aufklärung: Wandlungen des honnête-homme-Ideals im 17. und 18. Jahrhundert* (Bonn, 1980), 20.

Despite some nobles' claim that the nobility of the robe consisted of bourgeois parvenus, Malherbe argued that social fluidity in fact characterized the military career. The military nobleman had chances of rising higher, but he had fewer rules and procedures to guide his advancement, and he faced a greater likelihood of failure. The seventeenth century's greatest exemplars of military success seemed to suggest that it resulted from forms of genius that could change little with age or experience. Contemporaries viewed both Condé and Turenne as geniuses who regularly violated the rules of warfare but nonetheless succeeded. Few military nobles could hope to follow their example. Within the magistracy, in contrast, advancement followed clearly marked paths. The new arrival might encounter difficulty in buying an office and having himself accepted by the court he sought to join. Once he had entered on his career, however, both his work and his advancement fell under clear rules. Collective traditions and procedures determined nearly all activity within the courts, and rules of seniority governed most advancement. Once one had entered such a career, the question of ambition had essentially been solved.

The essayist Saint-Evremond spelled out the social and psychological consequences of this divergence. "Those who spend their youth in the companies, in assemblies," he wrote, "learn order, forms, and all the matters that are treated there. Passing then to the embassies, they instruct themselves in foreign affairs, and . . . with effort and experience there is little they cannot do." As young men, magistrates might make themselves ridiculous by trying to imitate the manners of the court. "But in the end awareness of their interests brings them back to their profession, and, having become adept over time, they find themselves in important positions, where everyone needs them." By contrast, the courtier's knowledge and abilities depended on youth, and advancing age meant only a decline in ability to please: "Whether from lack of effort or from believing that positions where one learns about public business are beneath them, they are equally ignorant of all serious matters; and as their charms fade with age, nothing brings them consideration and credit. They grow old in the antechambers, exposed to the mockery of the young."[22] Like Malherbe, Saint-Evremond saw regularity and steady advancement as characterizing

22. Charles de Marguetel, seigneur de Saint-Evremond, *Oeuvres en prose*, ed. René Ternois, 3 vols. (Paris, 1962–66), 2: 65–66, 67–68.

the magistrate's career, whereas the courtier and military noble had only the brief opportunities that his youth offered.

Ideas about ambition and career thus fitted with powerful images about youth and age, and about the patterns of an individual's life. These images were widely shared in seventeenth-century society, partly because they incorporated elements of Aristotelian thought. Aristotle had viewed the passage from arms to counsel as the natural accompaniment to old age. The old were natural governors, their impetuosity calmed by the coldness of age. The young were suited to fight; and their expectation of acquiring more civil power as they aged would curb their impatience at the army's control by civil authorities.[23]

Sixteenth-and seventeenth-century French men and women transformed these associations between social roles and age groups, by associating gravity and self-restraint with a specific social class, the magistracy. Dressed in long robes, subjected to rigid principles of seniority, and held to standards of decorum outside as well as inside the courtroom, young magistrates seemed to have voluntarily adopted the appearance and behavior of old men.[24] Not all easily adopted the role, yet even their refusals to do so suggested its force. Retz, who sneered at the leaders of the Parlement of Paris as "oldsters drowned . . . under the forms of the law courts," advised that the best way to achieve political results from the judges was to appeal to the young and incite them against the old.[25] The distinguished early-seventeenth-century magistrate Bernard de La Roche Flavin worried about "an evil in this kingdom; the young men, as soon as they have returned from the universities, because of an uncontrolled ambition . . . want to become magistrates and hold the first positions of justice."[26] Clearly, ambitious young magistrates could be found, and seventeenth-century circumstances brought them to the fore. They played a large role in the Fronde, and the fashions of court life had

23. Aristotle, *The Politics*, trans. T. A. Sinclair (London, 1962), 273–74 (7: 9). See also the discussion of age below, Chapter 4.

24. For the importance of images of age to the magistrates' understanding of their professional lives, see Jonathan Dewald, *The Formation of a Provincial Nobility: The Magistrates of the Parlement of Rouen, 1499–1610* (Princeton, 1980), 21–22.

25. Cardinal de Retz, *Mémoires*, ed. Maurice Allem and Edith Thomas (Paris, Pléiade, 1956), 615, 179.

26. Bernard de La Roche Flavin, *Treze livres des Parlemens de France* (Bordeaux, 1617), 308.

considerable appeal for them. Yet other norms and expectations governed the group. Ambition and uncertainty were central to the life of the military nobleman; the magistrate was expected, in La Roche Flavin's words, to "control himself and . . . condemn completely everything having to do with passion. And because of this he lives in peace, moves gently along in all matters, and never has cause to repent, to withdraw what he has said, or to change."[27] Unlike Campion and Bussy-Rabutin, the magistrate could never offer the passion of ambition as a guiding thread for understanding his life.

Military nobles thus saw ambition as one of the norms that defined their social group, setting it apart from such others as the nobility of the robe. Some nobles extended the contrast further, using ideas about ambition and youth to define the differences between their own monarchical society and the more republican societies they encountered in Holland and England. They saw their own society as dominated by the court and its values, hence as a society of intense competition and equally intense uncertainties—hence also as a society especially suited to the young. Saint-Evremond congratulated himself in the 1660s on living his last years "in the freedom of a republic, where, if there is nothing to hope for, at least there is nothing to fear. When one is young, it would be shameful not to enter the world with the design of making one's fortune; when one is in decline, nature recalls us to ourselves; and having relinquished ambition in favor of repose, it is sweet to live in a country where the laws protect us from the will of men, where to be sure in everything we need only be sure of ourselves."[28] Saint-Evremond used almost the same language to describe differences between France and Holland as he had used in contrasting sword and robe nobilities. On the one side he saw uncertainties, passion, ambitions, youth; on the other, the control, sobriety, and limits suited to age.

Montesquieu seems to have inherited this intellectual legacy, and early in the eighteenth century he offered these observations as broad political principles. In properly functioning republics, he argued, the young must subordinate themselves to the old, and all must subordinate themselves to ancient custom; frugality and self-control must dominate economic life. Monarchies, in contrast, require no such

---

27. Ibid., 441.
28. Saint-Evremond, *Oeuvres en prose,* 2: 24.

repression of impulse, and they work to undermine the authority of the old. "Paternal authority," Montesquieu argued, "ended at Rome together with the republic."[29] For Montesquieu as for Saint-Evremond, youth, ambition, and insecurity made up the background of monarchical life; republics represented stability, law, and the authority of old age.

Ambition as a social model gave a particular edge to a second component of this cultural system: an acute sensitivity to time. Such sensitivity reflected in part the fact that change inhered in court life itself. "These changes in the court are too ordinary an effect of fortune and of princely humors to cause surprise," reflected Montrésor, as he thought about his failures.[30] Because humors and people changed so quickly, nobles who hoped for success at court needed to make their way within narrow chronological limits, while they were young enough to be fashionable and while those they were connected to held power. The comte de La Châtre, disgraced in 1643, realized that his political life was over; "[W]hen our king becomes old enough to govern himself, there will be such disproportion between his age and mine, that I will never be able to claim access or familiarity with him."[31] La Rochefoucauld could draw consoling conclusions from the same principles, when Richelieu ordered him from court in 1641: he was young, both minister and king were ill, and he had everything to hope for from a change of regime.[32] La Châtre had made the same calculation a few years earlier: "[S]eeing that there was nothing for me to hope for so long as the Cardinal de Richelieu was all-powerful," he had attached himself to Anne of Austria, with the thought that "the regency would infallibly, in a very few years, fall into that princess's hands."[33]

Just as important as changing political constellations were the changing fashions of court life, which quickly excluded from society

29. Charles-Louis de Secondat, baron de Montesquieu, *The Spirit of the Laws*, ed. David Wallace Carrithers (Berkeley, 1977), 137–40.

30. *Mémoires*, in Michaud and Poujolat, eds., *Nouvelle collection des mémoires relatifs à l'histoire de France* . . . , 27 (Paris, 1854), 213.

31. Comte de La Châtre, *Mémoires*, in Michaud and Poujolat, eds., *Nouvelle collection des mémoires relatifs à l'histoire de France* . . . , 27 (Paris, 1854), 296.

32. François de La Rochefoucauld, *Oeuvres complètes*, ed. L. Martin-Chauffier (Paris, Pléiade, 1957), 63.

33. Comte de La Châtre, *Mémoires*, 271.

those who failed to keep pace with its evolution. Those who have been away, wrote Saint-Evremond in the 1650s, "come back to the court like people from the other world; their dress, their manner, their language are no longer in style; they pass for foreigners in their own country, and for ridiculous among the young courtiers. There is no one whose patience they do not exhaust with their tales of times past, their stories about the old wars."[34] Violation of tradition was at the center of court life, and the power of change extended to gesture, language, modes of thought.

But preoccupation with time also reflected the nobles' understanding of both youth and old age. Old age aroused aesthetic disgust because of the infirmities it brought. "The most dangerous folly of old people who have been charming," wrote La Rochefoucauld, "is to forget that they no longer are."[35] Saint-Simon offered a series of portraits to illustrate the repellent qualities of old age. Madame de Soubise, for instance, was struck by scrofula "as old age began" and had to "stay home during the last two years of her life, rotting over the most precious furnishings deep in the vast and superb hotel de Guise."[36] Partly because of physical decay, old age was believed as well to bring a narrowing of social attachments, a withdrawal from civic life. "They become indifferent to friendship," wrote La Rochefoucauld of the old. "[T]heir taste, stripped of useless desires, turns to mute and inanimate objects; buildings, agriculture, household management, study—all these things are subject to their will."[37] By this time, such ideas had spread so widely through upper-class Parisian society that Molière could mock them in *Dom Juan* and expect audiences to laugh as Sganarelle retails clichés about old age: "[S]torms wrack ships; ships need a good pilot; a good pilot is prudent; the young have no prudence; the young ought to obey their elders; the old love riches; riches make men rich; the rich are not poor," to which Dom Juan responds "O fine reasoning!"[38] As seventeenth-century wisdom presented the matter, youth was the time for attachment to others, old age the time for attachment to things.

34. Saint-Evremond, *Oeuvres en prose*, 2: 147.
35. La Rochefoucauld, *Maximes et réflexions diverses*, 80 (no. 408).
36. Saint-Simon, *Mémoires*, 3: 32.
37. La Rochefoucauld, *Oeuvres complètes*, 399–400. Cf. Aristotle's similar belief that the old lack capacity for friendship, discussed below, Chapter 4.
38. Molière, *Dom Juan*, Act V, Scene 2; in Molière, *Oeuvres*, ed. Eugène Despois and Paul Mesnard (Paris, 1880), 5: 196.

The contrast between youth and age thus overlapped those between sword and robe and between courts and republics. Each set of contrasts touched on the nature of the individual's attachment to a social order. The young founded attachments on passionate, often-changing, and disorderly connections to others; the old attached themselves to inanimate objects and thus could regulate their personal involvements. A *parlementaire* writer such as La Roche Flavin could present this contrast in simple ethical terms, setting the disorder of youth against the sagacity of age, but writers from the military aristocracy inverted or blurred such ethical judgments. If youth was the age of disorder and change, it was also the age of civic connectedness, the time when the individual involved him/herself with other people rather than with lifeless things—among which, it should be noted, La Rochefoucauld included economic life.

Ideas about ambition and time, I have suggested, had real social uses for French nobles. They helped individuals to understand the unfolding of their lives, and they helped to define social and even national differences. But ambition as a social model also posed difficult problems, some of them resulting from inherent contradictions, others from tensions between these and other important aristocratic values. Some of these evoked only mild anxieties. That ambition contradicted important demands of Christian ethics seems to have disturbed very few—perhaps because ambition's association with youth allowed for repentance during the calm of old age; the later seventeenth century saw a long series of well-publicized conversions, with well-known political figures withdrawing to pious retirement. That the individual's ambitions might contradict his family's demands could pose more serious difficulties (some of which we will consider in Chapter 3). But nobles could cope with these also, by attaching their ambitions to dynastic tradition. De Pontis hoped that ambition would lead the young men about whose education he had been asked "to imitate the fine actions of monsieur le maréchal their grandfather"; the future Grand Condé spoke of the "holy ambition" that his father's achievements had given him. Nobles could reconcile personal ambition with respect for dynastic traditions, though (we will see) significant latent tensions remained.

But other difficulties could not be so easily concealed. Linking civic engagement with images of passion, ambition, and change posed an immediate problem, by placing the individual's civic attachments in the realm of emotion, an area of life that (so important intellectual traditions taught) had less reality, less permanence than the domain of reason. Insofar as aristocratic civic life rested on youthful emotions, it acquired the instability, illusions, and moral uncertainties of love. And in fact aristocratic political actors spoke of their choices in highly emotional, even erotic terms. Pierre Lenet, devoted agent of the Condé during the Fronde, described his choice to follow the Condé into rebellion: "A great love [*amitié*] such as I had for the prince, a great desire for vengeance, or a great concern that I had only for him—only these could involve me in such an affair."[39] Retz too described political engagement as a form of passionate love: "Men forget themselves during these fevers of state, which resemble frenzies. I knew in those times substantial citizens who were persuaded to the point of martyrdom . . . of the justice of the princes' cause. I knew others . . . who would have joyfully died defending the court."[40] Henri de Campion described his "zeal and affection for [the duc de Beaufort] that no amount of bad treatment has made me lose"; and Montrésor claimed that "from childhood I had the honor of giving myself to M. le duc d'Orléans . . . by my own inclination," with no other object "than his glory and my duty."[41] Entry to political life, as these men described it, resulted from passionate feelings appropriate to youth.

Others stressed the more concrete role of passionate feelings in political life. "Ambition and gallantry formed the soul of that court," wrote Madame de Lafayette of the court of Henri II, "and preoccupied men and women equally. There were so many interests and so many different cabals, and the women had such a large part in them, that love was always mixed up with business and business with love."[42] Directly as well as metaphorically, political life might turn on affections and passions. Political choices and love had inherent similarities; at the royal court, so Madame de Lafayette and others suggested, they overlapped and reinforced each other.

A second problem strengthened this association of politics with the irrational: the problem of defining rational objectives to which noblemen might direct their ambitions. For poor country gentlemen like

39. Lenet, *Mémoires*, 191–92.
40. Retz, *Mémoires*, 703.
41. Henri de Campion, *Mémoires*, 279; Montrésor, *Mémoires*, 215–16.
42. Madame de Lafayette, *Romans et nouvelles*, ed. Emile Magne (Paris, 1961), 252. The issue of ambition lies at the center of A. J. Krailsheimer, *Studies in Self-Interest, from Descartes to La Bruyère* (Oxford, 1962).

Monluc or de Pontis, ambition and self-interest had clear directions. These men sought to acquire positions, property, and the honor that went with them. For nobles like Condé, who already enjoyed high position and enormous wealth, the meanings of ambition and interest were less clear.

The problem worried contemporaries and led them to speculate on the nature of ambition itself and on the illusions that surrounded it. Ambition might appear a straightforward pursuit of self-interest, but to seventeenth-century observers both the drive and its objects lacked clarity. Thus for La Rochefoucauld, the cardinal de Retz "seems ambitious without being so; vanity and those around him led him to undertake great things."[43] Retz himself offered lengthy analyses of how participants in the Fronde had misunderstood self-interest, had indeed acted directly contrary to it.[44] The conspirator Montrésor had the same vision of his patron Gaston d'Orléans; the prince's personal weakness had made him "ingenious at fooling himself about his own interests."[45] Christian morality taught that ambitious pursuit of self-interest sacrificed spiritual reality for impermanent and illusory ends. Seventeenth-century aristocratic writers offered more troubling questions in purely secular terms. Illusion might cloud even the most worldly self-interest; ambition itself might be fraudulent, a deceptive counterfeit of the drive for achievement.

Most important, their preoccupation with ambition forced nobles to think about the problems of success and failure and to seek explanation of failure in the nature of the polity itself. The result was a deeply pessimistic vision of the political community. A strikingly large number of the noble memoir writers described failed ambitions—an especially striking number given that most memorialists used their remarkable achievements to justify writing about themselves. Of course, the collapse of so many aristocratic political calculations during the Fronde gave particular impetus to thoughts about failure. Retz, La Rochefoucauld, and their fellow conspirators had to reflect on the uncertainty of events and the downfall of their plans.[46] But the theme of

43. Quoted in Retz, *Mémoires*, xix.
44. Ibid., Pamphlet 6, 986ff.
45. Montrésor, *Mémoires*, 215.
46. A point emphasized by Marc Fumaroli, "Les mémoires du XVIIe siècle: Au carrefour des genres en prose," *XVIIe Siècle* 94–95 (1971): 7–37.

failure had held a prominent place in aristocratic writing since the six-teenth century, and it reflected more than particular episodes or the affirmation of royal power after 1652.

In this as in much else, Monluc offered a pioneering example. Though proud of his successful career and eager that others follow his example, he could not avoid expressing bitterness at the neglect he had suffered since the death of Charles IX; and he assumed that his audience, the future captains to whom he directed his reminis-cences, "will say to me: 'And what will we do if we don't save and profit from the soldiers' pay? When the war is over, we'll go to the poorhouse: for neither the king nor anyone else will worry about us.' "[47] Like Monluc, de Pontis offered his life story as one of ascent from humble beginnings, but he too expressed bitterness at the result of his efforts. "I could scarcely persuade myself," he wrote, "that they could possibly forget an officer who had grown old in the army, and whose long services were known by the whole court. . . . [T]he long experience that I had of the world had not yet taught me that the service one gives to princes often seems to them well repaid by prison or by the death that one suffers for their glory and for that of their states."[48]

De Pontis was not alone in attributing his failure to the ingratitude of the great. Nobles saw such ingratitude everywhere. Service to the great, all contemporaries agreed, provided the appropriate structure for aristocratic political life, but such service involved no equality of commitment. The French princes, reflected Bussy-Rabutin, "know well that after giving a thousand vexations to a gentleman, the least of their caresses will bring him back and make him forget all the past."[49] Henri de Campion described the ill treatment he had received from several princes and concluded that "it is dangerous, with many princes, to be known as a man of the highest probity; the ingratitude natural to most of them prevents them from giving recognition for ser-vices received; and the assurance of not being deserted when in dis-grace removes the fear that would alone make them assist those they believe capable of finding employment elswhere."[50] Montrésor told

47. Monluc, *Commentaires*, 28–29.
48. De Pontis, *Mémoires*, 32: 411.
49. Bussy-Rabutin, *Mémoires*, 181.
50. Campion, *Mémoires*, 200.

how Gaston d'Orléans came to look on him "with all the indifference that a prince can direct to a gentleman in his service."[51]

Further down the social scale, petty nobles voiced comparable complaints about their aristocratic patrons. In 1618 a guard at one of the La Trémoille castles wrote to his patron's secretary complaining of ill health and that several letters had come to the castle "without even mentioning me, . . . which greatly surprised me, in view of the friendship that you always showed me during my prosperity; I beg you to continue it in my affliction. . . . Is there some means of making my need clear to Madame? . . . I am here far from relatives and friends."[52] A few years later, comparable complaints arrived from other La Trémoille dependents: one "is upset at not having had any news of you or of Monseigneur"; another "has always been ready to receive Monseigneur's commands, but he has not been willing to honor me with them."[53]

All of these complaints suggested the instability and fundamental inequality of political relations. Nobles described, in language suggestive of seduction and sexual submissiveness, giving themselves willingly and completely to those they served. But, so they claimed, they received no comparable emotional commitment in return; the great used them coldly, then neglected and finally abandoned them. Political failure, in other words, derived from a moral failure at the heart of the social hierarchy. Nobles suffered for the unwillingness of the great to honor their obligations to their dependents.

Comparable criticisms were directed at the king himself: he too, as disappointed aristocrats described the matter, refused to honor obligations to those who had served him, instead showering gifts on the disloyal. Henri IV's reign displayed the problem with special clarity, for he subdued his extreme Catholic opponents with bribes and gave them an important role in his reign. The La Trémoilles, Protestants and closely allied to the families who had followed Henri through his years of trouble, preserved among their correspondence a satirical manuscript entitled "Defense of the King Against Those Who Criticize Him That He Gives More to His Enemies Than to His Servants." "You acknowledge that he loves his enemies—join them," counselled the pamphlet. "[H]e caresses those who rob him—spare no effort to

51. Montrésor, *Mémoires*, 215–16.
52. AN 1 AP 642, Aubespin to M. de Chandol, 28 April 1618.
53. AN 1 AP 648, Chateauneuf to Madame, 12 November 1621, 9 March 1622.

do likewise." There was more to be won in this way "than . . . you might ever gain by your cowardly ambitions, which he so scorns." Monarchical ingratitude, the pamphlet argued, derived from the principle that the king stood above ordinary bonds of obligation and reasoning. The pamphlet mockingly dismissed those "feeble minds that judge only by appearances and lack sufficient vision to penetrate the secret cabinet of this prince's intentions."[54] Like the great aristocracy, the king could not be trusted to reward loyal service.

The La Trémoilles and their circle had of course special reasons for bitterness. But their pamphlet accurately captured elements in the monarchy's own descriptions of its actions. The Crown did in fact claim to stand above legal restrictions, and it stood still more clearly above the expectations of its servants. It offered both rewards and forgiveness as it chose, according to standards of judgment that only the king himself could fully understand. This is the stance that Corneille defends in concluding both *Le Cid* and *Horace* with instances of monarchical grace, moments in which rulers dramatically place other considerations before those of legality. Thus the conclusion of *Horace:* "The art and power of defending the Crown / Are gifts that heaven gives to few. / In such servants consists the power of kings, / And such servants stand above the power of law."[55] In appearance a justification of aristocratic privilege, at deeper levels Corneille's argument subordinated both privilege and law to monarchical need. Against this need, apparently reasonable claims for reward and recognition could have no force. The Crown's secret reasoning did not lead to a larger rationality of political structure; on the contrary, it meant that the Crown would often fail its most loyal servants.

Other criticisms emerged as aristocrats interpreted political failure. That politics depended on language and opinion led to dark thoughts about the political actor's vulnerability. His standing depended on what others said, and so he was constantly vulnerable to slander.

54. AN 1 AP 397, 43, 45. For discussions of Henri IV's reign as a turning point that disturbed many of his supporters, see Dewald, *Formation*, 40–54; Robert Descimon, *Qui étaient les Seize?* (Paris, 1984); Marc Fumaroli, *L'âge de l'éloquence: Rhétorique et "res literaria" de la Renaissance au seuil de l'époque classique* (Paris, 1980).

55. *Horace*, lines 1751–54, in Pierre Corneille, *Oeuvres complètes*, ed. André Stegman (Paris, 1963), 267. Corneille here follows the ideas that the French monarchy actually applied in its pardons: see Natalie Zemon Davis, *Fiction in the Archives* (Stanford, 1987).

Complaints of malicious talk appear throughout seventeenth-century correspondence. They suggested both that reputations were fragile and that an array of enemies surrounded the political actor. "I cannot imagine," wrote the prince de Tarente to the minister Brienne in 1658, "that our enemies' slander can render our best actions criminal and useless to the king and the state." Six months later he denounced "those who drew this disgrace on me . . . their malice . . . so full of passion."[56] Because political life rested on language, so Tarente and others believed, political standing was subject to irrational and unjust reversals. Virtuous actions risked misrepresentation or concealment, because enemies surrounded the political actor and could turn language against him.

Such misrepresentations contributed to a larger problem, the play of irrational or entirely unpredictable forces in frustrating efforts and expectations. Political society, so these discussions of the unexpected suggested, had ultimately no understandable structure. La Rochefoucauld made the point when he considered the career of the duc de Bouillon: "The duc de Bouillon's ambitions rested on all the qualities that ought to have secured its success. He was valiant and had a perfect knowledge of warfare. He had an easy, natural, ingratiating eloquence. His mind was clear, inventive, and capable of untangling the most difficult matters. . . . But such great advantages were often of no use to him, because of the stubbornness of his fortune, which almost always opposed his prudence." For La Rochefoucauld, this was only one instance of the larger phenomenon, "the care that fortune takes to raise and lay low men's merit."[57] La Rochefoucauld's turn to fortune as an explanatory tool typified the fascination Machiavelli held for seventeenth-century nobles and the extended commentary his writings received in seventeenth-century Paris.[58]

Implicit in such comments were doubts about the possibility of political knowledge, a sense of the difficulty of understanding the polity. Fortune seemed to govern political life because real knowledge of the polity was so difficult to attain. There were, first, practical and social obstacles to knowledge, about which Retz expanded complacently: "There are points in public affairs that escape . . . the most clear-

56. AN 1 AP 396, Prince de Tarente to Brienne, 9 August 1658, 37.

57. La Rochefoucauld, *Maximes et réflexions diverses*, 151.

58. Discussed by William Farr Church, *Richelieu and Reason of State* (Princeton, 1972), 44–80.

sighted and that we would encounter much more often in the histories if they had all been written by those who were in on the secrets of things and who, consequently, would have been above the ridiculous vanity of those impertinent authors who, born in the barnyard and never having moved beyond the antechamber, pride themselves on knowing everything that happens in the cabinet. I am amazed in this regard by the insolence of those nobodies who, imagining they have penetrated the hearts of those most involved in these matters, leave no event without claiming to have explicated its origins and consequences."[59] Knowledge could be a social prerogative, limited to those able to participate in political life and to those with the largeness of soul to understand the motivations of political actors.[60]

But the nobles also saw a deeper problem: the inherent limits on any knowledge of political affairs. As most noblemen described it, reality lay in particulars and often could not be captured in more general formulations. "Those who write the fat histories," wrote François de La Noue in the 1580s, "having so many facts to present, more numerous than the leaves of a great oak, cannot always do so by noting all the particulars that go with them."[61] Despite his claims for the participant-author, Retz too could take a skeptical stance, arguing that "even those who are the closest [to political events] cannot prevent themselves, on an infinite number of occasions, from taking for realities appearances that are sometimes false in every respect."[62]

A further problem for political knowledge lay in the evolving nature of reality itself. Retz made the uncertainties of political reality the central theme of his memoirs; and though his explanations for uncertainty varied widely, ultimately he emphasized the inadequacy of either the past or common sense as a guide. People's expectations of the possible, Retz argued repeatedly, touched only a small part of what might actually happen: "What I've seen during our troubles has made clear to me, on more than one occasion, what I had not been able to imagine in the history books. One finds there facts so opposed to one another that they are unbelievable. But experience teaches us

59. Retz, *Mémoires*, 485.

60. See Orest Ranum, *Artisans of Glory* (Chapel Hill, 1980), for the seventeenth-century idea that only a military nobleman could write about war.

61. François de La Noue, *Mémoires*, in Michaud and Poujolat, eds., *Nouvelle collection des mémoires relatifs à l'histoire de France . . .* , 9 (Paris, 1854), 593.

62. Retz, *Mémoires*, 609.

that what is unbelievable is not false."[63] Reason did not always govern political actions; there might be errors, "so obvious that people with common sense could not have made them."[64] Neither abstract principles nor past experience could capture realities that were so various, so large, so susceptible to change.

The seventeenth century's great examples of political success strengthened this conviction that the polity was fundamentally impervious to rational understanding. Richelieu's successes, both within France and within Europe as a whole, seemed as inexplicable to contemporary nobles as their own failures. Montrésor, one of the cardinal's failed opponents, turned for explanation to the familiar notion of fortune: Richelieu's success, he wrote, came, not from "his wise choices [*sa bonne conduite*], which I have not noticed, . . . nor from a far-seeing mind, nor from personal greatness, but simply from his being a very lucky man, sustained in the difficulties that he encountered rather by fortune than by the prudence that many have wished to see in him."[65] Henri de Campion debated Richelieu's character and situation with some friends shortly before the cardinal's death, coming to the more interesting conclusion that neither could be understood in rational or human terms. "What I call genius," concludes the dialogue's leading figure, "is nothing other than the grandeur and nobility [*générosité*] of certain exalted natures, that you might say have come to earth with an absolute right to command others. In fact this genius carries an indefinable impression of such absolute power over those who let themselves be guided by it, that it is only with an effort that one opposes its will."[66] Richelieu could only be compared to such other political geniuses as Alexander and Caesar, and neither moral nor even intellectual judgment really applied to him. Such leaders, Campion and his friends concluded, transcended normal analysis.[67] Turenne seemed to Retz a comparable example, a political actor whose choices placed him above most people's understanding:

63. Ibid., 601.
64. Ibid., 593.
65. Montrésor, *Mémoires*, 215; see also 202: "[T]outes les considérations qu'un sage ministre auroit eues et toutes les mesures qu'il auroit prises lui tournèrent à mépris, emporté par son impétuosité naturelle, que je ne saurois nommer que fureur désespérée, et lui un fléau de Dieu pour le châtiment des hommes. . . ."
66. Campion, *Mémoires*, 281.
67. Ibid., 279–81.

as someone of extraordinary merit, he could succeed with what would be mistakes for others.[68]

Seventeenth-century nobles employed a variety of metaphors as they sought to convey their vision of political situations as unstable and deceptive. We have seen the readiness of some to turn to the notion of fortune. Others used religious images. Thus Madame de Sévigné, in speaking of the disgrace of her friend, the minister Pomponne: "[W]e saw him leave this house a minister and a secretary of state; he returned that same evening to Paris stripped of everything and a private citizen. Do you believe that all these actions occur by chance? No, no, avoid such thoughts; it's God who guides it all, and whose plans always command adoration, though to us they be bitter and hidden. . . . And if we lose sight of this divine Providence? Without it, one would have to hang oneself five or six times a day."[69] Retz too could use religious imagery, though with ironic intent. Political life displayed choices so contrary to the actors' interests and personalities that the "blindness of which Scripture speaks so often is, even in human terms, sensible and palpable in men's actions."[70] Such language emerged easily from contemporary religious concern, with its stress on the instability of human affairs and the hopelessness of prediction.[71]

But the most common metaphors for political life derived from the theater. Saint-Evremond managed to combine theatrical and commercial imagery to suggest the inevitability of misperception and failure in court society: "Everyone offers his merchandise as best he can, it's the buyer's fault if he always takes it for what it purports to be [*pour bonne*]; merit wears out, beauty passes, the world is a comedy, each comedian plays his part in it, but there is nothing so ugly as to show oneself when it's over."[72] Retz turned constantly to the theater to

68. Retz, *Mémoires*, 216.
69. Madame de Sévigné, *Lettres*, ed. Roger Gailly, 3 vols. (Paris, Pléiade, 1955), 2: 530, 6 December 1679.
70. Retz, *Mémoires*, 660.
71. See Antoine Adam, *Du mysticisme à la révolte: Les jansénistes du XVIIe siècle* (Paris, 1968); Lucien Goldmann, *Le dieu caché: Essai sur la vision tragique dans les Pensées de Pascal et dans le théâtre de Racine* (Paris, 1955).
72. Saint-Evremond, *Oeuvres en prose*, 2: 151. On the interaction of theater and money in early modern culture, see Jean-Christophe Agnew, *Worlds Apart: The Market and the Theater in Anglo-American Thought, 1550–1750* (Cambridge, 1986).

describe and explain his situation. It offered powerful images for the contrast that he perceived between the knowledgeable few and the deluded many, contrasting the inner workings of the political "machine" (an image that he took from the stage) with what the spectators in the audience could see and understand. His own move into the center of political life he described as a shift from having been "in the parterre, or at best in the orchestra, playing and chatting with the violinists," whereas now he was to "climb onto the stage [*monter sur le théâtre*]"; and repeatedly he contrasted the knowledge of those on the stage with the ignorance of those watching from the audience.[73] Bussy-Rabutin had a similar view: "Society and especially the court are nothing but pretense, and . . . every appearance that one saw there ordinarily could not have been further from reality."[74]

Even Retz's discussion of political possibility, his belief that reality was more varied than common sense might anticipate, derived from theatrical problems and language. This language echoed contemporary debate surrounding the *vraisemblable* and its relationship to both the possible and the real. " 'We have a natural tendency,' " so Corneille quoted Aristotle, " 'to believe that what has never happened could not happen.' " For the dramatist, as Corneille understood the matter, a central problem was precisely that of disentangling the plausible from the real. Corneille arrived at an opposite emphasis from Retz's: the dramatist concluded that the public's expectations about the likely demanded respect, for otherwise the play would fail.[75] But the set of problems Corneille had raised dominated Retz's thinking about political knowledge. Politics was the art of the possible, but the politician's task was to understand what *was* possible in larger terms than contemporary understanding of *vraisemblance* permitted.

However they were used, theatrical images of political life carried uncomfortable associations. Retz used the theater to stress the dishonesties that constituted political life. Pascal underlined another source of discomfort in metaphors of theater, contrasting the flimsiness of the theater-state with the straightforward realities of violence: "Soldiers are the only ones who do not disguise themselves . . . , because their role is really more essential; they establish themselves by force, the others by masquerade. That is why our kings have not attempted to

73. Retz, *Mémoires*, 45 and passim.
74. Bussy-Rabutin, *Mémoires*, 1: 179.
75. Corneille, "De la tragédie," *Oeuvres complètes*, 838.

disguise themselves. They have not dressed up in extraordinary clothes to show what they really are, but they have themselves surrounded by guards, scarred veterans. . . . They do not wear the trappings, they simply have the power."[76] By contrast, magistrates and doctors needed costumes to impose themselves. Theatrical power of the sort represented by the magistrate might function effectively, persuading some to follow its directions, for illusion and imagination have a grip on nearly everyone. The realities of power, though, lay elsewhere, in the instruments of violence. Pascal's vision of politics thus differed sharply from Retz's, but shared common emphases and language. Both pointed to the theatrical form of political and social life; both saw much of this life in terms of flux, imagination, deception.

Ultimately, then, theatrical imagery suggested a troubling view of the polity's moral stature. Contemporaries continued into the late seventeenth century to link the theater with a variety of vices: lust, falsehood, slander, freedom from restraints. There was no assurance that a Christian theater could exist at all. Even Madame de Maintenon's efforts to create one for her maidens at Saint-Cyr produced anxieties, as courtiers came to ogle the actresses rather than to seek edification;[77] and to the end of the century the pious argued that Christians should avoid the theater altogether. Clearly a state that functioned by means of theatrical trappings and trickery could not easily be understood as a Christian enterprise.

Even for the secular-minded, to view the state as a form of theater, in which all political actors adopted some form of disguise and a handful of insiders sought systematically to deceive the rest, undercut a moral vision of the community. If political life preserved a moral center, so aristocratic writers were led to suggest, it lay in the individual rather than the political community. For the theatrical vision of politics implied that the real individual stood beneath the costume that her/his political role demanded. And the individual had a continuity that the political drama lacked. Retz made this contrast between individual reality and shifting political drama one of the main purposes of his memoirs. He sought to show that he had remained constant, despite the political changes taking place around him. In this he

76. Blaise Pascal, *Pensées*, trans. A. J. Krailsheimer (London, 1966), 41.
77. Carolyn Lougee, *Le Paradis des Femmes: Women, Salons, and Social Stratification in Seventeenth-Century France* (Princeton, 1976).

expressed with special clarity an underlying theme in many of the seventeenth-century memoirs: a contrast between the continuity of the individual's life and the unpredictable swirls of public drama.

The political experiences and expectations that have thus far been considered centered on the royal court, where political ambition was fiercest and failure most painful. Yet provincial politics too had deceptions, disappointments, uncertainties, and calculations. Much of the rhetoric that has been examined thus far, though it applied most readily to the court, could as easily describe provincial relationships. This rhetoric, in other words, represented more than a response to the specific experiences of the royal court; it represented a deeper pattern in aristocratic culture.

To be sure, a lively rhetoric of provincial probity subsisted in the seventeenth century; and the powers that substantial landowners continued to exercise gave real content to their dependents' claims of loyal service. "I have been an official of the *maison* for thirty years, and my ancestors for more than one hundred years," wrote one of the La Trémoilles' employees, prefacing a request that his son be given a vacant position; "in continuing my service I would wish that it also be continued by my children."[78] Such language emphasized the stable loyalties that the family enjoyed at its provincial landed base. Generations of local notables had offered the family service and had recognized its leadership. The contrast between solid loyalties of this kind and the instability of the royal court gave rise to consoling reflections during times of political trouble. In 1656 the marquise de la Moussaye wrote to her sister after visiting the prince de Tarente, exiled to his estates for his role during the Fronde: "[S]eeing him," she wrote, "one must acknowledge that virtue in this age is an obstacle to happiness; were it otherwise, he would be in high favor. . . . He is perfectly honored at Laval and could do there (so they tell me) anything he wishes, winning hearts as he has and everyone praising his behavior."[79] For the marquise, provincial loyalty contrasted with the amoral character of the court. At court virtue might suffer slanders and the most capa-

---

78. AN 1 AP 645, Billaud to Chandor, 22 July 1621. For investigation of these loyalties in another provincial setting, see Jonathan Dewald, *Pont-St-Pierre, 1398–1789: Lordship, Community, and Capitalism in Early Modern France* (Berkeley, 1987), 199–207; and, more generally, Sharon Kettering, *Patrons, Brokers, and Clients* (New York, 1986).

79. AN 1 AP 435, Lettres de la marquise de la Moussaye, 70: 17 December 1656.

ble might fail, but no such opacity characterized provincial relations: there, appearance and inner reality coincided.

Yet the marquise herself could describe provincial politics in quite different terms, as a play of contending interests in which success demanded careful calculation and secrecy, and in which enmity and slander constantly threatened. Alert to all of these dangers in provincial politics, she sent her sister a coded report in 1645 describing the political factions within the Estates of Brittany, using numbers to represent the assembly's leading figures and some of the issues with which it dealt.[80] Two months later she again wrote from the Estates to her sister, this time of the effects of faction and deceit on her own family: "I would never have believed that the rage those who surround monsieur your husband feel toward mine could have led them to report such absolute falsehoods, wanting you to believe that he has abandoned your husband. Had they written you, my dear sister, that he has been deserted by everyone *but* Monsieur de la Moussaye they would have told you the truth. . . . He ought to have been believed in his counsels, which would have avoided all these difficulties, but some *gens de robe* were the instruments used to lead him into the traps that were set for him. . . . M. de la Moussaye continues to devote himself wholly to your interests."[81] Just as at court, political actors had constantly to be aware of the traps their opponents set; enmities were universal and led naturally to misrepresentation, destroying the credit of the most loyal. There was in fact no more transparency in provincial than in court politics.

Calculation, enmity, and disguise provided organizing themes that other nobles employed in thinking about provincial politics. Like the marquise de la Moussaye, the duc de La Trémoille used numerical codes in describing the interests and groupings within the Estates of Brittany. He was eager, he explained in a letter to his son, "to know whether 179 will attend the Estates, since from this we can infer whether 24 supports the interests of 59, for we haven't been able to learn it otherwise than by rumor, which goes against us."[82] The issue was La Trémoille's long-standing struggle with the Rohan family for precedence in the Estates. La Trémoille had mobilized his friends for the struggle, but traditional loyalties offered no assurance: "I am

80. AN 1 AP 435, 21, 8 January 1645.
81. AN 1 AP 435, 19, Rennes, 1 March 1645.
82. AN 1 AP 394, Letters of Henri de La Trémoille, duc de Thouars, 1643–1651, 30, to the prince de Tarente, 29 April 1651.

afraid that our friends here may cool off because of my absence. . . .
[O]ur near ones ought not to abandon us in our need."[83]

Other matters stimulated La Trémoille to even stronger complaints
about the disloyalty and self-interestedness of those who ought to
have served his family. In 1658, after an unfavorable ruling from the
Parlement of Rennes concerning one of his properties, the duc wrote
of his opponent: "[E]very possession that he has . . . comes entirely
from the kindness of my *maison,* which seems to have raised his
only to bring out its insolence and ingratitude." He had as well a
strong sense that the Parlement itself had failed in its duties toward
him. From now on, he wrote, he planned to have his cases moved
to another court, "since I am so badly treated by the one from which
I anticipated the most protection, and whose interests I can claim
to have best served and most suffered for."[84] A few years later he
had similar complaints about a formerly dependent cleric. He asked
that the cleric be treated "as the enemy of my person and my *maison,*
who employs the property he has received from us to injure me."[85]
Patronage networks might function effectively within the provincial
setting, but they could as easily collapse, producing an enraged disil-
lusionment with local loyalties. As a result, local politics demanded
the same continuous assessment of interests and intentions as the
royal court.

Such assumptions extended to the lower levels of the seigneurial
structure, affecting relations even within the apparently stable world
of local loyalties: petty nobles and officials too described their conflicts
in terms of disguised enmities and slander, in other words, as requiring that political analysis push beneath the level of superficial politeness to underlying interests and conflicts. When one of the La Trémoilles' seigneurial clerks found himself threatened and insulted by a
local captain, he decided that the captain "was pushed to this by some
of our enemies, [having been] induced to say what he did without any
reason, because otherwise they would not have dared."[86]

At some point in the 1620s, the duc de La Trémoille had his secretary
copy out the views of an anonymous political analyst. "Man's life on

83. AN 1 AP 394, 31, 16 April 1651.
84. AN 1 AP 396, to comte de Villeneuve, 25 October 1658, 51.
85. AN 1 AP 396, 23 October 1664, 385.
86. AN 1 AP 645, La Trémoille correspondence, Billaud to Madame, 20 February
1622.

earth," wrote this author, "is a perpetual war; hence he who does not fight or is indisposed to fight lives either badly or not at all. Either the enemies who surround us strangle us or we advance at their expense; they are strong only because of our weakness and cowardice. To lack resentment is to be thought either cowardly or stupid, as lacking the wit to perceive an offense or the heart to avenge it; thus one remains exposed to violence as long as one does not oppose it, [inspiring] fear being the most suitable means of protecting oneself against it."[87]

La Trémoille's interest in these ideas illustrates one of this chapter's principal contentions: French nobles readily viewed their society as a collection of intensely competing individuals rather than an organic whole, organized around a stable hierarchy or effective traditions. Seventeenth-century nobles, this chapter has argued, interpreted their lives in terms of individual ambition. Ideas about hierarchy and tradition stood in the backgrounds of these lives and might be employed during moments of ideological debate; nobles often professed to believe that both social and natural worlds had orderly structures and that these structures provided the basis for their privileges. In the foreground of their lives, however, was constant emphasis on change, conflict, and personal ambition. Ambition, it was thought, specifically characterized the *noblesse d'épée* and the courtly society within which it moved. With ambition went a sharp sensitivity to time and a belief in the importance of engaging in public life. Society constantly changed, so that neither traditional attachments nor established practices necessarily retained their validity. Withdrawal to a private role drew almost entirely negative moral judgments, as a sign of impotence and failure. Nobles defined their lives in public terms; at least until age left them unsuited to be political animals, they viewed themselves as participants in a public world.

Yet seventeenth-century aristocratic culture, so I have argued here, also rendered the political world morally problematic. To Christian belief, of course, ambition itself was a vice, but anxiety in this regard rarely surfaced. Of more concern to contemporaries, ambition almost inevitably failed, as the soldier and courtier aged and ceased to be either useful or pleasing, or as superiors merely turned their affections elsewhere. Even those who praised ambition treated it as a passion, which reason could not entirely govern and which might easily attach to illusory objects.

87. AN 1 AP 397, 64–65.

Failures of this kind led French nobles to troubling questions about the political community in which they acted. As stress on ambition contrasted with belief in dynastic continuities, so contemporary visions of politics stood in tension with confidence in the monarchical order. The public world, as the nobles presented it, was dominated by the play of the irrational and the illusory. Theatrical metaphors were a favorite mode of describing these qualities and suggested the moral doubts that accompanied political life; the political actor readily saw himself as manipulated by invisible stage managers. Much else in public life suggested its lack of rational order. Civic attachments rested on passionate emotional attractions, analogous to sexual attractions and sometimes deriving immediately from them; participation in public life brought the dangers of enmity and slander. Nobles interpreted even the long-standing relations of local politics in terms of repeated betrayals and disguises. Ultimately, so Machiavellian a view of civic life made the individual seem more real than the community. Seventeenth-century nobles continued to write of an organic, unified society of orders, but their most vigorous cultural contribution lay elsewhere, in an autobiographical literature that sought to display the continuity of the self within an often irrational, fluctuating political environment.

# 2

# The Profession of Arms

"Since every man has to choose a profession . . . , it seems to me that there is none more honorable or more essential to a gentleman than that of arms. . . . [N]obility is acquired by arms; it is by arms also that it ought to be maintained." Thus Nicolas Faret, in his enormously popular depiction of how the *honnête homme* ought to make his way in the world.[1] In fact, most sixteenth- and seventeenth-century nobles never ventured into war but instead lived quiet lives as country gentlemen.[2] But the wealthier nobles did expect to perform military service; and Faret's comment suggests the centrality of warfare as one of the myths that defined the early modern nobility even for those who stayed home. In public discussion, their sacrifices in war justified privilege and gave nobles the right to address the king in special terms. More privately, war offered a cultural reference point, a source of stories and a model of behavior. Even the pacific Gilles de Gouberville read chivalric tales in his quiet Norman manor. Such talk of war defined the outer limits of the *noblesse d'épée* as a social group. The language of the nobles' disputes with other social groups more often centered on the incomprehension of soldier for civilian than on questions of genealogy.[3]

---

1. Nicolas Faret, *L'honnête homme, ou l'art de plaire à la cour,* ed. Maurice Magendie (Paris, 1925; repr. Geneva, 1970), 12. It is worth noting that although the passage imitates Castiglione, Faret's emphasis is very different; what Castiglione makes a preference between two acceptable courses, Faret makes virtually obligatory. The work's popularity is suggested by its reprintings in 1630, 1631, 1633, 1636, and twice in 1639 (ibid., li).

2. A point emphasized by James Wood, *The Nobility of the* Election *of Bayeux, 1463–1666: Continuity Through Change* (Princeton, 1980); and Jean-Marie Constant, "Nobles et paysans en Beauce aux XVIe et XVIIe siècles," Thèse d'Etat, University of Paris IV, 1978.

3. For a vigorous statement of the nobles' claim that they paid an *impôt de sang,* see François Bluche, *Louis XIV* (Paris, 1986). For other discussions of nobles' military involvement and attitudes, see Jonathan Dewald, *Pont-St-Pierre, 1398–1789: Lordship, Community, and Capitalism in Early Modern France* (Berkeley, 1987), 168–78; Ellery Schalk, *From Valor to Pedigree: Ideas of Nobility in France in the Sixteenth and*

This chapter attempts to define some of the meanings that war had for sixteenth- and seventeenth-century nobles. Such meanings may seem obvious, in view of the role arms had played in aristocratic self-perceptions through the Middle Ages; and historians of the early modern nobility have not hesitated to contrast the calculating, self-controlled mentality of the educated magistrate with the backward outlook of the warrior.[4] Yet, so this chapter argues, warfare as practiced during the sixteenth and seventeenth centuries in its own ways corroded traditional forms of thought. For seventeenth-century nobles, the experience of war was only partly an inheritance from the Middle Ages. The changing technology, expanding scale, and increasingly bureaucratic organization of seventeenth-century warfare required specific forms of calculation and political reflection. Just as important, military careers unfolded in ways that detached nobles from inherited settings and forced them to confront intellectual and moral novelties.

Warfare, as Nicolas Faret made clear, was a professional choice, a focus for the ambition which (the previous chapter argued) offered seventeenth-century nobles a guiding theme for understanding their lives. That ambition had an important place in military careers seemed obvious to contemporaries. We have heard the poet Malherbe contrast the moderate ambitions appropriate to a robe career with the lofty but uncertain ambitions appropriate to warfare.[5] Others used comparable language. Arnauld d'Andilly described his military uncle as governed by "wild ambition [*une ambition démesurée*]."[6] Henri de Rohan made ambition central to his view of proper government policy toward the army. Worried that young men might satisfy their ambitions elsewhere, he proposed that government "encourage men of honor and ambition to enroll, both by [giving them] hope of advanc-

*Seventeenth Centuries* (Princeton, 1986); Madeleine Foisil, *Le sire de Gouberville: Un gentilhomme normand au XVIe siècle* (Paris, 1981); and (with a very different analysis from the one presented here) Denis Crouzet, "Royalty, Nobility and Religion: Research on the Wars in Italy," *Proceedings of the Annual Meeting of the Western Society for French History* 18 (1991).

4. George Huppert, *Les Bourgeois Gentilshommes: An Essay on the Definition of Elites in Renaissance France* (Chicago, 1977), 45.

5. Above, Chapter 1.

6. Robert Arnauld d'Andilly, *Mémoires*, in M. Petitot, ed., *Collection des mémoires relatifs à l'histoire de France*, 33–34 (Paris, 1824), 33: 326.

ing to other honors if they embrace the craft of warfare and by closing off any other means of advancing [*parvenir*]."[7] Even those most delicate in their social discriminations accepted that advancement through military service was commonplace. "Bourgeois manners can sometimes be lost in the army," conceded the snobbish La Roche-foucauld, "but never at court."[8]

Basic realities of military practice underlay La Rochefoucauld's assumption that bourgeois families would use military service as a means of social mobility. Already by the late sixteenth century, the French army needed a substantial number of commoners as officers.[9] The linkage of war with economic advancement was still older. Froissart had described the straightforward economic motives of fourteenth- and early fifteenth-century captains. The Bascot de Mauléon, whom he met at the comte de Foix's court, immediately impressed Froissart with the worldly success he had attained: "He arrived with plenty of followers and baggage. . . . He had as many pack horses with him as any great baron, and he and his people took their meals off silver plate." Froissart promptly set out to understand this success story, drawing from the Bascot a tale of unpredictably changing fortunes: "Sometimes I have been so thoroughly down that I hadn't even a horse to ride, and at other times fairly rich, as luck came and went." Military life in the late Middle Ages was crudely oriented to financial success, and indeed was one of the great avenues to success.[10] But, in contrast to the language of the sixteenth and seventeenth centuries, Froissart and the Bascot placed images of fortune at the center of their understanding of success. Triumphs and reverses succeeded each other without apparent order, not as part of a coherent strategy of advancement. For most late medieval nobles, actual experience of war was more haphazard still; it involved only very occasional service in the enormous, unruly hosts the French kings led into battle.[11]

7. Henri de Rohan, *Le parfait capitaine ou abrégé des guerres des Commentaires de César*, new ed., expanded (n.p., 1757), 176–77.

8. François de La Rochefoucauld, *Maximes et réflexions diverses*, ed. Jacques Truchet (Paris, 1977), 79 (no. 393).

9. André Corvisier, *Armies and Societies in Europe, 1494–1789*, trans. Abigail T. Siddall (Bloomington, Ill., 1979), 163.

10. Jean Froissart, *Chronicles*, ed. Geoffrey Brereton (London, 1968), 280, 288. See Philippe Contamine, *Guerre, Etat et société à la fin du moyen âge* (Paris, 1972), 441–48, and K. B. Macfarlane, *The Nobility of Later Medieval England* (Oxford, 1973), for discussions of the economics of medieval warfare.

11. Contamine, *Guerre, Etat et société*, 44–45.

Although the sixteenth and seventeenth centuries brought alternative models of what it meant to be noble, they also brought a greater demand for soldiers, as armies grew in size and war became more ferocious. The army also became increasingly professional, providing long-term careers rather than occasional marauding.[12] In these circumstances, advancement within the army had a meaning that had not been possible in the years around 1400. Experience of battle was probably more common among the seventeenth-century nobility than among their sixteenth-century ancestors, for after 1635 the French army began a breathtaking expansion. The army had numbered 50,000 in the mid-sixteenth century. By the end of the religious wars it had reached 80,000, and it nearly doubled after 1635, when France entered the Thirty Years' War; after a small decline in the later seventeenth century, it swelled to 360,000 by 1710.[13] Its numbers alone assured that the army would be a mechanism of social mobility.

For nobles and bourgeois alike, service began very young, at the age of sixteen or seventeen.[14] Early experience of war gave a decisive turn to their views of the world, leaving many eager to fight throughout their lives and shaping even ideas about youth itself. After a few years in Jesuit colleges, his parents sent Bussy-Rabutin to war at age sixteen, then brought him back to Paris for some training at an academy: "[B]ut having for a certain time commanded a regiment, I had difficulty lowering myself to the obedience of a schoolboy and only stayed there eight months."[15] Military life meant early adulthood and reduced education, and it early left nobles disinclined to accept many forms of authority.

Nobles' enthusiasm for military activity suffered only from the relative peace that France enjoyed during the first third of the seventeenth century. Between the peace with Spain in 1598 and the formal French entry into the Thirty Years' War, only a few occasions offered the experiences and profits of warfare. During these years, nobles who

---

12. Ibid., 536–46.
13. Geoffrey Parker, *Europe in Crisis, 1598–1648* (London, 1979), 70; William Doyle, *The Old European Order, 1660–1800* (Oxford, 1978), 242.
14. For examples, Charles de Saint-Evremond, *Oeuvres en prose*, ed. René Ternois, 3 vols. (Paris, 1962–66), 1: xxiii–xxiv; Roger de Bussy-Rabutin, *Mémoires*, ed. Ludovic Lalanne, 2 vols. (Paris, 1857; repr. Westmead, 1972), 1: 5–8; Sieur de Pontis, *Mémoires*, in M. Petitot, ed., *Collections des mémoires relatifs à l'histoire de France*, 31–32 (Paris, 1824), 31: 213–14; Blaise de Monluc, *Commentaires, 1521–1576*, ed. Paul Courteault (Paris, Pléiade, 1964), 50; Dewald, *Pont-St-Pierre*, 168–69.
15. Bussy-Rabutin, *Mémoires*, 1: 8.

wanted experience of war had often to seek it abroad, and they did so in large numbers, traveling first to Holland and then to Germany. War was yet another characteristic seventeenth-century impetus to mobility, reinforcing the effects of duels and political miscalculation in creating exiles. "France being at peace, he went off to serve in Holland," as a genealogist wrote of one early-seventeenth-century nobleman.[16] Arnauld d'Andilly used almost the same words of his uncle: "[S]ince at that time there were no wars elsewhere, M. Arnauld went to seek it in Livonia," under Gustavus Adolphus.[17] The baron de Sirot, who eventually played a distinguished role in the Grand Condé's campaign of 1639, served for two years in France, then entered Maurice of Nassau's army, then fought in Piedmont, then in Hungary, and then under Wallenstein in Germany; after a brief stay at his estate, he fought in the Swedish army against Wallenstein, before rejoining the French armies at the time of the French entry in the Thirty Years' War. At that time, having served in a half-dozen armies across Europe, he was twenty-nine years old.[18] The connection between war and travel was not new. At the age of seventeen, wrote Monluc, "desire to go to Italy overtook me, from the rumors circulating about the fine fighting [*beaux faicts d'armes*] there"; he discussed his plans with a neighbor of his father's, "who told me so many things and recounted so many fine exploits, happening there every day," that the young man immediately set out to cross the mountains.[19]

Especially in the uncertain international politics of the early seventeenth century, such careers posed problems of moral choice. The comte de Souvigny recalled his uncle's experience: "Since there was peace in France, he went to the siege of Ostend, preferring to serve the king of Spain rather than the Dutch, because he was a good Catholic." Two of Souvigny's brothers, a few years later, went off "to learn to serve the king in Holland," but returned when they were told "that they could not attain their salvation so long as they served the heretical Dutch against the Catholic king of Spain."[20] Conversely, Henri de

16. François-Alexandre Aubert de La Chesnaye-Desbois, *Dictionnaire de la noblesse . . .*, 15 vols. (Paris, 1770–86), 9: 290.

17. Arnauld d'Andilly, *Mémoires*, 33: 326–27.

18. M. le duc d'Aumale, *Histoire des princes de Condé pendant les XVIe et XVIIe siècles*, 6 vols. (Paris, 1885), 4: 15.

19. Monluc, *Commentaires*, 30.

20. Comte de Souvigny, *Mémoires*, ed. Ludovic de Contenson, 3 vols. (Paris, 1906–09), 2: 44, 278.

Campion found himself in the Spanish armies in the Netherlands in 1634, on the eve of French entry into the Thirty Years' War and long after French opposition to Spain was clear, a situation he justified by the fact that "in truth I was just a poor younger son trying to make my way [*à faire fortune*]."[21] National and religious interests balanced uncertainly in such cases, leaving the individual nobleman very much on his own. He was seeking experience and skills, not responding to demands from the state or expectations generated by feudal tradition. "I was, at that time, in Germany, whither the wars, which had not yet finished there, had called me": so begins the century's most famous exploration of the individual's fundamental separation from society's moral and intellectual orders.[22] For early-seventeenth-century noblemen, Descartes's experience of voluntary exile, war, skepticism, and moral relativism must have carried familiar echoes.

Of course military careers might lead to immorality for simpler reasons, because of the brutality that camp life and fighting involved. This was one reason that notable families sometimes sought to discourage their sons from entering "the profession of arms." To seventeenth-century social theorists, military service was unquestionably the most glorious pursuit in French society, and for high aristocratic families it offered the only conceivable choice of career.[23] But this hierarchy of values was not so clearly established that families always welcomed their sons' choice of the military life. On the contrary, they often sought to direct their sons elsewhere. Early in the seventeenth century, the président de Nicolay received a letter from a provincial cousin whose son had decided on a military career. The son had made his choice despite his father's wishes; a military career was here an assertion of individuality. "The efforts I had made to follow in the traces of our forefathers and the advice you have always given me to set my children to studying," wrote the boy's irritated father to Nicolay, had led him to have the boy educated with care; "but I have been frustrated in these plans because he has entirely departed from my intentions in order to take up the path of arms. I have placed ex-

21. Henri de Campion, *Mémoires,* ed. Marc Fumaroli (Paris, 1967), 48–49.

22. René Descartes, *Discourse on Method,* trans. F. E. Sutcliffe (London, 1968), 35. For Descartes's self-conscious use of the genre of aristocratic autobiography, see Georg Misch, *Geschichte der Autobiographie,* 4 vols. (Frankfurt am Main, 1969), 4: 736–37.

23. For instance, Roland Mousnier et al., *Problèmes de stratification sociale: Deux cahiers de la noblesse pour les Etats généraux de 1649–1651* (Paris, 1965).

amples before him, and above all of you, my lord, who hold the finest dignities in France; but these have not changed his opinion; I am therefore compelled to send him to Paris to be trained at the academy, so that (God willing) he may appear among men of honor at least through arms, if he does not wish to through letters."[24] In this family, as in many others, there was nothing obvious about the superiority of arms to letters. Rather, a military career violated paternal ambitions and expectations.

Nicolay's cousin believed that letters offered surer hopes of advancement than arms (a point discussed above, Chapter 1). The squalor and uncertainties of camp life likewise encouraged hesitation. The brother of Madame de La Trémoille's secretary served in Holland in the 1620s, and a friend described his circumstances and concerns. When his father sent money, he immediately spent it all. "I advised him to save that money for his needs," reported the friend, "but he told me that he preferred to spend part of it, since he might lose it or have it stolen in the disorder and license of war. Such caution makes me think that he is not at all debauched, and that he wants to make something of himself. . . . [H]e told me that he has decided to go to Amsterdam and place himself with some merchant, a plan that I approved all the more fully because I see that the soldier's lot is very miserable."[25] The young man's father agreed. He commanded him to "continue in the army in that land if he cannot find some merchant with whom to apprentice himself. . . . [His father] orders him also to learn mathematics, as do several persons in his situation."[26]

The exchange illustrates again the complex cultural lines that met in a military career. There was little visible glory here. The young man was on his own, far from home and subject to the "license of war." Relatives and friends watched him closely, but they could only hope that readiness to spend frivolously actually betokened good sense and resistance to temptation. The young man was expected to use his time in Holland as an apprenticeship, to acquire the mathematical skills he would need whether merchant or soldier. The young man's social

24. AN 3 AP 59, 3F 4, 21 July 1605. See also Huppert, *Les Bourgeois Gentils-hommes,* for stress on the self-confidence of the robe and its dislike of military values; and John Hale, *War and Society in Renaissance Europe, 1450–1620* (Baltimore, 1985), for the demilitarization of aristocratic values in sixteenth-century Europe.

25. AN 1 AP 648, dossier Champdor, March 1626.

26. Ibid., 25 May 1626.

position was strikingly fluid: he came from the lettered milieu of seigneurial officials and secretaries; he served in the military; but he and
his family were quite ready for him to undertake a mercantile career—
which, surprisingly, proved to have intellectual affinities with the military. Even without the dangers of battle, military life posed worri-
some threats to the young man's well-being: theft, debauchery,
uncertainty.[27] The end of a military career was still less attractive, as
even its enthusiasts acknowledged. "The fear of finding oneself poor
and crippled, after having long served," wrote Henri de Rohan, "is a
powerful bridle holding back [enlistments]." Rohan's solution was to
encourage "men of ambition and ability [*vertu*] to enroll freely, by
closing the door on any other means of advancing."[28] Poverty was not
a real concern for the high aristocracy, but they too could fear the
scars and decrepitude military life might bring.

To these doubts about the value of a military career the evolution
of tactics during the seventeenth century added further anxieties.
"Nowadays we wage war as foxes rather than lions," observed Rohan, "and it is founded rather on sieges than on battles."[29] As Geoffrey Parker has pointed out, even the great battles of the sixteenth and
seventeenth centuries demonstrated the prominence of siege warfare,
for they arose from confrontations between besiegers and relief
columns.[30] With the development of both artillery and fortifications,
soldiers spent much of their time in trench warfare, amid horrors that
(because of their authors' focus on glorious events) receive only casual
mention in military memoirs.

Even without life in the trenches, there were horrors. Henri de
Campion described the siege of Saverne, in Alsace, which its defenders
had fortified brilliantly. After a disastrous full-scale assault, the army
settled down "to attack the besieged foot by foot." When a sortie by
the besieged killed five hundred attackers in one day, "the stench of

27. Cf. Hale, *War and Society,* for further stress on the unpleasantness of military
life; similarly, James Wood, "The Royal Army During the Early Wars of Religion,
1559–1576," in Mack P. Holt, ed., *Society and Institutions in Early Modern France*
(Athens, Georgia, 1991), demonstrates the very heavy losses that the French nobility
suffered in sixteenth-century combat.
28. Rohan, *Le parfait capitaine,* 177–78, 179; cf. Monluc's awareness of captains'
fear of poverty in old age, quoted above, Chapter 1.
29. *Le parfait capitaine,* 207; see Geoffrey Parker, *The Military Revolution: Military Innovation and the Rise of the West, 1500–1800* (Cambridge, 1988), 16, for the
circulation of this remark in England.
30. Parker, *Military Revolution,* 16.

their corpses, which we could not remove, and which were all on top of one another, was one of our great inconveniences during this siege." After forty days and two thousand deaths among the attackers, a lack of food finally forced the defenders to surrender. The next year, half of Campion's army died of plague "because of the multitude of women and children who were there and the pillage and, I believe, as punishment for all the evils that we did"; he himself contracted dysentery and, after five months of dragging illness, recovered only after leaving the army.[31]

Military life thus embodied a paradox obvious to thoughtful contemporaries. On the one hand, this was the pursuit for which the nobility existed, and which writers commonly presented as society's most glorious activity. On the other hand, warfare involved moral discomfort and physical squalor. War itself became steadily less glorious, as firearms and siege tactics increasingly dominated its practice. More profoundly, the pursuit of military experience required young men to leave the control of parents and feudal superiors, and it often led them to strange lands and heretical religions. It is not surprising that fathers hesitated to encourage their sons to pursue such a career.

Because contemporaries saw so clearly that warfare *was* a career, they gave considerable thought to the training and behavior that a young man needed to make his way successfully in it. Warfare did not demand the formal education of the future magistrate, but it did require a broad effort of self-formation. Social relations between magistrates and military nobles, whether at the level of seigneurial servants or at the more exalted level of the président de Nicolay and his cousin, ensured that such awareness touched the robe milieu as well as purely military families. Three years after his father had first complained to the président de Nicolay, Nicolay's cousin was ready to begin his military career, and Nicolay offered some worldly advice: "Now that he has chosen the profession of arms, it seems to me that you ought to have him learn the trade at the start among the foot soldiers: among the king's guard, which is full of nobles and young men eager to get ahead [*qui ont volonté de parvenir*], and be known by the king and his captains; or else in a good garrison, like that of Calais, under Monsieur de Vic, a very wise governor." After this year of apprenticeship,

31. Campion, *Mémoires*, 79–88.

Nicolay recommended a place in the light cavalry, "who are always on duty, . . . well paid, and it suffices to have two horses, for the master and his valet." In the heavy cavalry, expenses would be higher and income less certain, "and, in addition, a young gentleman who wants to get ahead [*parvenir*] should not launch himself immediately into the heavy cavalry."[32] For Nicolay and his cousin, the problem of success was at the heart of the military career; a young man who had chosen it needed to learn the métier and to place himself among others who were striving to advance. War required both formal training and more delicate choices about surroundings and companions.

Some years later, the comte de Souvigny likewise reflected on the kinds of knowledge a military career demanded. Having overcome his father's opposition, Souvigny spent nine months serving in the army with his uncle; then, during the winter, the uncle "boarded me at Lyon to learn mathematics and fortifications, from M. Le Beau, and dancing and marksmanship." This was in 1613, when Souvigny was sixteen years old. Near the end of his life, he urged a more formal version of the same program on his sons: if they were to enter the military, he urged them, "use your time carefully to learn history, all sorts of arithmetical rules, which are absolutely necessary to a man of war, the general rules of fortifications, to draw up plans of forts, battles, and camps, to form battalions, and even the orders of battle and camps. I have some knowledge of these things from practice more than from theory. . . . Thus I have not built on a good foundation and have only a confused knowledge [*science*]." In place of such empirical confusion, he urged on his sons formal study of Euclid, recently translated into French; he also urged that "if in your garrison there are also masters to teach you to shoot and to dance" they should take advantage of the opportunity, but not to the neglect of other duties.[33]

Long before Vauban, thus, war was a science, requiring special forms of knowledge and a high degree of precision. Knowledge of ancient authorities counted as well. The Grand Condé was famous for his knowledge of ancient military writings. "His genius and experience are helped by everything that can be known of warfare," wrote Saint-Evremond. "[T]he arrangements [*discipline*] of the ancients are

32. AN 3 AP 59, 3 F 5, 7 June 1608.
33. Comte de Souvigny, *Mémoires*, 1: 17; 3: 63–64.

as well known to him as those of the last centuries, and those of the last centuries as those of our own. That is to say that there has been no great siege or battle whose smallest details he does not know. The wars of Alexander and the *Commentaries* of Caesar move him enormously."[34] "No one could be better instructed than he in the *discipline* of the Romans. . . . [H]e had determined to follow them whatever the cost," wrote Arnauld d'Andilly of his military uncle;[35] Henri de Rohan thought ancient military knowledge sufficiently important that he translated and analyzed Caesar's *Commentaries,* specifically justifying its relevance to the age of artillery;[36] and William Louis of Nassau based his innovations in arranging troops on Roman military writings.[37] Military careers encouraged close study of the ancients and a belief that ancient knowledge had enduring, universal usefulness.

But this humanist belief in the value of literary study coexisted with an empiricist strain in the rhetoric surrounding military life. For war demanded sensitivity to particular circumstances and historical change, and an appreciation of progress. As much as in any area of seventeenth-century life, its practitioners used the rhetoric of Baconian science to describe the changes around them. Thus Rohan urged the aspiring captain to read the numerous treatises that had appeared on the science of fortification, but, "even better, [to learn] from the exercise of war, where every day experience adds something."[38] Arnauld d'Andilly praised his uncle for having "so deeply studied every aspect of war," but praised him above all as an innovator: "[S]uch exact discipline, and so many new formations invented by M. Arnauld, attracted from all sides . . . young gentlemen who came to learn their trade."[39] The successful warrior had to be something of an inventor. Everyone of course knew that firearms had changed military life, and in the 1570s Monluc offered conventional complaints about the harquebus's effects on the sociology of war: "I wish to God that they had never invented this cursed instrument! I wouldn't carry

---

34. Saint-Evremond, *Oeuvres en prose,* 1: 110; see also Philippe Ariès, *Centuries of Childhood: The Social History of Family Life,* trans. Robert Baldick (London, 1962), for discussion of the Grand Condé's education.
35. Arnauld d'Andilly, *Mémoires,* 33: 332.
36. Rohan, *Le parfait capitaine,* passim, esp. Epistle vi.
37. Parker, *Military Revolution,* 18–19.
38. Rohan, *Le parfait capitaine,* 219.
39. Arnauld d'Andilly, *Mémoires,* 33: 326, 336.

its marks, which still today leave me weak, and many brave men wouldn't be dead at the hands of those weaker and more cowardly than themselves."[40] For better and for worse, war seemed to demonstrate as few other domains of seventeenth-century life could the inadequacy of rules from the past and the danger of excessive generalizations; it both demanded close study of the past and enforced belief in intellectual progress.

This sense of historical particularity reinforced a larger empiricism that military experience seemed to encourage. War, so the military nobles argued, created forms of knowledge inaccessible to others. "Those who have never left their well-carpeted studies or the dainty tables of the court can no more judge what war is or how diverse its effects are than a blind man can judge colors," wrote the baron de Villars in the early seventeenth century.[41] He referred not only to the violence but also to the mass of particular events that made up the experience of battle. Like Villars, other seventeenth-century military men stressed rejection of abstract and theoretical knowledge and suggested that real knowledge lay in particulars. This was a form of knowledge to which numerous noble memorialists laid claim, whether or not they spoke to the specific intellectual problems that fighting posed. "Those who write the large histories," wrote François de La Noue in the 1580s, "having so many facts to describe, more numerous than the leaves of an oak tree, cannot always do so while noting all the particularities that go with them."[42] "This is not a book for intellectuals," wrote Monluc in introducing his work. "They have enough historians; this is for soldiers and captains, and perhaps even a royal governor might find something to learn here."[43] Because so many particulars made up the reality of warfare, success in it (like success in court politics) remained uncertain, and this formed an additional element in the outlook that military life created. La Rochefoucauld viewed the military successes of the comte d'Harcourt as an instance of "the care that fortune has taken to elevate and cast down men's merits. . . . [S]he wishes to show the full extent of her powers when

40. Monluc, *Commentaires*, 35.
41. François de Boyvin, chevalier baron du Villars, *Mémoires*, in M. Petitot, ed., *Collection complète des mémoires relatifs à l'histoire de France*, 28–30 (Paris, 1822), 28: 349.
42. François de La Noue, *Mémoires*, in Michaud and Poujolat, eds., *Nouvelle collection des mémoires relatifs à l'histoire de France . . .* , 9 (Paris, 1854), 593.
43. Monluc, *Commentaires*, 22.

she selects mediocre figures [*sujets*] to set on an equal footing with the greatest men."[44]

This Machiavellian vision of human affairs came naturally to seventeenth-century military men, and so also did Machiavellian forms of political reflection. War required that the captain view himself as a political leader, mobilizing his followers and carefully analyzing his opponents; and like so much else in seventeenth-century culture, it encouraged close study of individual personalities. In the mid-seventeenth century the duc de La Trémoille copied into his letter book a portrait of the great late-sixteenth-century captain the duke of Parma: "[M]aking war rather with his wits and speeches than with the force of his arms; using with great acuity nations' weaknesses to conquer them, and carefully applying himself to learn their weaknesses, foibles, impatience, suspicions, and envies, manipulating them according to their characters, and never failing to use the opportunities that they gave him."[45] War in these terms was closely linked to a broader vision of politics, in which rational manipulation replaced pure violence. The La Trémoilles showed other signs of taking such advice seriously. The comte de Laval's library in the early seventeenth century included most of the available literature on military practice and its political dimensions: Machiavelli's *Art of War*, "le livre sur le maniement des armes," works on Caesar and Maurice of Nassau, and a striking number of histories and memoirs, including Pasquier, Froissart, and Commynes.[46]

Seventeenth-century warfare, in short, encouraged noblemen to adopt important values of Renaissance humanism. This was a realm in which Roman and Greek knowledge was thought to have direct contemporary pertinence: the well-trained captain needed to have read both Caesar's tactics and Euclid's mathematics. He was to have read history; he needed rhetorical skills to mobilize his own troops and political insight in dealing with others. At the same time, he needed sensitivity to the role of progress in human affairs. Whatever reservations nobles may have had about the role of gunpowder in early modern warfare, new military technology required that they recognize the particularity of historical circumstances, the degree to

---

44. La Rochefoucauld, *Maximes et réflexions diverses*, 151.
45. AN 1 AP 397, 70.
46. AN 1 AP 382, "Mémoire des livres et meubles. . . . "

which each age differed from the last. Warfare led nobles to a powerful engagement with contemporary intellectual life.

In the course of the seventeenth century, a further change strengthened these educative effects of warfare: the manners and practices of the court became an increasing presence in camp life. Writing in about 1660, the comte de Souvigny, it has been seen, assumed that his son might learn not only marksmanship but also dancing in his military camps. In this and other ways, seventeenth-century nobles increasingly sought to assimilate military life to models of courtly behavior. "I was certainly surprised in the evening," wrote Gourville of a visit to an army commander in 1654, "when supper was served, to see that it was done with the same elegance [*propreté*] and delicacy that he would have had at Paris. Up till then no one had taken his silver dishes to the army, or had thought to serve entremets or fruit. But this bad example soon spoiled others, and this carried so far that today there are no generals, colonels, or *maîtres de camp* who lack silver dishes, and they believe themselves obliged to do like the others, insofar as they can."[47] Earlier in the seventeenth century, Campion described carting around his books on campaign, "with which I occupied myself fairly often, sometimes alone, more often with three of my friends in the regiment, men who were clever and very studious." They would read aloud from "some good book, whose finest passages we would examine, to learn how to live and die well."[48] In the winter, when campaigning ceased, life at moments could hold still more pleasures. Lodged at Lautrec, remembered Campion, "I spent a very agreeable three months. I struck up a friendship with a well-born and clever young woman, . . . with whom I passed some lovely hours."[49] For Campion and others, war's effects in some ways paralleled those of life at court, with efforts at self-improvement and polishing playing a large role in camp life. Despite the squalor of the trenches, war could be a school of elegant behavior.

Like the court, war also had elements of theatrical performance, in which actions were carefully observed and evaluated. As at court,

47. Jean Hérauld, sieur de Gourville, *Mémoires,* ed Léon Lecestre, 2 vols. (Paris, 1894), 1: 108.
48. Campion, *Mémoires,* 95, 96; see Jean-Marie Constant, *Les conjurateurs: Le premier libéralisme sous Richelieu* (Paris, 1987), for discussion of the political significance of these discussions.
49. Campion, *Mémoires,* 120.

thus, the warrior had to exercise rigid self-control within a highly emotional setting. Monluc made the point in the later sixteenth century: "Those who want to gain honor by arms must resolve to shut their eyes to all dangers in the first battles where they find themselves. For everyone will be watching, to see what they've got inside. If at the beginning they carry out some striking action, to show their courage and toughness, they'll be marked and known forever after."[50] La Rochefoucauld likewise offered reflections on the ways in which war was a public performance. "Most men expose themselves enough in war to save their honor. But few want always to expose themselves enough to bring success to the plans for which they have exposed themselves," he commented; and "One does not want to lose one's life, and one wants to win glory; which means that brave men are more ingenious in avoiding death than are the litigious in preserving their property."[51] Despite the growing scale and ferocity of warfare, the seventeenth century brought only an increased awareness of its theatrical qualities. The development of journalism spread word of military achievements throughout society, and Louis XIV's eagerness to note and commemorate them had the same effect. At the end of the seventeenth century, war was still far from being an anonymous enterprise.

Even wounds and death carried these theatrical overtones: they were watched by a large public. In the 1620s the dowager duchesse de Longueville wrote to Madame de La Trémoille to congratulate her on "the news of the wounds of M. de Laval, your son, and the marvelous deeds he has done in Germany. . . . Praise God that his life is not in danger and that he will return to you full of glory and esteem."[52] Turenne's death (he was hit by a cannonball as he observed the preparations for battle) offered seventeenth-century writers an example of the completed military life: a death "so suited to such a fine life, surrounded by so many striking circumstances and coming at so important a moment," in La Rochefoucauld's words.[53]

The awareness that the warrior acted in a theatrical setting, observed by his fellows and commented on at court, encouraged contem-

50. Monluc, *Commentaires*, 31.
51. La Rochefoucauld, *Maximes et réflexions diverses*, 64 (nos. 219, 221).
52. AN 1 AP 649, dossier Catherine de Gonzague de Clèves, duchesse douairière de Longueville, 26 XI, n.d. See also Madame de Sévigné, *Selected Letters*, trans. Leonard Tancock (London, 1982), 143–48, for Parisian and court perceptions of the crossing of the Rhine (17, 19 June, 3 July 1672).
53. La Rochefoucauld, *Maximes et réflexions diverses*, 130 ("Des modèles de la nature et de la fortune").

poraries to take a complex view of the emotions of battle itself. Like life at court, the experience of war offered yet another stimulus for nobles to view human personality as infinitely complex, inadequately comprehended by generalizing formulations. Human feelings, concealed by the role-playing that battle demanded, might vary enormously. "Perfect valor and cowardice are extremes that rarely occur. The space between them is vast, and contains all the other kinds of courage: there are no fewer differences among them than among faces and temperaments," noted La Rochefoucauld, and he went on to list some of these, distinguishing men who were brave at the start of battle, fatigued thereafter; those who allowed themselves to be swept up by "general terrors"; those who were more afraid of bullets than of swords; and so on.[54]

Finally, warfare was connected with the court and with civil life more broadly, by the economic calculations that the captain needed to make. Economic concerns touched military careers at the outset, for, like positions in the judiciary and the financial administration, military positions were purchased, and positions of any consequence commanded high prices. In 1618, Jean Nicolay, first président in the Chambre des Comptes of Paris, spent just over 66,000 livres to buy a position as councillor in the Parlement of Paris for his oldest son; two years later a heavy cavalry position for his younger son cost him 75,000 livres.[55] These were enormous sums at a time when a wealthy provincial nobleman's yearly income rarely exceeded 15,000 livres and a substantial landed estate cost about 50,000 livres. This scale of investment meant that economic calculations immediately assumed a central place in a military career.[56]

But investment in office represented only a start. Thereafter arose the problems of recruiting soldiers, equipping them and assuring their wages, and surviving long periods of governmental neglect. "A captain should never be miserly," counselled Monluc in the later sixteenth century. "Miserliness brings a captain troubles at least as great as any other vice. For if you let yourself be dominated by greed, you'll never have decent soldiers around you. All the good men will flee, saying that you love silver more than a valiant man."[57] But the captain often

54. Ibid., 63 (no. 215).
55. AN 3 AP 20, 14 C 3, 14 C 10.
56. See below, Chapter 5, for the functioning of venality in military offices.
57. Monluc, *Commentaires*, 25–26.

had to be generous with his own money, and this remained the case well into the seventeenth century. "We are in garrison without having touched any of the king's money, and with no assurance of doing so," wrote one of Nicolay's relatives from his camp near La Rochelle. "I've had to maintain my company for the past three months out of the money you loaned me, buy arms, and raise [troops]. . . . I don't see any prospect of prosperity, and they remain indifferent to me [*l'on ne me veut aimer*] no matter what I do, . . . at least [so it seems] by the effects that appear in our purses."[58] The same complaints echoed lower in the military hierarchy. In 1602 one of the La Trémoilles' agents asked that the profits of a shipwreck near the family's château of Talmont be given him, so that a family guard could "receive recognition for his vigilance at your castle as I promised; he has received nothing for three years, and I could be reimbursed for the advances I've made to the soldiers that I maintain there for your service."[59] Whatever the level, monetary calculations could never be far from the captain's mind.

Such conditions required that the captain act as both courtier and entrepreneur. He needed to make himself loved at court, to maintain his relations with the high officials who would secure the payment of his troops and his other financial needs; in 1653 Campion had to spend a month at court "soliciting payment of our winter wages" for his regiment.[60] Even in camp or in battle he needed to evaluate carefully the economic dimensions of his actions—sometimes to the point of comical involvement in local business affairs.[61] It was thus important that captains be "persons well-born and rich . . . being rich, they can keep their companies intact [*faictes*]": so an aristocratic author reflected near the start of his "Treatise on the Light Cavalry."[62] Military profits might be high, but they came only after heavy initial investment and with continuous effort thereafter. At all levels of the military hierarchy, warfare involved the nobleman in complicated economic networks and exchange relations.

58. AN 3 AP 21, 21 C 68, Vieupont to Nicolay, 25 November 1625.
59. AN 1 AP 645, "mr Bessay" to Monseigneur, February 1602.
60. Campion, *Mémoires*, 213.
61. For an extreme example see Dewald, *Pont-St-Pierre*, 179–80. Saint-Evremond told a friend that he had turned a profit of 50,000 livres from his two years' service in Guienne during the Fronde (*Oeuvres en prose*, 1: xxvii).
62. AN 1 AP 397, 4.

Failure to negotiate these relationships could be costly, in terms both of military effectiveness and of the nobleman's political standing. When the prince de Tarente could not assure his troop's payments in 1650, he was warned that his failure "leaves your company dying of hunger and ruins it from top to bottom."[63] The sums of money were often very large: in the same year Tarente borrowed 50,000 livres in order to raise troops to support the crown against the Bordelais frondeurs—a sum that required the prince's agents to turn to friends and bankers in La Rochelle.[64]

The Crown in fact used such nobles as Tarente for precisely this money-raising function, employing their financial credit with local merchants and their political credit with local nobles to raise armies it could not raise directly. When financial problems delayed his levies of troops in 1650, Tarente was warned about "the impatience that the court feels about your levies. My lord, I believe that it is very important for you to have some troops appear under your name before the peace with Bordeaux is concluded—very soon, it appears"; and his correspondent urged him to make as much use as possible of his followers within the local nobility in putting together these corps.[65] Failure to engage one's resources—both money and reserves of patronage—in military levies meant risking favor at court. Even in the mid-seventeenth century, the Crown could not do without the independent military power of such families as the La Trémoilles; such families' power to mobilize followers provided an important element in the royal army itself. Money and political maneuvering were central to a military career; they tended to overshadow the animal ferocity of combat and the chivalric traditions of military service.

In all of these ways, seventeenth-century war was a far from atavistic enterprise. It demanded of its aristocratic practitioners economic and political calculations, and some classical and mathematical learning. The successful captain had in certain ways to be a courtier, and even in the field his experiences in some ways paralleled those of the court. Like the court, war was a stage for carefully controlled performances, and, as at court, successful performance might lead to social

63. AN 1 AP 443, no. 36, Beaugendre to prince de Tarente, 28 September 1650.
64. Ibid., no. 10, "Estat des sommes empruntez par monseigneur . . . "; no. 30, St.-Maurice to prince de Tarente, 20 September 1650.
65. Ibid., no. 30, St.-Maurice to prince de Tarente, 20 September 1650.

advancement. La Rochefoucauld even thought that army life improved manners, polishing away "*l'air bourgeois*."

But war of course also stood outside established social norms. By its very nature violence represents destruction of order and the disruption of daily life, and seventeenth-century soldiers experienced especially savage forms of violence. Possibly the divergence between daily life and battlefield was less great than in our own time, given that violence was a more common element in seventeenth-century daily life; but seventeenth-century writers stressed the special forms of perception and behavior that war demanded—and the difficulty anyone who had not experienced war had in understanding what it was like. Seventeenth-century observers could cite impressive examples both of ferocity and of the reasonings that lay behind it. "When he took prisoners," claimed Tallemant of a sixteenth-century nobleman, "he had them killed by his son, who was only ten years old, to accustom him early to bloodshed and carnage."[66] This was an extreme and perhaps mythical instance, but in some degree all warriors were expected to share this combination of rage and indifference to blood. Bussy described the Grand Condé fighting hand to hand in the trenches, moved by a terrifying animal rage.[67]

But even rage and fear were also tactical instruments, elements in the highly rational conduct that seventeenth-century war demanded. Three generations before Richelieu, Blaise de Monluc used the term *raison de la guerre* to summarize the approach to violence that he advocated. Thus he described one massacre that he had directed and emphasized the example's broad relevance: "Don't think, those of you who read this book, that I ordered that execution so much to avenge my wound as to spread terror through the whole countryside," he wrote; " . . . and it seems to me that any captain at the start of a campaign of conquest ought to do the same against those who dare to hold out against him; he must close his ears to any talk of negotiation or truce. . . . [Y]ou need rigor (call it cruelty if you wish)."[68] Even in its violence, warfare for Monluc involved special forms of calculation. In such passages, he argued for a Machiavellian vision of the warrior's

66. Gédéon Tallemant des Réaux, *Historiettes*, ed. Antoine Adam, 2 vols. (Paris, Pléiade, 1960–61), 1: 153.

67. Bussy-Rabutin, *Mémoires*, 1: 143.

68. Monluc, *Commentaires*, 409, 784.

situation. He had detached political from personal morality, so that his good captain could not be an entirely good man.

Monluc's vision required a comparable sacrifice of chivalric values. Though he worried about the socially corrosive effects of gunpowder, which seemed to eliminate honor from the battlefield and allow the cowardly to kill the brave, he also urged captains to relinquish honor as a measure for evaluating battlefield choices. Thus he offered strong defense of night-time retreats against the scruples of captains who might believe this to be cowardly behavior: "Have no shame about covering yourself in darkness. Far from being shameful, it's honorable to trick and mock the enemy who awaits you, and who at daybreak finds only your camp. It would be much more dishonorable and shameful to be beaten while you retreat, if you're so fussy. For God's sake, fight knowing what you're doing [*à bon escient*]; stay in your position, if it's even slightly advantageous, and there wait for your enemy either to grow tired or to attack you, and you'll play with all the cards on your side."[69] War as Monluc conceived it demanded absolute rationality, an adjustment of means to ends that permitted the use of deception and every other possible advantage. Effectiveness rather than honor became an increasingly exclusive standard for judging military actions.

The seventeenth century brought some mitigation of this calculated ferocity, but no real diminution. Commanders themselves participated, rather than merely directing others' violence. Henri de Campion described the comte de Harcourt, one of the century's most successful commanders, in battle against the Spanish, in 1639. Having routed the enemy, a French officer sought to save a wounded enemy officer; Harcourt arrived, apparently also to help the man but in fact to finish him off, "cutting off half of his head." Campion, with his sensitivity and stoical morality, thought this an act "of pure cruelty" and "unworthy of so highly reputed a prince," but his own delicacy had its limits. When a French village violently refused to lodge his troops, he encouraged his soldiers to march on it, promising that "we would overwhelm them and that our troop could then pillage the town." He likewise described without comment having hanged the governor of a fort "for having held out in a fortress that couldn't withstand can-

---

69. Monluc, *Commentaires*, 273. There were of course also practical reasons to avoid night-time retreats. Campion pointed out that darkness allowed frightened, retreating soldiers to escape the control of their officers and thus risked turning a retreat into chaos: *Mémoires*, 109.

non"—in other words, in what he knew to be a helpless situation.[70] For Campion as for Monluc, the captain was expected to employ techniques of calculated terror, whatever his personal morals. Like his travels, his planning on the battlefield detached the warrior from inherited ethics.

Contemporaries were impressed by the special psychological impact of the experience of warfare and by the ways this experience separated nobles from other social groups. In combat as in other aspects of his life, the military nobleman was expected to regulate his passions in ways quite unlike other men. Passion was not to be entirely repressed. It was also to be used and even encouraged, for peasants and garrison commanders alike could thus be frightened into following the army's needs. But ferocity could recede as quickly as it had come. The day after Harcourt killed the Spaniard, a treaty allowed the Spanish to leave their besieged fortress; Harcourt and the Spanish commander "embraced each other on horseback."[71] Shifts between ferocity and gentleness formed part of the experience of battle and testified to the extraordinary psychological state that the combatant entered. Henri de Rohan offered more general reflections on the psychological impact of battle, but he too stressed that warfare involved a changed state of mind, something beyond ordinary social experience: "It's a maxim that any troop, no matter how big, if it has fought, is in such disorder that the smallest fresh troop arriving can absolutely undo it. . . . [I]t is a long and difficult task to try to restore in good order an army that has fought, to fight again: some amusing themselves by pillaging, others upset at returning to the peril; and all of them so excited that they don't understand or don't wish to understand our orders."[72] Entering combat meant a changed state of mind, a state of emotion from which there was no rapid or easy return. Seventeenth-century fascination with duelling, so François Billacois has suggested, reflected a similar sensitivity to extraordinary experience. Both the duelist and the warrior were men who had stepped beyond the normal limits of social behavior.[73]

70. Campion, *Mémoires*, 131, 132, 77, 89.
71. Ibid., 132.
72. Rohan, *Le parfait capitaine*, 211. My understanding of these issues owes much to John Keegan, *The Face of Battle* (London, 1976).
73. François Billacois, *Le duel dans la société française des XVIe–XVIIe siècles: Essai de psychologie historique* (Paris, 1986).

Seventeenth-century writers saw this psychological experience as founding a basic social distinction between military men and even the highest-born civil magistrates. Seventeenth-century writers had all about them examples of the mingling of military and robe families. Yet belief in the special experience that war constituted led them to treat the distinction between robe and sword as fundamental, resting on different visions of the world. Pascal took up this theme in the mid-seventeenth century and presented the contrast as one of divergent epistemologies. The world of the robe, as we have seen, represented for him a world of illusions and appearances, in contrast to the realities of warfare and violence: whereas magistrates used theatrical trappings to create power over people's imaginations, soldiers exercised power directly, with physical force.[74] Pascal placed the judicial apparatus of the state, its ceremonies, laws, and costumes, on the side of imagination. Reality lay with the soldiers; they held real power and provided the real basis of monarchy. Fascination with deception and illusion permeated seventeenth-century thought. The contrast that Pascal drew between judges and warriors gave the contrast between reality and illusion a social dimension.

The belief that they inhabited a separate mental world gave military nobles a powerful sense of their distance from the educated officials of the robe nobility. The sense of difference could generate intense bitterness. Thus Henri de Rohan, in the 1630s: "Most states today are founded rather on administration [*police*] than on war, and try to maintain themselves rather than to grow. As a result, we have seen letters flourish and arms decay. . . . [M]en of letters nearly everywhere have occupied the governments of states, who, because they hate men of war, always mistreat them, and even advise using mercenaries rather than their subjects, a very pernicious maxim."[75] Rohan held these views despite the learning evident in the very work where he expressed them, his commentary on Caesar. His dispute with the "men of letters" concerned, not letters, but their lack of sympathy for violence. La Rochefoucauld suggested a comparable gulf of understanding when he described bravery as inappropriate to a magistrate, "even though he can be resolute in certain circumstances; he should appear firm and confident during a sedition that he must calm, with-

---

74. Blaise Pascal, *Pensées*, trans. A. J. Krailsheimer (London, 1966), 40–41. See above, Chapter 1.
75. Rohan, *Le parfait capitaine*, 175–76.

out fear of being false, and he would be false and ridiculous to fight in a duel."[76] By this point, differences between robe and sword had little to do with *race;* but they rested on a sense of difference that was nonetheless very powerful. Violence defined a special knowledge of the world; it gave the military noble access to realities that were closed to others.

In this common experience of violence, warfare represented probably the most visible tie between seventeenth-century nobles and their medieval past. At the level of ideologies, the ability to fight provided one foundation of the society of orders itself. Nobles claimed that the blood they shed in war compensated for their failure to contribute to the state's finances. At deeper levels, fighting gave nobles common experiences with ancestors and detached them from other social groups. We have seen how far this sense of special experience extended, setting the nobles in some ways outside the norms of civil society.

But seventeenth-century warfare involved more than these impulses, for it upset inherited situations. There was, first, the experience of social mobility, which contemporaries believed was an important, perhaps necessary, component of military success. Ambition was so central to military strength, in the view of Henri de Rohan, that the army could thrive only if other avenues of advancement were closed off. Even those born to high positions found that warfare detached them from their settings, by encouraging them to wander throughout Europe in search of experience and offices; especially during the early seventeenth century, these wanderings included contacts with religious heterodoxy, as young men journeyed to the Dutch and German "schools of war." Even without such specific intellectual dangers, wandering in search of military office was thought to have unsettling effects on ideas and morals (as we shall see in detail in Chapter 3). In these ways, war involved nobles in situations of social fluidity and individualistic calculation. Money's role in a military career had similar effects. Any significant military career forced the nobleman into large monetary transactions, and it typically required extensive borrowing as well.

Such monetary calculations reinforced the other ways in which, contemporaries thought, military careers demanded knowledge and

76. La Rochefoucauld, *Maximes et réflexions diverses,* 126–27 (13, "Du faux").

reflection. There were the forms of numeracy and literacy that warfare demanded. Captains needed a certain level of mathematical education, in order to deal with firearms and fortifications, and knowledge of the ancients, whose teachings were still closely followed despite the advent of firearms. They also needed some knowledge of more recent military theorists. More important, there were the broader forms of thought that accompanied military activity: alertness to historical change and the particularity of events; interest in the political calculations that increasingly were thought to determine military outcomes in an age when warriors needed to be "foxes rather than lions." The seventeenth-century warrior had to think in terms of purposive and controlled action, with scant regard for ethical or social restraints.[77]

Underlying these specific perceptions and intellectual demands was the warrior's peculiar moral position, as a man acting at the limits of social order. Warfare involved the calculated release of passions, and even such thoughtful moralists as Henri de Campion found themselves deliberately terrorizing civil populations. Ultimately, it was this experience of savagery that separated nobles of the sword from the society around them; military nobles claimed to have experienced a separate mental world.

77. For an illuminating discussion of the issue of purposiveness in seventeenth-century politics, see Elizabeth Marvick, *The Young Richelieu: A Psychoanalytic Approach to Leadership* (Chicago, 1983), 3–13.

# 3

# Family, Education, and Selfhood

The ethic of *race* presented the family as a unified entity, organized around cohesiveness of political action and continuity from one generation to the next. Such ideals had enormous force in the later sixteenth and seventeenth centuries, but they coexisted with apparently antithetical forms of thought and action. Contemporaries, this chapter will argue, were continually impressed by the disruptions of family life, the conflicts that set generations against each other and undercut assumptions about unity. Seventeenth-century familial practices forced young men and women to think of themselves as separate from their families—and, often, at odds with them. Such tensions derived in part from the very importance of the family's dynastic functions, for these often required bending individual wills to collective aims. The process produced painful situations in real life, and it stimulated striking symbolic representations by seventeenth-century dramatists. Other practices and beliefs also undercut the family's unity. Educational theory encouraged separation of children from parents, because of anxieties that at home children would receive too little discipline; and foreign residence, voluntary or not, was common in the seventeenth century. Together these experiences removed young men from familial settings and forced them to think of their situations as in some sense personal creations, the outcomes of personal histories and choices rather than inheritance. Conflict within seventeenth-century families, this chapter argues, did not contradict the ideals of a dynastic society, but it did testify to the weight that these ideals placed on individuals, and to the large areas of life that individual choice necessarily dominated.

In the same way, conflict might coexist with intense love for children and with belief in children's individual qualities and development. Educators and parents alike spoke approvingly of children's expressing themselves freely, and they urged that each be allowed to develop at his/her own pace. At least some parents described the pleasure they took in their children's company, and they spoke with strong emotion of children's deaths. Such beliefs and practices further contributed to the tendencies toward individualism that, I have argued, were central to seventeenth-century ways of perceiving the world and acting within it. Yet this attention to the child's specificity (so runs a further argument of this chapter) added its own tensions to family life. Concern with individuality sharpened siblings' sense of distance from one another and, above all, conveyed the belief that parental love was earned and conditional, rather than natural and universal; seventeenth-century men and women expected children to acquire their parents' love by their abilities, and they expected many to fail at the task. Familial affections and attentions thus sharpened the anxieties that the seventeenth-century social order created.

Expectations of familial conflict had a long history within the French nobility. Early in the fifteenth century, Jean Froissart described the events that led Gaston de Foix—in many respects Froissart's pattern of chivalric behavior—to murder his own son. The murder itself was accidental, Froissart concluded. But Gaston had long raged at his son, in a history of conflict that had included his wife's flight from home and his son's unwitting participation in an attempted poisoning, masterminded by Gaston's father-in-law. In this instance, conflict derived partly from aristocratic politics and partly from the nature of the family itself. Because Gaston had married to forge political alliances, his son found himself torn between the interests of his paternal and maternal lineages; inevitably the son mirrored his father's interests imperfectly, and inevitably struggle ensued.[1] But underlying this political conflict were anxieties that might arise in any patrilineal family: with each marriage it admitted a foreign influence to the household, and thus each new generation acquired a set of loyalties slightly different from those of the last. Froissart's tale implied an unavoidable tension within the ideology of *race*, between children's obedience to the paternal line and the fact that they were equally members of the mother's family and subject to its influences.

---

1. Jean Froissart, *Chronicles*, ed. Geoffrey Brereton (London, 1968), 266–74. Some of the evidence and arguments in this chapter appear in Jonathan Dewald, "Deadly Parents: Family and Aristocratic Culture in Early Modern France," in Barbara Diefendorf and Carla Hesse, eds., *Dialogues with the Past* (forthcoming).

In the next century, Michel de Montaigne more explicitly stressed the inevitability of familial conflicts, but he also viewed them in narrower terms, as a consequence of ideas about aging and money. The old, he wrote, envy their children's pleasure in the world as they are about to leave it; the young resent their parents' continuing control over the family's resources.[2] A century and a half later, Saint-Simon told much the same story through specific examples. Thus the prince de Conti: "His son, young as he was, he could not abide." The prince de Condé: "For monsieur le duc [his son], it was only politeness. They feared each other: the son, a difficult and capricious father; the father, a son-in-law of the king. But from time to time the son would trip up the father, and the father's attacks on the son were furious." The duc de La Rochefoucauld: "His feelings for his children were less than lukewarm; and though they served him well, he made their lives very difficult."[3] For Saint-Simon, as for Montaigne, parents and children struggled over scarce resources, and in the process they easily came to dislike each other.

These literary descriptions of familial tensions all aimed at public audiences, but families' private papers contain similar events and reflections. Antoine Arnauld recalled his father with a vivid sense of grievance: "He loved his friends enormously; but one can say that he always preferred new friendships to old. It is thus easy to see that his children were not what he loved the most." Of his nineteenth year, he remembered that "it was about that time that I received the first sign of the scant love that my father had for me, or at least of his indifference toward my position and advancement [*mon établissement et . . . fortune*]." His father had refused to spend the money needed to buy Antoine a military position. "It wasn't that he was miserly," Antoine remembered; "on the contrary, he could be accused of liberality and even prodigality; but alas for his children, this was only for himself and his new friends."[4]

A case of comparable anger arose in the La Trémoille family a few years later. In 1642 there died in exile in Venice the scapegrace comte

<hr>

2. Michel de Montaigne, *The Complete Essays*, ed. Donald Frame (Stanford, 1958), 280.

3. Louis de Rouvroy, duc de Saint-Simon, *Mémoires*, ed. Gonzague Truc, 8 vols. (Paris, Pléiade, 1953–61), 3: 55, 99, 142.

4. L'abbé Arnauld, *Mémoires*, in M. Petitot, ed., *Collection des mémoires relatifs à l'histoire de France*, 34 (Paris, 1824), 123, 144, 146.

de Laval, the duc Henri de La Trémoille's younger brother; the La Trémoilles dispatched a dependent to the scene to unravel the comte's affairs and recover what the family believed to be its property. After extended negotiations with the comte's wife, the messenger reported back to the duc that "M. de Laval carried off to the other world, and wanted to leave behind here, marks of the hatred and aversion he had for Monseigneur (his brother) and Madame." The comte's methods had included confiding to his wife important family papers, with the assurance "that by carefully keeping them, she would be able to out-maneuver Monseigneur, since they were so necessary to him that Monseigneur would be delighted to pay any price for them."[5]

A few years earlier, a relative of the président de Nicolay described family conflicts surrounding her son's choice of career, and again her language suggested the severity of the family's divisions: "Our perfid-ious stepfather has so won over my mother's mind with his malicious tricks that he uses her to fulfill his vicious aims against us, seeking with no justification to ruin our lives and properties. . . . [A]s for my son, one could scarcely imagine his perfidy and ill-will in this affair."[6] The marquise de la Moussaye, sister of the great Turenne, used similar language. "God give me the grace to pardon them," she wrote her sis-ter, "my brother's treachery is beyond anything, . . . however he seeks to hide it."[7] Four years later she offered more general reflections of this sort: "It's so common to receive neither pleasure nor satisfaction from anyone that it no longer surprises one, it seems to me," she wrote to her sister, "for those who have the greatest obligations of birth and friendship are those who take the greatest pleasure in upsetting us."[8]

But even descriptions of properly functioning families might stress the sacrifices that propriety demanded and the conflicts that might re-sult; muffled conflict between family members, in other words, ap-peared in praiseworthy as in pathological actions. In 1649 Nicolas de Nicolay expressed these sentiments in a speech to the Chambre des Comptes of Paris. His father had just resigned to Nicolas his presi-dency in the court, and the speech opened with tribute to this gener-osity. "When I consider," he began, "that I could not be a part of this illustrious body without my father—who has had the happiness of be-

5. AN 1 AP 642, Allard to Monsieur, 6 September 1642.
6. AN 3 AP 17, 13 C 281, 5 May 1618.
7. AN 1 AP 435, 77, 2 September 1657.
8. AN 1 AP 435, 92, 7 December 1661.

ing its leader—departing from it; that I could not have arisen to this place of honor without his lowering himself; that I could not climb to the glory of my ancestors save by the same steps that I see him descending; that my good fortune can only be built on the ruins of his; when I reflect that his fall is the price of my happiness . . ."[9] Nicolay used strong language to describe what was in fact an ordinary situation for seventeenth-century officials, the passage of office from one generation to the next. He spoke of the "ruins" of his father's situation, his "fall," his decline (*"il s'abaisse"*). With this language the young man sought to underline the generosity of his father's retirement, but generosity and potential conflict were closely joined. The father's sacrifice was a genuine "fall"—so much so that not all fathers accepted their loss. The generational conflicts that the Nicolays managed to deflect occasionally brought other robe families into public scandal. Early in the seventeenth century, a father and son of the Busquet family, notable Rouennais magistrates, disputed the possession of an office before the assembled Parlement. The father accused the son of attempting to "despoil him shamelessly of his position"; the son responded by claiming that the father sought "to reduce him to indigence."[10]

The ideology of dynastic continuity, so Nicolas de Nicolay's speech suggested, fitted easily with assumptions about potential hatreds within the family: because the family's continuity and development required the sacrifice of individuals' desires, family life inevitably produced tensions and rebellions. Other families used similar language and emphasized similar connections between demands for unity and the reality of conflict. In 1662 Henri de La Trémoille wrote in a fury to his forty-two-year-old son, following what he took to be a slight: "[A]fter God's service, serving myself and the family ought to be your principal object and employment. . . . [C]onsider that having received from us life, honor, and properties, you can give us nothing that is not infinitely beneath what you owe." Ten days later, following inadequate apologies from his son, La Trémoille's eloquence rose to further heights: "Know then, ingrate, that you do not deserve to be treated like the least of my servants, who has not merited as you have every sort of punishment. . . . [L]earn that except for my mercy you ought

9. AN 3 AP 256, "Harangues de mon grandpère," 73.
10. Jonathan Dewald, *The Formation of a Provincial Nobility: The Magistrates of the Parlement of Rouen, 1499–1610* (Princeton, 1980), 302.

to demand nothing but leave to die. . . . [T]he parricide committed by Cromwell and his colonels is a lesser crime than the ingratitude of an unnatural son, since it touches a father more keenly than the executioner's axe."[11] La Trémoille's patriarchal vision of his family made any violation of obedience an immediately dangerous challenge; beneath the language of dynasticism lay barely concealed assumptions about the family's potential for conflict—domestic equivalents of Cromwell's murderous revolution.

A more complex interplay of obedience and enmity characterized relations between the Grand Condé and his father, but again their language suggests the problems that dynastic ideology posed. Condé's adolescent letters to his father speak at length of obedience and deference. The young Condé made explicit the links among these patriarchal relationships, larger political relations, and personal ambitions and actions. "I am reading with great pleasure of our kings' heroic actions," he wrote at age fifteen, at a time when his tutor was having him read history, "while you accomplish great actions, leaving me a splendid example and a holy ambition to imitate and follow them, when age and ability will have made me such as you would wish." Yet obedience also threatened selfhood, with nearly equal explicitness. For political reasons, Condé's father married him against his will to one of Richelieu's nieces. Soon after the event the father wrote to the minister describing his view of the transaction: "[H]e is your nephew, your creature; do with him as you wish." Obedience, so the elder Condé proclaimed, came at the price of autonomy, and the young Condé's response indicated his sense of the loss. He spent the months following the enforced marriage first in illness and severe depression, then in slow recovery during which he did nothing but have novels read to him.[12] Condé's depression thus paralleled his father's words to Richelieu, emphasizing his passivity and even (since contemporaries already viewed novel-reading as in some ways a feminine pursuit) implying a renunciation of masculinity. But a different response soon followed: to his father's annoyance, Condé surrounded himself with dissipated young men, many of them actively bisexual, and embarked on

11. AN 1 AP 396, fol. 308, 12 December 1662; fols. 314–15, 12 December 1662.
12. Quoted by M. le duc d'Aumale, *Histoire des princes de Condé pendant les XVIe et XVIIe siècles*, 6 vols. (Paris, 1885), 3: 332, 441, 449. On assumptions about seventeenth-century novel-reading, see English Showalter, *The Evolution of the French Novel, 1641–1782* (Princeton, 1972), chap. 1.

a career of profligacy.[13] Condé's depression and subsequent dissipation, like the experiences of the La Trémoille and Nicolay families, illustrated difficult realities of the society of orders. For these families, society consisted of a single hierarchy of individuals, and no place within that hierarchy was exactly comparable to any other; this was as true within the family as in relations with outsiders.[14] In such circumstances, there could be no compensation for lost standing or powers. What the son gained, the father necessarily lost; the father's pursuit of familial standing threatened the son's identity. There could be no full accommodation of these diverging interests.

We can judge the frequency of such tensions and their emotional resonance by turning from isolated events to public representations of familial patterns, in seventeenth-century drama. If drama fictionalizes contemporary life, it presents versions of it that interest a large public—unlike most other literary forms, it cannot survive without engaging contemporaries, and seventeenth-century dramatists claimed with special vigor to appeal to their audiences.[15] And when seventeenth-century high society attended the theater, it received the lesson that transitions from one generation to the next were difficult and that they often occasioned violence. Foolish fathers and restive sons recur throughout Molière's comedies, of course, but these are in some degree only an inheritance from classical models. More surprising is seventeenth-century tragedians' fascination with the theme of parents killing their children, either symbolically or in reality. In Corneille's *Andromède*, a mother's impiety leads to her daughter's selection as sacrificial victim; the father oversees and defends the sacrifice, and the same play presents a goddess preparing to murder her stepson. In *Rodogune*, a mother stabs one son and seeks to poison another. In *Médée*, a mother kills her two children. In *Horace*, it is a brother who kills his sister, but with his father's vociferous approval; and earlier in the play the old Horace calls for his son's death, believing that the

13. D'Aumale, *Histoire*, 3: 453ff.; Georges Mongrédien, *Le Grand Condé: L'homme et son oeuvre* (Paris, 1959), 63ff. It is tempting to link Condé's episodes of homosexuality to such experiences of paternal humiliation, but they seem to have reflected larger patterns of seventeenth-century expectation: see below, Chapter 4.

14. A point brilliantly elucidated by Roland Barthes, *On Racine*, trans. Richard Howard (New York, 1977).

15. See below, Chapter 6, for discussion of these claims.

young man has dishonored the family: "[B]efore this day is done, these hands, my own, will cleanse with his blood the Romans' shame."[16]

Racine typically avoids such images of physical assault, but his plays too speak repeatedly of parents' potential violence against their children, and most of his plays explore the theme that parents destroy their children's happiness in other, less direct ways. *Mithridate* presents a father who has already killed two sons and whose efforts to kill two more dominate the plot. *Iphigénie* of course turns on a father's having to kill his daughter. In *La Thébaïde,* a father exults over his sons' deaths, which open the way for his acquiring both throne and beloved: "I lose much less than I expect to gain. . . . In depriving me of a son, the heavens eliminate a rival. . . . It's all like a dream: I was a father and a subject; now I'm a lover, and king."[17] In *Britannicus,* Nero can command during his mother's absence, but in her presence "my efforts are of no avail. / My genius trembles, stupefied, at hers; / And it's to free myself from this her hold / that I avoid her."[18] Neither Pyrrhus (*Andromaque*) nor Titus (*Bérénice*) can have the woman he loves, because of obligations each has inherited from a dead father; for Pyrrhus there is as well the threat that the boy he contemplates raising will eventually kill him, and that he risks his own life by allowing the child to live. Hippolyte (*Phèdre*) dies because of his father's curse, and from the play's outset he makes clear the mixture of admiration, moral criticism, and self-doubt that his father's example inspires in him; against his own priggish and unheroic youth, Hippolyte sets his father's sexuality, seductions, and heroic achievements.[19]

Though less concerned than Racine with the psychology of lineage, Corneille too had emphasized the oppressiveness of parental inheritance, the ways in which inheritance denies personal existence. This was the theme of *Le Cid,* in which fathers' quarrels demand that children renounce love, and the theme reemerged in *Rodogune:* "Can you not allow us to reign in innocence?" asks a son of his mother, and the play concludes with the mother's decisive answer: "[B]ecause of one

16. Pierre Corneille, *Oeuvres complètes,* ed. André Stegman (Paris, 1963), 437 (*Horace,* lines 1049–50).

17. *Oeuvres complètes.* Volume 1: *Théâtre-poésies,* ed. Raymond Picard (Paris, Pléiade, 1950), 166 (Act V, Scene 4).

18. Jean Racine, *Andromache, Britannicus, Berenice,* trans. John Cairncross (London, 1967), 157 (lines 505–7).

19. Racine, *Oeuvres complètes,* 1: 751–52 (Act I, Scene 1).

crime and then another, there you are, finally king. For you I've killed a father, a brother, and now myself. May the heavens take you both for victims, and rain down on you the punishments for my crimes!"[20] Inheritance here follows crime, and with his property the heir receives the guilt of what his parent has done to enrich him.

This mixture of inheritance, violence, and guilt comes with a persistent preoccupation with incestuous or otherwise forbidden sexuality. There are of course the Oedipus plays, of which both Corneille and Racine wrote versions; Racine's displays the mixture of prohibited sexuality and generational conflict with special clarity, because he adds to the oedipal story rivalry between Creon and Hemon for Antigone's love. In *Mithridate* two brothers are in love with their father's bride, and the bride has been in love with one of them since before the father's proposal. Corneille's *Rodogune* presents the same pattern: two virtuous brothers are in love with their dead father's bride. In Racine's *Phèdre*, there is not only the heroine's incestuous love for her stepson but Hippolyte's love for a girl whom his father has adopted and to whom he has forbidden marriage. Less directly, his *Andromaque* and *Bérénice* likewise focus on forbidden loves, cases in which young men fall in love with women for whom they should have inherited enmity. *Bajazet* centers on a wife in love with her husband's brother, and the expectation of fratricide is essential to its plot: "You know the harsh practices customary to our sultans. They rarely allow their brothers long to enjoy the dangerous honor of descending from blood that places them too close to the throne."[21] The tragedians' recurrent interest in incest suggests the intensity of the emotions that familial competition mobilized. In the tragedies, family members long violently for the same objects, sexual as well as material. The tragedies teach that proper family life demands renunciation of such desire, ultimately under the threat of parental violence. In the tragedians' vision, the continuity of the *race* rests on a series of losses and conflicts that reach the bases of family itself. Parents sacrifice their children, heirs their younger siblings. As in the Grand Condé's experience, self and inheritance cannot fully coexist.

In these plays, a second line of tension makes the problem of *race* all the more difficult. Both Racine and Corneille set the tensions

20. Corneille, *Oeuvres complètes*, 437 (Act V, Scene 4).
21. Racine, *Oeuvres complètes*, 1: 536 (Act I, Scene 1).

surrounding inheritance within the context of division between public and private spheres of life. The paternal demands and prohibitions that weigh on Titus, Pyrrhus, Horace, Andromède, and so many others are demands that they accept a public role at the expense of private feeling: love and public duty lead in contradictory directions, and the burden of paternal inheritance normally pushes toward the public— hence toward renunciation of personal wishes. This of course is also the theme of Corneille's *Le Cid*. Likewise, Horace *père* insists that "It is wrong to weep for domestic losses, when one sees them producing public victories."[22] *Horace* presents public and private realms as more than simply distinct. They oppose and threaten each other, in gendered terms: the public presented as male, the private as female. Father and son in the play insist on the superiority of public obligations, whereas sisters and daughters call for the primacy of private affections and denounce the sacrifices that public virtue demands. The family in these plays works as the agent of public virtue, demanding that individuals sacrifice personal happiness for some larger good.

In thus celebrating the father's role as guarantor of public virtue, the dramatists spoke for an increasingly significant line of political thought in early modern France. From Bodin in the sixteenth century through Montesquieu in the eighteenth, theorists argued that the authority of the polity rested on properly functioning families, and above all on proper respect for fathers.[23] Order in the small, familial polity would lead to order in the polity at large and to respect for its father, the king. Such a vision of interlocking orders obviously comforted many early modern Europeans, by suggesting the solidity of monarchy, its affinity with the natural order of families. But the parallel with the family also suggested the anxieties that monarchy might evoke; and indeed the dramatists were not alone in suggesting the violence that underlay paternal authority. Like Corneille and Racine, Jean Bodin thought that public virtue rested on the threat of familial violence; and he, too, developed images of paternal violence at startling length. "In any rightly ordered commonwealth," he wrote, "that power of life and death over their children which belongs to them under the law of God and of nature, should be restored to parents. . . . If this power is not restored, there is no hope of any restoration of good

22. Corneille, *Oeuvres complètes,* 262 (Act IV, Scene 2).

23. Nanerl O. Keohane, *Philosophy and the State in France: The Renaissance to the Enlightenment* (Princeton, 1980), 68–69; and forthcoming work by Sarah Hanley on what she terms the "family-state compact" during these years.

morals, honor, virtue, or the ancient splendor of commonwealths. . . . Nowadays, fathers having been deprived of their paternal authority, and any claim to property acquired by their children, it is even suggested that the son can defend himself and resist by force any unjust attempt at coercion on the part of his father. . . . [I]f a father is not out of his mind, he will never be tempted to kill his own child without cause, and if the son has merited such a fate, it is not for the magistrate to intervene."[24] The violent father was a political as well as a dramatic image.

When tragedians placed threatening fathers on the stage, then, they expressed a complex mixture of contemporary anxieties. Audiences would have recognized the realities of conflict between parents and children, and they would have responded to the further suggestion that submission to family needs involved renunciation of strongly felt desires, that inheritance brought with it loss. Audiences would also have noted that these images implied a vision of public life. Like the family, the polity was seen as resting on the repression of personal desires, enforced by threats of paternal violence.

Disjunctures and difficult emotions, I am arguing, had long characterized relations within the aristocratic family. In important ways, aristocratic educational patterns responded to these tensions. But aristocratic education also brought its own tensions, for it typically functioned to separate children from their families and to stress the autonomy of their development. In this sense, education too challenged the solidity of the family, while clarifying the boundaries between the individuals who formed it.

Aristocratic parents of the seventeenth century took education seriously.[25] In keeping with Renaissance thought on the matter, fathers often expressed the wish that their sons acquire more learning

24. Eric Cochrane et al., eds., *Early Modern Europe: Crisis of Authority* (Chicago, 1987), 232, 233, 234. It is worth noting that Bodin (and, with him, much French thought during the Old Regime) here dissents from Aristotle's division between the private world of the family and the public world of the state. For Bodin and his followers, the two displayed the same virtues and vices, in effect blended into each other. As Sarah Hanley has pointed out, this equivalence echoed important sixteenth- and seventeenth-century practices: the increasingly clear dynastic foundations of both the monarchy and its principal servants, for whom public office was increasingly a matter of inheritance.

25. The standard work on aristocratic education during these years is now Mark Motley, *Becoming a French Aristocrat: The Education of the Court Nobility, 1580–1715* (Princeton, 1990). This study uses some of the materials discussed here, but for rather different purposes and arguments.

than they themselves had, so as to play a large role in public affairs. The duc de Bouillon, one of the La Trémoilles' cousins, addressed his memoirs to his son and described the three benefits he wished to leave him: piety, a well-established fortune, and, "for the last, it is to leave you capable . . . of acquiring the moral and political virtues. There are numerous books for these, written by all sorts of people, for which you should learn Latin." The duc's own education had been cut short, "to my great disadvantage," and he thus had lost "the means of learning languages and philosophy, which has been a great weakness in the positions that I've held." Bouillon professed the educational objectives of Renaissance humanism: aristocratic education was to prepare the young man for public action, and for this purpose it was to center on politics, ethics, and language itself.[26] The Grand Condé expressed versions of these ideas in the course of his education and underlined the connections that contemporaries saw between humanist education and leadership. He reported to his father: "I've also written . . . various conversations on the prudence of the prince, with examples of those who have been great and prudent captains, so that I may learn from their conduct to become such as you would desire. I hope to become capable of rendering you the services that God and nature demand of me."[27] Condé's education employed a range of commonplace humanist techniques—dialogue form, historical examples, examples of the prudence of the prince and the captain—and he presented these as exercises that would especially please his father. The upper aristocracy clearly had absorbed many of the assumptions and aims of humanist reformers.

The La Trémoille family (like their cousins the Bouillons, mainly Calvinists) displayed their concern with education in a minute inspection of what their children learned. It was Madame de La Trémoille herself who commanded that her fifteen-year-old son begin instruction in mathematics, despite a tutor's anxiety that the subject might prove too difficult for him.[28] She received numerous reports about her children's intellectual and moral progress, and they regularly sent her examples of their writing.[29] Some Latin and other languages figured

26. Henri duc de Bouillon, *Mémoires*, in Michaud and Poujolat, eds., *Nouvelle collection des mémoires relatifs à l'histoire de France* . . . , 21 (Paris, 1854), 1.

27. Quoted in d'Aumale, *Histoire*, 3: 341.

28. AN 1 AP 648, Chamizay to Madame, 14 April 1635.

29. See below, Chapter 6.

in their educations as well. Women too might receive a good education. During her family's exile in the 1660s, the thirteen-year-old Charlotte Amélie de La Trémoille had "masters in writing and arithmetic, a dancing master, one who taught me German, and in addition I was required daily to repeat lessons on maps, the globe, ethics, music, and the other little things that I'd learned in France." Of her earlier childhood, she wrote that "in truth my hours were regulated from morning to evening."[30]

Standards of aristocratic education rose visibly over the seventeenth century. In 1600 the tradition of military scorn for learning still remained lively. Thus, having explicated a Greek verse too difficult for several magistrates, the maréchal de Biron fled the scene, "so ashamed was he of knowing more than the *gens de robe;* for, to fit in with his era, one had to have the reputation as rather a brute than a man conversant with literature."[31] But Tallemant, writing in the 1650s, made it clear that Biron's anxiety about his learning derived from his times and that attitudes toward learning had changed. By this time a certain degree of learning had become a normal adornment of the polished nobleman. Saint-Evremond quoted the elderly commandeur de Jars lamenting the prevalence of such standards: "In my time, one made gentlemen study only to join the church; even they were mostly satisfied with just the Latin needed for their breviary. Those destined for the court or the army went to the academy. They learned to ride, to dance, arms, to play the lute, to leap, and that was all."[32] He complained that now—the letter dates from 1656—all had changed, and military nobles were expected to be polished and knowledgeable as well.

Military nobles thus took learning seriously, and they steadily acquired more of it as the seventeenth century advanced. Yet there remained clear limits to nobles' educations that sharply distinguished them from relatives intended for the church or the legal professions. Already by his early teens other educational tasks awaited the young man who planned on a military career, and the role of tutors and books had soon to end. Henri de La Trémoille (1598–1674) displayed

30. AN 1 AP 444, 35, 16.
31. Gédéon Tallemant des Réaux, *Historiettes*, ed. Antoine Adam, 2 vols. (Paris, Pléiade, 1960–61), 1: 16; cf. Dewald, *Formation*, 106–9, for discussion of this tradition.
32. *Oeuvres mêlées de Saint-Evremond*, ed. Charles Girard, 3 vols. (Paris, 1867), 2: 259 ("De l'éducation et de l'ignorance").

the progress of his learning and its abrupt reorientation in a series of letters to his mother. "I would indeed like to learn Latin; I humbly beg you to send me some handsome and well-bound books," he wrote at age eight;[33] three weeks later he thanked her for some Latin books that she had sent and praised some letters that he had received from his cousin—already at this age the exchange and evaluation of letters had an important place in his daily life.[34] Somewhat later he thanked his mother for more books and for a map of France she had sent.[35] But a few years later, now apparently in his teens, Henri described the very different routine that he planned to follow in Paris: "[M]ornings I shall devote to dancing and target practice, sometimes to riding; afternoons, to learning mathematics; late in the day there will be visits and time at court, so the time will pass, along with several exercises that we are practicing, . . . which we'll have to put into practice this winter," in military campaigning.[36] After his bookish childhood at home, Henri's adolescent learning included only preparation for war and the court: mathematics, arms, and horseback riding for the one, dancing lessons and visits for the other.

Such focus on practical training at the expense of literary education formed a typical pattern. Henri de Campion's family, in delicate financial circumstances, knew that they had to husband educational expenses. Because his mother "wanted me to follow the soldier's trade . . . she sought only to have me read and write well, and to give me for reading only books that would form my mind and inspire in me good sentiments."[37] When Antoine Arnauld moved from a clerical to a military career in the 1630s, his literary education came to an end, and he was sent for six months to M. Benjamin's famous Parisian academy, to learn horsemanship and other military skills; late in life, he justified the literary style of his memoirs with the comment that "I left my studies and took up the military life too early to pride myself on learning."[38] Bussy-Rabutin, proud of his Latinity and elegant French style, attended Jesuit schools until the age of sixteen, then left for war;[39] the future Grand Condé ended his schooling at age fifteen.

33. AN 1 AP 393, fol. 4, 4 May 1606.
34. Ibid., fol. 8, 26 May 1606.
35. Ibid., fol. 25, n.d.
36. Ibid., fol. 39, n.d.
37. Henri de Campion, *Mémoires*, ed. Marc Fumaroli (Paris, 1967), 42.
38. L'abbé Arnauld, *Mémoires*, 130, 134–35, 119.
39. Roger de Bussy-Rabutin, *Mémoires*, ed. Ludovic Lalanne, 2 vols. (Paris, 1857; repr. Westmead, 1972), 1: 5–8.

As a student, Condé had written Latin letters to his father, but once he left school he shifted to French—a symbol, his biographer suggests, of independence and adulthood.[40] Like Arnauld, both young men added to their literary educations with the Jesuits time at Benjamin's academy. But in each case problems arose, reflecting tensions between ideals of independence and the submission demanded of the student, even in this setting designed for military training. Bussy, as noted above, could not accept his return to schoolboy status after his military experiences.[41] For Condé, later serious study was limited to mathematics, a subject with practical military applications.[42] It is perhaps because of this familiarity with mathematics that several military nobles moved into the position of *surintendant des finances,* a transition that was apparently easy both intellectually and psychologically, with none of the social uncertainties that surrounded judicial careers.[43]

Military nobles, so these examples suggest, devoted considerable attention to their children's educations—but literary education clearly had a secondary role in their lives, and this became clear by the time young men reached their mid-teens. In this respect, educational practices sharply divided the French nobility between robe and sword. The contrast was evident in reading patterns: compared with the *nobles de robe,* military nobles before the eighteenth century owned few books, and the difference probably reflected real differences in reading habits.[44] More important, young men destined for military careers received much of their education in a loosely structured apprenticeship in arms; those preparing for the magistracy were expected to continue their education, under close supervision, until their early twenties. Such an education anchored the future magistrate firmly to his family and social milieu. "I've been to La Flèche," wrote one of the président de Nicolay's agents, "following the command that it pleased you to give me to see Monsieur your son. I found him in his study with his robe and his bonnet, which is great testimony to his eagerness to

40. D'Aumale, *Histoire,* 3: 329, 332.

41. Bussy-Rabutin, *Mémoires,* 1: 8; and see above, Chapter 2.

42. D'Aumale, *Histoire,* 3: 358–59.

43. Examples include the marquis d'O, surintendant from 1578, the duc de Sully, surintendant from 1599, the maréchal de Schomberg, surintendant from 1618, and the maréchal d'Effiat, surintendant from 1626.

44. Henri-Jean Martin, *Livre, pouvoirs, et société à Paris au XVIIe siècle,* 2 vols. (Geneva, 1969), 1: 481, and passim; Jonathan Dewald, *Pont-St-Pierre, 1398–1789: Lordship, Community, and Capitalism in Early Modern France* (Berkeley, 1987), 189–90; Kristen Neuschel, *Word of Honor* (Ithaca, 1989); Motley, *Becoming a French Aristocrat,* 77ff.

content you. The Jesuit fathers are very proud of him." As the only in-
terruption in this round of effort, the son tentatively proposed an occasional game of tennis.[45] Such an education had to be followed from
an early age. The principal of the Jesuit college of Pont-à-Mousson
wrote to the discouraged stepfather of a young man studying there, a
cousin of the président de Nicolay, that the student "is accomplishing
something, but among other things I see clearly that his age causes
him many difficulties that a little child would not have, and principally
because of his weak memory."[46] At this age—twenty-three—it was
too late to shift from a military career to one that required Latin,
though the principal's judgment concerned an especially incompetent
student.

If anything, robe education became more structured over the period. From the early seventeenth century, the Jesuit colleges took the
dominant role in educating the *noblesse de robe,* leaving to the universities mainly the formal process of certifying minimal legal compe-
tence. Most sixteenth-century universities had been rickety institutions, with students and instructors alike commonly wandering from
one to another; and they offered relatively lax moral control of their
students. The Jesuit colleges functioned quite differently. The président de Nicolay described his expectations of the college system in a
letter to the principal at Pont-à-Mousson, again concerning his unfortunate young cousin. He hoped that the cousin's "mind might awaken
when carefully guided, watched over, and considered by the good Jesuit fathers, charitable and insightful [*clairvoyans*]."[47] Jesuit education offered watchfulness and control within a clear-cut institutional
setting. By his mid-teens, the young *noble d'épée* had left this kind of
environment for the much more fluid setting of academies, camps, and
courts. In this respect as in many others, the contrast between sword
and robe was a contrast between uncertainty and a career within a
clearly defined official hierarchy. Unlike the future magistrate, the military nobleman had experienced a prolonged period of moral and personal uncertainty, uncertainties that might be deepened by voluntary
or enforced residence abroad but that were in any case inherent in the
educational demands made on young men.

45. AN 3 AP 17, 13 C 221, Bodin to Nicolay, 7 August 1611.
46. AN 3 AP 17, 13 C 276, 27 March 1618, principal, Pont-à-Mousson, to M. de
Senillac.
47. AN 3 AP 17, 13 C 285, 6 June 1618.

Even among the well-educated nobility of the later seventeenth century, writers continued to stress the specific psychological and intellectual orientations that the *noblesse d'épée* ought to seek. Saint-Evremond himself denied the worth of speculative and scientific learning; he concluded: "I find none of the sciences especially relevant to *les honnêtes gens* save ethics, politics, and the knowledge of *belles lettres.* . . . The one teaches us to govern our passions; by the next you instruct yourself in affairs of state and regulate your conduct in the face of fortune; the third polishes the mind and inspires refinement and pleasure."[48] The sieur de Pontis used very similar terms. A young gentleman should learn "to reason and to speak well in public," skills suited "to those who, because of their high birth, their tasks, and their positions, may need them in countless circumstances." These needs required an education that differed sharply from that of the *noblesse de robe,* who required a genuinely scholarly education and technical expertise. "One must distinguish clearly between a child destined for the robe and one to be raised in the profession of arms. The first ought never to discontinue his studies; whereas it suffices that the other study until the age of fifteen or sixteen, in order to learn philosophy, ancient and modern history, and the principal maxims of politics, so as to regulate his conduct in society." This was to be followed by two or three years at an academy, to learn the basic skills and graces of the military profession, and then by foreign travel, "to learn languages and the ways in which different peoples govern themselves."[49]

For de Pontis as for so many others in the seventeenth century, the differences between robe and sword were cultural rather than genealogical. The education that he proposed for the military nobleman was explicitly civic and unspecialized, designed to prepare the young nobleman for a role in public life, in contrast to the future magistrate, who ought ideally never to leave the structured cultural world of the college and university. De Pontis, like Saint-Evremond, Condé, and the duc de Bouillon, had adopted assumptions of Renaissance humanism, especially its concern that young men be formed for public life and its claim that rhetoric and ethics offered the best training for such

48. Charles de Marguetel, seigneur de Saint-Evremond, *Oeuvres en prose,* ed. René Ternois, 3 vols. (Paris, 1962–66), 2: 12.

49. Sieur de Pontis, *Mémoires,* in M. Petitot, ed., *Collection des mémoires relatifs à l'histoire de France,* 31–32 (Paris, 1824), 32: 488.

a life.[50] But his comments also suggested suspicion of excessive learning as a barrier to civic action. The La Trémoilles shared these views. They copied into one of their letter books an anonymous political tract emphasizing the value of the active life and the dangers of retreat from the world, in particular the danger of excessive study: "Study is a form of idleness . . . it weakens minds and bodies. . . . [T]o be always among books is to be dead to the living and to live among the dead—or to be dead to both, and live only for oneself. . . . It is incompatible with service to princes . . . but to be ready to serve them, it is necessary to have studied." Action and service to the prince were the point of aristocratic education; any educational program that distracted from these ends was to be avoided, and excessive immersion in studies would have this effect.[51]

Magistrates such as La Roche Flavin largely accepted the divergence of educational programs that military nobles perceived. La Roche Flavin stressed the young magistrate's slow acquisition of the "secrets of the palace," his need for technical learning, and the importance of age to real learning. He even called on magistrates to devote less of their time to historical studies of Roman law, more to the techniques they would need in the practice of their profession. He framed his warning in terms of the moral consequences of humanistic thought: excessive preoccupation with history, he wrote, served only to relativize the student's vision of the laws that he would have to apply as a magistrate.[52]

Both military careers and educational aims required an early end to humanist learning. For a variety of reasons—involving educational theory, political accident, and personal ambition—such careers also typically demanded early departure from home and early exposure to adult life. Whereas the future magistrate's education in some ways more firmly attached him to the parental milieu, the future soldier encountered experiences that distanced him from older generations and left him to develop without much outside guidance.

50. My understanding of Renaissance humanism rests heavily on the views of J. G. A. Pocock, *The Machiavellian Moment: Florentine Political Thought and the Atlantic Republican Tradition* (Princeton, 1975); and of William Bouwsma, most recently developed in *John Calvin: A Sixteenth-Century Portrait* (Oxford, 1988), 113–27 and passim, and *A Usable Past: Essays in European Cultural History* (Berkeley, 1990).
51. AN 1 AP 397, "Extrait du Pol__ Cris__," 64.
52. Discussed in Dewald, *Formation,* 26–27.

Travel was the clearest form taken by this urge to detach individuals from their native settings. French nobles traveled through Europe in the early seventeenth century: in search of military experience, in hopes of making a fortune abroad, and often involuntarily, because of political pressures and legal difficulties at home. Henri de Campion described the large émigré population in England, *grands* who, under Louis XIII, had "retired to shelter themselves from the hatred of the Cardinal."[53] Milder political disappointments and simply the lack of political opportunities continued to have the same effect throughout the seventeenth century. In about 1650 Henri de La Trémoille wrote to his mother with praise for "the resolution that my brother has taken ... to travel to Flanders ... since the times promise nothing, given that he has no position here; during this time he'll find diversions which, even if they lead to no concrete results, at least distance him from the evils that solitude and other things (better to perform than to mention) may bring him."[54] His brother himself described the similar role of disappointment in driving another young man to Holland: "[H]e was a gentleman of quality and ability [*mérite*] who had enjoyed the friendship and favor of Monseigneur le Duc d'Orléans and who had lost them."[55] Henri himself described the role of youthful ambition in driving him to Holland. Frustrated that his tutor had delayed his entry on a military career, "I developed the idea of leaving his care to withdraw to Holland, to be with M. le Prince d'Orange my great uncle."[56] Duelling too regularly led to voluntary exiles, as those involved prudently waited outside France for the royal pardons that typically concluded these affairs; and each year in the early seventeenth century saw about thirty-five duels, almost all of them (because of the French custom of duelling in groups) involving numerous combatants, and hence numerous exiles.[57]

Above all, young nobles traveled because contemporaries believed separation from home to be an important element in education. Such ideas touched all social classes,[58] but they affected the *noblesse d'épée*

53. Campion, *Mémoires*, 144.
54. AN 1 AP 394, no. 46, n.d.
55. AN 1 AP 381, no. 78, 10 April 1628.
56. AN 1 AP 441, fols. 1ov, 3r.
57. François Billacois, *Le duel dans la société française des XVIe–XVIIe siècles: Essai de psychologie historique* (Paris, 1986), 190, 407.
58. See Alan Macfarlane, *The Family Life of Ralph Josselin, a Seventeenth-Century Clergyman: An Essay in Historical Anthropology* (Cambridge, 1970).

with particular force because of assumptions about the personal qualities and experiences that the military noble would need. In the later
sixteenth century, Montaigne had encountered large numbers of
young French nobles who had come to Italy to acquire the skills and
manners of courtly life.[59] In the early seventeenth century, attention
had shifted to northern Europe, as young men sought experience in
the great theaters of the Thirty Years' War. From his correspondence
with his mother, we may follow the teenaged duc de La Trémoille as
he traveled through Europe in the early seventeenth century. At age
fourteen, La Trémoille accompanied his cousin the duc de Bouillon on
an embassy to London; two years later he was at Metz and then Sedan, in the duc's territories; in January of the next year he visited Venice and Geneva, and at about this time he traveled also to eastern Europe. He reported the gracious reception that the emperor accorded
him and his acquaintance with "the flower of the lower Austrian nobility and an infinity of fine ladies, with whom I dance allemands to
the sound of trumpets until daybreak." From there he went "to see the
fortifications of Hungary, where I was very magnificently received by
the governors."[60]

La Trémoille's younger brother the comte de Laval—born in about
1600—traveled as widely, and the impact of his travels was ultimately
deeper. His experiences illustrated in extreme form the complex mixture of freedom, parental control, and personal ambition that such
journeys might involve. Before he was ten years old Laval had been to
Germany, and as a teenager he too spent considerable time at Sedan.[61]
In 1619 he was at The Hague, pursuing both military training and a
position with the Dutch armies. He did not travel alone: eight paid
subordinates accompanied him to Germany in the early 1620s, including an apothecary, an argentier, two lackeys, a page, and two
gentlemen.[62] Their numbers assured that Laval's mother received a
continuous flow of detailed reports about his experiences and disposition; his family wanted to retain close control over him even as it
sent him far from home.

59. Michel de Montaigne, *Oeuvres complètes*, ed. Maurice Rat (Paris, Pléiade, 1962), 1182, 1204.
60. AN 1 AP 393, fols. 32–43; 1 AP 394, 53, 95.
61. AN 1 AP 381, 5–16.
62. AN 1 AP 382, Comte de Laval, "Dépenses," "Estat des gages que Madame a ordonne estre paiez par chancun an a ceux qui sont a la suite de monseigneur le comte, en son voiage d'Allemagne . . . "

His family showed particular concern that he make the most of his opportunities to secure a distinguished position, but Laval found his situation discouraging: "I must say that there is no chance here for military exercises, and it's difficult to get anywhere with Monsieur the prince of Orange because of the quantity of business that occupies him."[63] The Dutch diplomat François van Aerssen gave more detailed reports to the comte's anxious mother. Her son, he reported, "is doing well as to both his health and his conduct, without neglecting any respect that he owes both to your Excellency and to my lord the prince of Orange, to whom he pays his respects at the appropriate hours, employing his remaining hours for his instruction."[64] Two months later there was more reassurance: "[H]e is doing well, in both body and mind; there is certainly great pleasure for those who wish your happiness to see him so well-governed in his actions and words, showing on every occasion great interest in gaining knowledge of things appropriate to his rank, and thus I dare hope that his stay here will succeed, to his great profit."[65] Despite his assurances, Van Aerssen's language conveyed the young man's uncertain situation within the foreign court, the combination of self-control and inquisitiveness that his situation demanded. La Trémoille was in Holland to learn both politics and warfare, to establish connections with leaders of the Dutch state, perhaps to acquire a position, even to learn to handle the discomforts of military life: his mother received encouraging reports that "he spent last night in the trenches, under a continuous rain . . . but he endured this trial without complaint, since he was in an honorable position."[66] His inherited social position, his *qualité*, demanded that he acquire suitable knowledge; *qualité* went easily with words like "succeed" and "profit."

But soon after, the episode ended badly. Just a month later, Van Aerssen wrote again, now to report that the comte was returning to France. "I see," he wrote to the anxious mother, "that they have alarmed your Excellency with the lubricity of his age and acquaintances [*conversation*], without there being sufficient care to . . .

63. Ibid., 17.

64. AN 1 AP 642, 16 January 1619.

65. Ibid., 25 March 1619.

66. AN 1 AP 648, dossier Chateauneuf, to Madame, 8 October 1622; cf ibid., same to same, 12 November 1621: "Lincommodité que ceste armée recevoit a dornic l'a contrainte de desloger mais monseigneur le Conte en a sy bien supporté sa part que graces a Dieu il sest rendu en ce lieu en tres bonne disposition."

control him. But, Madame, when your Excellency sends him back the same considerations will always arise—unless you decide to throw him straight into action, and to start him with a company."[67] Here were the dangers of exile and travel: involvement with doubtful friends and immorality. But the risks and purposes of such travel were intimately bound together. The point was precisely to separate the young man from the constrictions of home and to teach him to handle himself in an unsettled situation.

Thus Laval's failures and unsuitable associations did not put an end to his travels. Early the next year Van Aerssen encouraged Laval's mother to send him again to Holland: "[I]t will now be time that you direct him to the profession to which the service of his king and his rank call him; hence if he is to stop here—since he could not possibly find a better school—I want to take on the responsibility, Madame, of supervising not only his health but also his actions."[68] Instead, Laval and his retinue spent much of the next year in Czechoslovakia and Germany, but in 1621 he was back in Holland, again worrying about the difficulty of finding suitable employment and the intricacies of court life, and again worrying his mother.[69] She asked about a report that Laval had declined an advantageous position, but, so Laval's companion sought to reassure her, the Dutch had offered nothing solid: "We must start over, and help ourselves. [Laval] scarcely considers minor positions . . . he finds mediocre ones more acceptable, but . . . with all his heart he aspires to something great; and his servants upset him when they speak of accepting anything less."[70] Laval, his friends, and his anxious mother all viewed his stay in terms of the difficult problems of ambition. The same companion sought to reassure Madame about Laval's morals: "[H]e says that he is strongly resolved to gamble no more, both for the respect that he owes your orders and for several personal reasons."[71] But he had also come to the brink of fighting a duel with a young prince visiting The Hague, an event that the prince of Orange forestalled when the two young men were seen leaving the palace together.[72]

67. Ibid., 21 April 1619.
68. Ibid., 19 January 1620.
69. AN 1 AP 648, dossier Chateauneuf, 3 August 1620, 17 September 1620, 8 August 1621, 25 May 1622.
70. AN 1 AP 648, Chateauneuf to Madame, 25 May 1622.
71. Ibid., same to same, 13 December 1621.
72. Ibid., 25 March 1621.

In the end Laval spent three years in Holland, his ambitions repeatedly frustrated. Even to leave the country required delicate manipulation of the political situation in which he found himself: exile proved a political as well as a military school. An anonymous memorandum "On the Departure of My Lord the Count" described the steps needed to leave "with good will and some sort of advantage." To do so required, first, discussion with the prince of Orange, "whose approval one must have; and for prudence's sake one must act in such a way that one seems to be following his orders entirely." The comte needed to show similar deference to the Estates and perhaps to the exiled king of Bohemia as well. Through the whole process, the comte was to "take the greatest care not to give any cause for annoyance to anyone, but to come away with everyone's good will and to leave behind such a reputation that he will be missed."[73] On his own in a complicated, foreign political setting, Laval needed self-control and an intense effort to shape others' responses; the comte had to measure each act against not only immediate but also long-term consequences.

Laval's wanderings continued all his life, with just the disquieting moral consequences that his mother had anticipated. In 1627 he received a commission from the king of Denmark to raise and lead 3,000 French soldiers.[74] He involved himself in several of the military uprisings that marked Louis XIII's early reign, and he spent his last years in Venetian exile. In 1642 he was killed in a duel, following a secret marriage with a lady of doubtful standing.[75]

Laval's was hardly a typical life or fate, yet in some ways he was a paradigmatic figure. His wanderings illustrated the moral risks of education that detached young men from familial controls and required them to make their way in alien settings; his mother's worries echoed those of an earlier generation about the effects of Italian vices on young men studying there. Foreign settings posed political as well as moral dangers, for they often brought young men into contact with alien religions and quasi-republican forms of government. Contact with republican ideas generated fear in early-seventeenth-century England,[76] and such fear was even stronger in seventeenth-century

73. AN 1 AP 382.
74. AN 1 AP 383, 25 March 1627.
75. AN 1 AP 382, 22 February 1642.
76. S. L. Adams, "Foreign Policy and the Parliaments of 1621 and 1624," in Kevin Sharpe, ed., *Faction and Parliament: Essays on Early Stuart History* (Oxford, 1978), 139–72, 141.

France, especially after the awful example of Cromwell pointed to the danger in any criticism of monarchy. Yet Laval's experiences displayed also families' readiness to subject their sons to a large degree of dislocation and independence. Despite their concern at his moral development, Laval's family placed him in these difficult situations, and they sent him back after an initial failure. Clearly these choices betokened neither indifference to the child nor moral laxity. Laval's mother followed his development closely and anxiously, and she displayed characteristically Calvinist views of the dangers that surrounded him. The family's choices reflected their sense that autonomy and ambition were necessary components of the young man's education.

Families took these risks also because of their sense that excessive familial closeness posed greater dangers for children's development. In 1618 a relative of the président de Nicolay wrote to him about an unsuccessful son: "[M]y mother is the first cause that he is incapable of entering society [*n'est pas propre pour le monde*], having always wanted to have him next to her."[77] And the consequences of such a failure were, it was thought, obvious to all. "It must not be expected," wrote the Jesuit principal of the young man's school, "that this young man will succeed either in letters or in arms, but he is much more, even altogether, incapable of entering society, lacking the strength, the grace, and the judgment to govern himself there; he would be a laughing-stock, the disgrace of his family."[78] The principal readily equated "arms" and "society," and he made clear the totality of training that such a career demanded. A life in the world, the principal believed, demanded strength, self-control, and ability. A young man lacking these qualities endangered not only his own career but also his entire family's standing.

Even without travel abroad, acquiring these qualities demanded liberty and the consequent dangers of disorder. In 1637 yet another relative of the président de Nicolay wrote asking him to watch over his grandson, who was coming to learn military skills at a Parisian academy, "since in this century the young often liberate themselves" from familial discipline.[79] The young man was coming to Paris, so his father explained, "so that he may attempt to become an *honnête homme* and worthy of the name that he bears and capable of rendering you his

77. AN 3 AP 17, 13 C 187, 10 June 1618, Mme de Senillac to Nicolay.
78. Ibid., 13 C 285, 6 June 1618.
79. AN 3 AP 59, 3 F 9, 5 October 1637.

very humble services."[80] Time at the academy was necessary, so the father's comments implied, because the youth needed to form himself. The président de Nicolay agreed: "[Y]ou will scarcely believe the pleasure I feel in your expectation of my concern for your son's advancement; he is well born, and shows promise [*& promect quelque chose de bon*], if God gives him the grace to continue from good to better."[81] The young man's birth mattered to Nicolay, but it provided only a start toward his development into *quelque chose de bon*. It was amid the moral uncertainties of the academy that the young man would try to become the *honnête homme* that his birth demanded; birth and becoming were not contradictory but complementary aspects of the self, both of them needed. The problem of youthful liberty was comparable. Youth needed to be prevented from "emancipating itself," but it also required situations of freedom as a normal stage of education.

The Condé family likewise experienced the tensions between parental moral control and independence in education. At age fifteen, the future Grand Condé thus found himself brought to court and to M. Benjamin's academy, on the one hand expected to acquire the graces of courtly life, on the other subject to the close scrutiny of his father, who, fearful of the morally corrosive effects of elegant Parisian society, sought to limit even Condé's visits to his mother.[82] Lesser nobles might in some degree resolve these contradictions by sending their sons to serve as pages in the households of wealthier patrons, a practice that survived well into the seventeenth century. Madame de La Trémoille received a request from one nobleman to receive his son, "humbly begging you to accept him as he is—that is, with several faults; but these I hope nonetheless, with God's help and with the virtuous education that those nourished in your house ordinarily receive, will change into zeal, ability, and affection for your service as long as he lives."[83] Like Condé's father, the writer sought to resolve contradictory expectations. He wanted his son raised away from home, but he worried about the boy's moral development. In a local version of the comte de Laval's experiences in Holland, the boy was expected as well to acquire the patronage connections that would serve his ambi-

80. Ibid., 3 F bis, same day.
81. AN 3 AP 59, Nicolay to Nicolay de Languedoc, 7 June 1608.
82. D'Aumale, *Histoire*, 3: 335–41.
83. AN 1 AP 649, Chevratière to Madame, 31 October 1635.

tions later in life. Ability to navigate such situations formed an underlying objective of this kind of education.

Despite their commitment to humanist learning, I have argued, aristocratic parents in the seventeenth century attached more importance
to other educational objectives: they sought—despite the moral risks
entailed—to place their sons in situations that detached them from
household and family and taught them to deal effectively with the social world. Underlying this pattern was a concern with young men's
personal development, and this concern recurred in other aspects of
seventeenth-century childhood and youth. Even in dealing with young
children, tutors and parents directed their main energies to developing
the child's personal qualities, and they showed surprising sensitivity to
differences between children. "Monsieur the prince's mind strength-
ens a little in science and reasoning, which I try to have him acquire
rather than any other thing," wrote a somewhat discouraged tutor to
Madame de La Trémoille in 1633, about her thirteen-year-old son;
"and I hope with God's help that we will succeed, at least when he
thinks about what he is undertaking. I assure you, Madame, that he
surpasses by far the expectations one might have of those of his
age. . . . [I]f he had the outlook [*le fond de l'humeur*] of Monseigneur
his brother he would be an angel, for I swear to you that when he controls himself and reflects, he sometimes says things that astonish me,
far beyond his age. What he lacks for that outlook is little in itself, but
important in regard to that free spirit that children need to have; that
of Monseigneur le comte [the prince's younger brother] is just as it
should be . . . he speaks continuously. . . . [T]ake some time, if you
please, Madame, to examine his letters. . . . [H]e sometimes includes
some rather good things for a child, for I assure you that no one puts
a hand to them but he. He takes pleasure in everything."[84]

The tutor's educational program gave a considerable place to notions of liberty and expression: that the comte de Laval chattered constantly was desirable; his older brother's silence needed correction.
The older brother needed more reflection before he spoke, but he also
needed to have "*l'esprit libre.*" This language of directness and freedom of expression echoed comments during these same years about

84. AN 1 AP 642, Allard to Madame, from Paris, 23 January 1633.

the value of a direct, informal style of writing.[85] Although formal attainments certainly had a significant place in this educational program, the main objective was to encourage the child to speak and write easily. Children were expected to progress at different rates toward this goal, and the goal itself demanded attention to individual differences.

Ease of physical motion had equal importance and called forth similar assumptions about the educational process. "Monsieur your son," wrote another observer to Madame de La Trémoille, "is in fine health and begins to have an idea of dancing; but he certainly needed [his dancing master], for he alone could have achieved what you will soon see for yourself, not only for the dance, but for all manner of bodily movements; as for movements of the intellect, I hope that they will develop with time, attention, and association with groups who will contribute to this project."[86] Intelligence, it was here assumed, would develop with sociability.

The same tutor described his hesitancy regarding mathematics, "to which I haven't yet dared to introduce him, for fear of straining his mind, which weakens with too much work; it is still too weak in reasoning, but before May is out I'll have him beginning arithmetic and the sphere, which are the bases of fortifications, and maps, then gradually to other things, so that I can see how his mind deals with this work, which I'll assign only according to his ability."[87] Yet again, there was concern for the child's specific abilities and a readiness to adapt tuition to them. With its clear practical relevance to an eventual military career, arithmetic and geometry formed an appropriate bridge between early education in letters and the practical skills acquired in later adolescence. At the same time, arithmetic was clearly viewed as a difficult subject, whose introduction had to await the pupil's developing mental strength.

Emphasis on liberty and on individual development recurs throughout the La Trémoilles' correspondence about education, from the start of the seventeenth century. Already in 1609 a visitor to the household noted with approval that the young duke's tutor "proceeds according to his pupil's temperament" and with respect for the fact

---

85. Discussed below, Chapter 6.
86. AN 1 AP 648, Chamizay to Madame, 16 May 1633.
87. AN 1 AP 648, Chamizay to Madame, 14 April 1635; as noted above, Madame insisted on a faster educational pace.

that "this boy wants to know the reasons for everything that he is asked to learn. . . . In sum, he's being very well brought up. I advised them not only to allow him to play when he wishes, but to invite him to play when he hasn't asked."[88] Liberty, leisure, and responsiveness to the child's character each had an important place in this vision of education. The tutor had to respect the child's character even when the child demanded justification for the tutor's requirements.

Two generations later these ideas remained vigorous within the La Trémoille family. Charlotte Amélie de La Trémoille described the degree of liberty that she had been allowed during the 1650s. Her grandmother, she wrote, raised her according to the "maxim that as long as I did nothing contrary to the respect I owed God and the modesty that a girl ought to have, the rest would take care of itself with time; beyond those two points, she thought that one had to leave children in complete liberty, in order to get to know their character [*humeur*], and that otherwise they would disguise themselves before others, and act badly in private."[89] Her grandmother's methods did not preclude educational seriousness: Charlotte Amélie, as we have seen, faced rigorous educational demands. But her grandmother's belief in freedom was no mere personal whim. Her German mother, wrote Charlotte Amélie, "couldn't endure me, since I'd been raised in the French style in complete liberty, and she wanted her children much more restrained; so she never saw me without saying something harsh about my being dirty or misbehaving."[90] Liberty of upbringing was *la manière de France*," for men and women alike.

Such comments include significant assumptions about how children developed and about the interplay of nature with external cultivation. Children's true natures had to be allowed to emerge, and this could not happen if excessive constraints were placed on them. Teachers had to allow their charges play and leisure, and they had to adjust their methods to individual children, for temperaments differed widely. Early education thus worked in the same directions as later travels: in childhood as in adolescence, it was thought important to

88. AN 1 AP 651, La Trémoille, Jacques de Constant to duc de Bouillon, 22 April 1609.

89. AN 1 AP 444, La Trémoille, "Vie de la princesse de La Trémoille comtesse d'Aldenburg, écrite par sa propre main en forme d'instruction à son digne fils" (Marie Amélie was the daughter of the prince de Tarente and lived 1652–1732), 2.

90. Ibid., 9.

give enough freedom to allow personal qualities to develop. As a result, there could be no certainty about patterns of eventual development. All children were different, and all needed to develop their specific abilities.

Such educational practices, with their stress on children's distinct personalities and vigorous natural qualities, accorded well with strong emotional attachments to children. Attachment was not necessarily the rule, but it formed part of an expected pattern of behavior, an aspect of the appropriate. A glimpse both of a family's real feelings and of the wider conventions from which they emerged comes from a manuscript compiled at the death of the twelve-year-old Elisabeth de La Trémoille, sister of the prince de Tarente.[91] Elisabeth died in 1640, with exemplary courage and faith after months of uncomfortable illness. The family composed a fifteen-page account of her "death and last words" and circulated copies among friends and family. Their intent was partly pious edification: "I'll try to profit by her fine teachings, and will often reread the discourse that you've sent us, not without bitter tears," so responded one recipient. But the description also included concrete details about the girl's eating, described her loss of weight and other symptoms, and quoted her moments of misery and discouragement.[92] The account sought to capture a real moment as well as moral lessons. The narrative's existence and its wide circulation both suggest the importance that a child's death might have.

In response came ninety-one letters of condolence, from a wide range of eminent figures, among them the Condé family, Richelieu, Mademoiselle (the king's niece), the duc de Rohan, Mademoiselle de Rambouillet, Mademoiselle de Gournay, Voiture. Elisabeth's death brought into action a wide social network, one that cut across important contemporary divisions: the letter writers included both Protestants and Catholics (fittingly, in that Elisabeth and her mother were Protestant, her father a Catholic convert for the past decade); and they came from the high *noblesse d'épée*, the Parisian magistracy, and the literary world. Despite these differences, most of the writers emphasized their close connections with the family, an indication of how tightly upper-class society continued to hold together in the face of

91. AN 1 AP 433, "Lettres de consolation escrites à Madame la Duchesse de La Trémoille sur la mort de Mademoiselle sa fille."
92. Ibid., fols. 9r, 87r–94r.

significant strains. Fifty-five of the ninety-one were women, and some of the letters hinted at the feminine quality of grief at such a moment: all were addressed to the girl's mother, and the duchesse d'Aiguillon added to her consolation a request "to assure Monsieur your husband of my share in his grief, I haven't dared write him for fear of importuning him"; the girl's grandmother wrote to the mother that "after you, no one can have lost more than I," leaving father and brothers at a lower position. Yet the father had spent the night before she died in the girl's room and had tearfully granted her request that her sister be raised a Protestant.[93]

The letters themselves are at once formulaic and intensely emotional—again, suggesting that contemporaries believed intense emotion to be an appropriate response to the loss of a child. All stressed the wild grief that both the mother and her friends would feel at the loss. "Truly I cannot express to you my grief," wrote the princesse de Condé; "with all my heart I wish that I could be with you, to mingle my tears with yours." Extreme pain at the loss was expected, but all of the letters move on to stress the countervailing wisdom that was to bring grief under control. Such wisdom was, in the words of the duchesse d'Aiguillon, "to preserve you for the people who have some share in the honor of your friendship."[94]

Intense love, grief, and—in formulaic antithesis—self-controlled wisdom thus mingled in these appreciations of what a child's death meant. So also did admiration for the child's precocious abilities and spiritual state. Elisabeth had shown her extraordinary qualities, wrote the marquise de Duras, "by her admirable end, so extraordinary for her age; all who have seen the description are amazed, and shed tears along with yours." Elisabeth's grandmother agreed: "We are amazed at what she said; it's a lesson for even the oldest."[95] Such comments bound love for the child with appreciation of her capacities, in ways reminiscent of friends' and tutors' assessments of other La Trémoille children. In spiritual as in intellectual matters, children were to be evaluated, in particular on a scale of age. The La Trémoilles and their friends valued precocity, so that love of children, as of friends, sprang at least partly from "merit." But emotion also had value, at least among the formulas of polite expression; desperate grief at the loss of

93. Ibid., fols. 7r, 8v, 88r.
94. Ibid., fols. 3r, 7r.
95. Ibid., fols. 36r, 9r.

a child was a natural and expected impulse, one that required the teachings of religion and philosophy to control.

The mid-seventeenth-century military nobleman Henri de Campion described similar affections and grief—and like the La Trémoilles, he explained his love by his child's special merits. In 1649 his wife gave birth to their first child, a daughter "so beautiful and so delightful that from the moment of her birth I loved her with a tenderness that I cannot express." Two years later, during an interlude from his political maneuverings, he spent "part of my time in reading, or in playing with my daughter, who, despite her youth, was so amusing that everyone who saw her felt enormous pleasure, and I more than all the rest together." Two years later the child died, at the age of four, and Campion felt his life blighted: his affliction was such "that since then I've felt no real joy. I had so firmly convinced myself that my daughter would be the consolation of my last years, and I had begun so to associate her with all my actions, that I feel it a form of theft to take any pleasure without her." Campion too presented these emotions as tending to the feminine ("I would play the role of a woman if I bothered everyone with my sorrows," he wrote), and like the La Trémoilles' friends he thought in terms of a balance between grief and wise self-control. "Many will criticize me for weakness," he wrote, "and for lacking constancy in an event that they will not rank among the most grievous." Thus Campion too treated his emotions as unusual and ambiguous in moral standing, and he linked his sense of loss to the girl's specific qualities; her beauty and charm had initially created his love, and the survival of another child offered no consolation or even much interest. Yet Campion also offered a defense of emotion: "Insensibility and coldness are often taken for constancy, just as love and friendship are often taken for weakness."[96] Campion did not present his feelings for his daughter as universal, but neither were they shameful eccentricities. They represented intense versions of a normal and proper engagement with others.

These were instances in which parental love functioned well. Yet the same ideas about childhood and parenting might produce entirely different outcomes. For ideals of naturalness, childhood individuality, and love based on merit allowed wide room for parental distance

96. Campion, *Mémoires*, 199, 201, 212. Cf. Lawrence Stone, *The Family, Sex, and Marriage in England, 1500–1800* (New York, 1977), for the argument that play with children was essentially an eighteenth-century phenomenon.

from children—and for intense consciousness of rejection on each side. Charlotte Amélie de La Trémoille described these complex emotions with exceptional acuity. Raised at the family's estates by her loving and liberal grandmother, Charlotte Amélie rarely saw her parents, and such interviews as they had went badly. Early on, she wrote, "my mother couldn't endure me," because of the liberal way in which she had been raised. Yet a halting relationship between them developed, a by-product of the pressures which Protestant families like the La Trémoilles faced after mid-century. A Catholic uncle sought through court influence to have the thirteen-year-old Charlotte Amélie and her brother placed under his care; to avoid this enforced conversion, Charlotte Amélie's mother suddenly appeared at the estate of Thouars to carry them off to Holland. "I awoke, I looked at her," recalled Charlotte Amélie in her memoirs, "and thinking that I was dreaming (which had happened to me several times) I rolled over and tried to get back to sleep." The poignancy of the moment lay both in the child's longing for her mother and her awareness of the mother's indifference. "I knew that my mother had never loved me, but things improved somewhat; for seeing that she received my little efforts well gave me courage, and I gained ease with her much sooner than I would ever have hoped; and this truly won my mother's heart in my favor, so that she did sincerely what she had resolved to pretend—that is, to treat me well and to love me."[97] Parental love emerged only in response to the child's ease of manner and openness. Even then, however, "my brother . . . stood way above me" in their mother's heart.[98]

With their father (who first set eyes on Charlotte Amélie when she was two or three years old, and who saw her only a few times in the following decade), the situation was reversed—but anxieties and tensions were equally present. He "displayed the greatest joy in the world at seeing me again, and a love as strong as I could have wished. In this he distinguished sharply between my brother and me; for since he was always timid and serious, and I very bold and gay, [our father] had a preference for me, which followed the sentiments that he had had from the start."[99]

Ideals of childish naturalness and directness thus placed their own burdens on children and on familial relations. Parents responded

97. AN 1 AP 444, 28.
98. Ibid., 36.
99. Ibid., 34, 35.

badly to timidity or gravity, apparently because these raised doubts about their connections to their children. The La Trémoilles demanded that their children feel natural with them despite long separations. Tarente's relations with his son became still more complex as the family's religious history changed. In 1667 the prince abjured his Protestantism and sought to encourage his son to do the same. The son's resistance provoked furious rage; Tarente threatened "to place him between four walls, on bread and water for the rest of his life." When the son finally yielded, he was sent to a Parisian academy for two years.[100] Others in these years placed comparable weight on children's spontaneity: when his son displayed anxious reserve toward him, Louis XIII threatened to remove the boy from his mother's care.[101]

From all of these experiences, Charlotte Amélie de La Trémoille drew a striking picture of the conditional nature of parental love; it needed to be earned by the child's behavior and personality, and the potential for coldness was very great. To the end, children could not take affection for granted: "[A]ssuredly," reflected Charlotte Amélie as she thought about her childhood, "I believe that blessings or curses from fathers and mothers, and especially at the hour of their deaths, have great importance, and draw to their children benefits or sufferings; that's why every child ought to seek religiously to observe the fifth commandment, as something of great importance."[102] Parents were dangerous, a source of blessings if placated, of efficacious curses if treated with disrespect. Both Charlotte Amélie's experiences and her reflections paralleled the images of dangerous parental presence seen in the classical dramatists. The parallel is the more striking in that Charlotte Amélie understood parenting in broad terms. She did not see her father and mother simply as sources of authority; she worried about their love and analyzed its strengths and failures. But the existence of parental love merely exacerbated tensions within the family.

Clearly, then, love for children existed in aristocratic milieux. As significant, there were powerful societal conventions about love for children. At their deaths, intense grief was proper and expected, not merely from the parents, but from a wide range of relatives and

---

100. Ibid., 51.
101. A. Lloyd Moote, *Louis XIII, the Just* (Berkeley, 1989), 283; Ruth Kleinman, *Anne of Austria, Queen of France* (Columbus, Ohio, 1985), 114.
102. AN 1 AP 444, 21.

acquaintances. Like educational patterns, though, emotional responses to children focused on differences among them, on their specific qualities; not all children were lovable. Both Campion's daughter and Elisabeth de La Trémoille were loved partly for their superiority to other children and for their precocity—in other words, for their closeness to adult forms of thought. Charlotte Amélie's brother, because of his reserve, failed to please their father. Emotion attached to the child's individuality. And neither expectations about love nor ideas of individuality lessened tensions between generations.

Such emphasis on individuality, with all the discomforts and conflicts that it generated, gave aristocratic education its principal coloring. In contrast to nobles destined for careers in the magistracy, young men preparing for military careers received educations that allowed considerable freedom of personal development and that regularly placed them in situations of moral ambiguity. To be sure, families of the *noblesse d'épée* worried about their sons' moral development and dangerous associates, and expected from them deference to family needs. Yet both ideals and practices gave young men great freedom from such controls: by encouraging travels from home, early departure from school, and the experience of independence; by directing education toward the rhetorical and skeptical emphases of Renaissance humanism; by insisting that both boys and girls needed to develop personal qualities of directness and self-expression. These rather than specific educational accomplishments were what parents wanted for their children.

Such educations took place within a larger context of familial tensions. The very ideology of the society of orders intensified conflicts between generations, by requiring individuals to view their own rise to adulthood as coming at their parents' expense. As a result, conflict between generations occurred frequently, both in reality and in seventeenth-century literary representations; conflict was both a typical experience and a cultural norm. By itself this experience of conflict with elders encouraged a sense of the individual's separation from his family, but even the experience of familial love had comparable effects. Some aristocratic parents described great love for sons and daughters, but they did so in terms that made clear how specific and conditional their love was. Love was expected to go to individual children, not to all, and it was earned by the children's grace and abilities, by their "merits." Both its tensions and its affections, in other words, assured that the aristocratic family would sharply define the individual's differences from others, a process that seems to have applied equally to men and women. Within the family and in education outside it, intense anxiety surrounded the development of aristocratic selfhood.

# 4

## Friendship, Love, and Civility

The apparent unity of the aristocratic family, I have argued, concealed powerful tensions and anxieties. The family's successes came at visible expense to its individual members, whose wants the family sacrificed to its larger needs; at the same time, educational practices encouraged young men (and, to a lesser degree, young women) to think of themselves as distinct individuals, specific in character and life histories, and brought up far from parental controls. Such tensions within the family help to explain the intensity with which seventeenth-century nobles turned to other kinds of relationships, to friendships and love affairs. These offered emotional attachments based on choice and little affected by family demands. Passionate friendships and love affairs, what contemporaries called gallantry, thus formed an important element in seventeenth-century lives, women's as well as men's. These relationships filled needs that other kinds of relationship failed to meet. At the same time, by their nature they further disrupted efforts to make the ideology of dynasticism a functioning reality.

To claim an important role for either friendship or love in seventeenth-century society runs counter to an important tradition of historical thought. Lawrence Stone and others have argued for the superficiality of most such emotions before the eighteenth century. When seventeenth-century men spoke of friendship, it is claimed, they typically referred to the self-interested bonds of clientage; when they spoke of love, they meant chiefly the sexual impulses generated by a courtly society and a system of arranged, loveless marriages. Seventeenth-century practices, so Stone and others have argued, so damaged children as to leave them as adults incapable of much feeling toward either friends or lovers.[1]

1. Lawrence Stone, *The Family, Sex, and Marriage in England, 1500–1800* (New York, 1977). Sharon Kettering is currently preparing a study of friendship in early modern France. For another interpretation of some of the issues taken up here, see Roger Chartier, ed., *A History of Private Life*, vol. 3, trans. Arthur Goldhammer (Cambridge,

This chapter argues instead for placing such affections at the center of seventeenth-century culture. Partly because of the very child-rearing practices to which Stone and others have drawn attention, seventeenth-century men and women had enormous needs for affection from others, needs so strong as to blur the distinction between sexual and nonsexual relations. Thus the forms of friendship and its complicated manifestations occupied a very large place in seventeenth-century thought.

Medieval French law recognized friendship, but mainly as an appendage to familial ties, and relics of this view survived into the early modern period. Sixteenth- and seventeenth-century legal commentators needed to make sense of the phrase *parents et amis,* which they encountered in the provincial law codes. The customs used the term regularly to describe the group that was to formulate decisions about orphans: that is, the group that was to step in when patriarchal authority was absent or incompetent. The phrase, the lawyers concluded, referred, not to friends in the classical sense, but to well-disposed family members, those who were friends as well as relatives. In the medieval tradition thus interpreted, friendship by itself had little independent existence. It was mainly an appendage to family.[2] Friendship in this tradition served to replace paternal relations, and the same held true of another form of friendship, that based on patronage. Through the seventeenth century, writers commonly used the term "friend" to refer to protectors and patrons. This was friendship not as intimacy but as a means of organizing political and social life. Thus the former minister Villeroy began his memoirs by stressing the importance to an *homme de bien* of being well regarded by "those to whom he has promised *amitié et service.*"[3] Olivier Lefebvre d'Ormesson recalled at about the same time that "my father was greatly loved and ever since greatly favored by M. de Morvilliers [a relative of his wife's], from whom we still have several letters, testifying to the affection he felt."[4]

Mass., 1989), 163ff. In general, these accounts stress the radical difference between seventeenth- and eighteenth-century emotional lives (see, for instance, 371–75).

2. J. Brissaud, *Manuel d'histoire du droit français* [Paris, 1908], 1821.

3. Monsieur de Villeroy, *Mémoires d'estat,* in M. Petitot, ed., *Collection des mémoires relatifs à l'histoire de France,* 44 (Paris, 1824), 19.

4. Olivier Lefebvre d'Ormesson, *Journal,* ed. M. Chéruel, 2 vols. (Paris, 1860), 1: viii.

Medieval traditions of this kind received further strength from classical thought about friendship. Just as feudalism had presented political bonds in the guise of personal friendship, so also ancient theorists had presented friendship as the basis for the collective life of the polis. They had seen the polity as essentially a web of friendships within its ruling class. Because the political stakes of friendship were in this view so high, friendship's rational and ethical content counted heavily. For Cicero, only the virtuous could enjoy real friendship, and it developed slowly and thoughtfully, rather than from immediate attraction.[5]

These opinions remained vigorous through the sixteenth century. In the middle of the century, Antoine du Saix cited Aristotle to the effect that friendship held together the monarchy, "for loyal service comes from *amityé,* not money."[6] Even Michel de Montaigne reflected this tradition, despite the intensity of his friendship with Etienne de La Boétie. He and La Boétie, he reported, had sought each other out because of reports of each other's excellence. Friendship had preceded personal acquaintance, because it began in universally acknowledged virtues; thus Montaigne quoted with approval Cicero's dicta on the necessary overlap of virtue and friendship.[7] Villeroy made the same point. Men in his situation needed to justify political choices to their friends, "in order not to cause them to change the good opinion that they have . . . , which is the chief foundation of friendship, since it is impossible for us really to love someone whom we do not esteem."[8] Friendship here rested on rational choice and ethical behavior. It reinforced civic and ethical responsibilities, serving as a motive for the efforts and self-sacrifices that civic life demanded.

By the eighteenth century, these connections among friendship, family, and politics had largely broken down. Friendship no longer complemented blood relations but, rather, opposed them as a competitor for the individual's emotional and material resources. "[O]ught

5. Cicero, *De Amicitia,* in *De Senectute, De Amicitia, De Divinatione,* trans. William Armistead Falconer (Cambridge, Mass., Loeb Classical Library, 1964), XXVII; see also Aristotle, *Ethics,* trans. J. A. K. Thomson (London, 1953), 227–57, for friendship as essential to the functioning of the polis. My understanding of early modern friendship owes much to studies of medieval friendship by Brian Patrick McGuire: see *Friendship and Community: The Monastic Experience, 350–1250* (Kalamazoo, 1988).

6. Robert Aulotte, ed., *Plutarque en France au XVIe siècle: Trois opuscules moraux, traduits par Antoine du Saix, Pierre de Saint Julien, et Jacques Amyot* (Paris, 1971), 18–19.

7. Michel de Montaigne, *Oeuvres complètes,* ed. Maurice Rat and Albert Thibaudet (Paris, Pléiade, 1962), 186–87 ("De l'amitié").

8. Villeroy, *Mémoires d'estat,* 20.

not friends to be preferred to relatives in intestate successions?" asked an eighteenth-century author. "Friendship is often placed above the ties of blood relationship [*parenté*]." He ultimately concluded against such a procedure, but that he could raise the question suggests the role friendship had acquired.[9] The same author offered an extended definition of the bases of friendship, and in doing so he suggested why friendship and family now stood in conflict. Whereas familial relations (even those between siblings) rested on difference and subordination, between older and younger or male and female, our author situated the sources of friendship in likeness and equality: "[F]riends are those who resemble each other in their temperament, their inclinations, their passions, their professions, their age, their way of thinking, etc., and their relationship is always a function of this resemblance. Man is always his own greatest friend; to approach him in this respect, and substitute so to speak for him someone comparable, the latter must resemble him in everything; and it is only then that one can say that he has found a true friend, another self."[10] Medieval friendship had in some measure been a substitute for patriarchy. The *parents et amis* of the law codes replaced the absent father, and the friends of patronage relationships supplemented paternal protection; these forms of friendship rested on inequality. Eighteenth-century friendship offered instead a second self, perfect equality.

Nor did eighteenth-century friendship fit so easily within the relations of civic life. For by the end of the eighteenth century friendship acquired much of its significance from its contrast with life in society. A friend was another self, with whom one could exchange the secret thoughts that social life excluded. What created friendship was, in Kant's terms, "the complete confidence of two persons in disclosing to one another their secret thoughts and feelings, so far as such disclosure is compatible with mutual respect."[11] Such disclosure, Kant believed, emerged from a basic human need: "Man is a being meant for society . . . ; and in cultivating social qualities he feels powerfully the need to *disclose* himself to others. . . . On the other hand, since he is also cramped and forewarned by the fear that others might misuse this revelation of his thoughts, he sees himself constrained to *lock up* in

9. M. de Félice, ed., *Code de l'humanité ou la législation universelle, naturelle, civile et politique . . . composé par une société de gens de lettres . . .* , 13 vols. (Yverdon, 1778), 1: 279.

10. Ibid., 1: 278.

11. Kant, quoted in H. J. Paton, "Kant on Friendship," *Proceedings of the British Academy*, vol. 42 (Dawes Hicks Lecture on Philosophy, 1956), 45–66, 54.

himself a good part of his opinions." Finding a friend with whom he can share these thoughts, Kant said, meant that "he is no longer entirely *alone* with his thoughts as in a prison, but enjoys a freedom which he cannot have among the common herd, where he must shut himself up in himself."[12]

Friendship, in this view, began with the individual's contradictory place in society: on the one hand, alone in a competitive situation, in which social masks provide a necessary defense; on the other hand, driven by a powerful need for exchanges with others. Except for his friendships, the individual survives in public life through his disguises. Again, these functions imply a need for equality between friends; the communication that is basic to friendship demands that the two friends share abilities and outlook, as well as affection. Such views also imply a difficult relationship between friendship and public life. Friends could express secret thoughts that would pose dangers elsewhere. Friendship expressed humanity's essentially social nature, but it also showed that society failed to satisfy that nature.

The seventeenth century uneasily combined elements of medieval, classical, and eighteenth-century visions of friendship—and precisely because the concept incorporated so many elements, friendship had an especially prominent place in seventeenth-century thought and sensibility. Talk of friendship was everywhere. The comte de Souvigny, a successful military man, concluded his memoirs with five basic rules for his children to follow through life. The first was "to maintain yourself constantly in God's grace"; the second, "to acquire a faithful friend, who can give you good advice."[13] The great Jansenist patriarch Arnauld d'Andilly similarly concluded his memoirs by claiming friendship as the central thread of his life, and he used the language of Montaigne or even Cicero: "My greatest passion, after my salvation, has been friendship with those persons whom I have known to be the most worthy of esteem; I believe that no one has had as many true friends as I, friends whose merits and virtues make it a great honor to have been loved by them."[14] Arnauld's fellow Jansenist Pierre Nicole

12. Ibid., 64; emphasis in original.
13. Comte de Souvigny, *Mémoires*, ed. Ludovic de Contenson, 3 vols. (Paris, 1906–09), 3: 69.
14. Robert Arnauld d'Andilly, *Mémoires*, in M. Petitot, ed., *Collection des mémoires relatifs à l'histoire de France*, 34 (Paris, 1824), 102. Arnauld's son, it will be re-

presented the related view that friendship formed the basis of society: "It is absolutely necessary, in order that human society subsist, that men like and respect one another. . . . An infinity of small things, all of them necessary for life, are given freely and, since they do not enter commerce, can only be bought with love."[15] For Adam Smith, of course, this was precisely not the essence of society; according to Smith, we rely for our needs on others' interests, not their altruism. For Nicole, friendship played the socially integrating role that liberal thought would accord to the market.

Such comments suggest the continuing strength in the seventeenth century of classical traditions of friendship, a friendship of rational choice and one that reinforced larger bonds of collective life; personal and public life here interlocked, and fitted well with moral and religious structures. But the seventeenth century also had other models of friendship, which fitted far less well with these other concerns. Aristocratic men felt driven to the intense intimacies that Kant described, and they often presented friendship as an alternative to the competition and insincerity around them. At the same time, they sought to preserve the idea that friendship could be based on inequality and could function within the unequal relations of patronage and political power. Nicole himself stressed the psychological as well as material needs that friendship fulfilled, and he sought to link the intensity of men's need for friendship to the weakness of the human condition itself. "Nothing is so natural to man," he opened one of his essays, "as the desire to be loved by others. . . . Our soul is so languishing and weak that it could not sustain itself were it not carried, as it were, by the approval and love of others. . . . [I]magine being forgotten by all men; who could endure such a vision without terror and melancholy?"[16] Friendship involved need as well as rational choice.

Monarchs displayed this need in extreme form. They experienced intense emotional involvement with chosen friends, but without the

---

called, bitterly agreed; his father's love for his friends meant neglect of his children (above, Chapter 3).

15. Pierre Nicole, *Oeuvres philosophiques et morales,* ed. C. Jourdain (Paris, 1845; repr. Hildesheim, 1970), 239. On the other hand, Nicole's essay "De la grandeur" virtually anticipated Smith: "Quelle charité serait-ce que de bâtir une maison tout entière pour un autre, de la meubler, de la tapisser, de la lui rendre la clef à la main? la cupidité le fera gaiement. . . . Il n'y a donc rien dont on tire de plus grans services que de la cupidité même des hommes" (398). I discuss this passage below, Chapter 5.

16. Ibid., 267.

possibility of equality. Both Henri III and Louis XIII depended desperately on favorites, to the point that contemporaries widely suspected them of homosexual practices. Even those who did not express such suspicions stressed the intensity of the kings' feelings, their ardor when relations went well and their despondency during quarrels. His physician Jean Héroard described Louis calling in his sleep for his friend Luynes and recorded Louis's dream of, in effect, marrying Luynes;[17] Tallemant des Réaux retailed stories of Louis in bed with his last favorite, Cinq-Mars; and Louis regularly confided to Richelieu his anxieties about the course of this and other friendships.[18]

Both kings evoked scandalized disapproval from some contemporaries, but in fact their infatuations typified larger patterns in seventeenth-century high society. Whether in the provinces or at court, noblemen often described friendships originating in immediate, nearly physical attraction, and they stressed the intense emotions that arose as friendships evolved: "The changes that arrive in friendship have about the same causes as those that arrive in love: their rules have a great deal of similarity."[19] This was La Rochefoucauld's view, and memorialists from the *noblesse d'épée* repeated the parallel in recounting the specific circumstances of their lives. Thus Jean de Mergey, in the mid-sixteenth century: a distant relative "took such an *amitié* for me" that he devoted himself to Mergey's education.[20] The maréchal de Bassompierre recalled that in the early seventeenth century, "Monsieur the constable at that time could not live without seeing me, so much did he love me, and he thought only of my advancement."[21]

Antoine Arnauld in his sixties still felt bitter at his father's enthusiasm for "his new friendships [*amitiés*], which in the case of another man might reasonably have have been termed love affairs [*amours*]."[22] The comte de Souvigny recalled his uncle's experiences

17. Elizabeth Wirth Marvick, *Louis XIII: The Making of a King* (New Haven, 1986), 135–36.

18. A. Lloyd Moote, *Louis XIII, the Just* (Berkeley, 1989), 285–86.

19. François de La Rochefoucauld, *Oeuvres complètes*, ed. L. Martin-Chauffier (Paris, Pléiade, 1957), 398.

20. Jean de Mergey, *Mémoires*, in Michaud and Poujolat, eds., *Nouvelle collection des mémoires relatifs à l'histoire de France . . .*, 9 (Paris, 1857), 559.

21. Maréchal de Bassompierre, *Mémoires*, in Michaud and Poujolat, eds., *Nouvelle collection des mémoires relatifs à l'histoire de France . . .*, 20 (Paris, 1854), 54.

22. L'abbé Arnauld, *Mémoires*, in M. Petitot, ed., *Collection des mémoires relatifs à l'histoire de France*, 34 (Paris, 1824), 146.

in the same years: a small town merchant "took such an affection for M. de Beauregard that he could not live without him," and for this reason arranged his marriage with his daughter.[23] Bussy-Rabutin mused angrily on the mystery of "whence came to the prince [de Condé] so much *amitié* for this boy [one of his followers], in the course of such a brief acquaintance." Condé, Bussy explained, "finding [the boy] to his taste, took an affection for him, and made his fortune."[24] Of two of the more notorious of Louis XIV's courtiers, Bussy likewise wrote, "[T]hey had by nature the same inclination to harshness and mockery, also they loved each other greatly, as if they had been of different sexes."[25] Tallemant des Réaux described the success of the handsome chevalier de Boisdauphin in his regiment: he "was not there long before making himself loved by everyone. . . . I tend to believe that his beauty did him no harm in this respect, for he was one of the most beautiful and well-built gentlemen in France." Having illicitly married the Chancellor Séguier's daughter, he soon found himself "in the good graces of his father-in-law. The chancellor could no longer live without him."[26] As Nicolas Faret, the early-seventeenth-century theorist of courtliness, summarized the matter, some men have such abilities that whatever they undertake, they "make themselves attractive [*agréables*] to anyone who has eyes to look at them."[27] Like love, friendship began in visual pleasure.

Novelists made the same point. In d'Urfé's *L'Astrée*, it is a female lover disguised as a male friend whose "beauty, youth, and affection" for the man whom they believe to be her friend "moved all those who were present"; onlookers take for male friendship the signs of what in fact is heterosexual love.[28] In *Francion* there is no ambiguity of gender, but physical attraction retains its power: soon after meeting Francion, Raymond tells him "that his good face, whence he had noticed streamed forth something noble and distinctive, was a charm that had

23. Comte de Souvigny, *Mémoires*, 2: 47.

24. Roger de Bussy-Rabutin, *Mémoires*, ed. Ludovic Lalanne, 2 vols. (Paris, 1857; repr. Westmead, 1972), 1: 159, 160.

25. Roger de Bussy-Rabutin, *Histoire amoureuse des Gaules*, ed. Paul Boiteau, 4 vols. (Paris, 1866), 1: 68.

26. Gédéon Tallemant des Réaux, *Historiettes*, ed. Antoine Adam, 2 vols. (Paris, Pléiade, 1960–61), 2: 347.

27. Nicolas Faret, *L'honnête homme, ou l'art de plaire à la cour*, ed. Maurice Magendie (Paris, 1925; repr. Geneva, 1970), 11.

28. Honoré d'Urfé, *L'Astrée*, abridged edition, ed. Jean Lafond (Paris, 1984), 95 (Part 1, book 12).

invited him to make him an infinite number of offers of his service";
having seen Francion's qualities in action, Raymond assures him,
"[M]y dear friend, it is now that I shall give you proofs of the affection
that I carry for you."[29] Pierre Marivaux took up the theme in the early
eighteenth century. "There's no need to thank me for what I have
done," explains his Jacob to the man whose assailants he has just
driven off. "I was only too pleased, and I took to you at once just from
your looks."[30] Such stress on personal attraction fitted easily with the
ideology of nobility. Jacob's friend, Francion, and d'Urfé's heroine all
attract strangers because they are of noble birth; indeed, their attractiveness serves as an outward sign of social standing, which their new
friends will learn of only as the plot unfolds.

Like these literary depictions, Furetière's late-seventeenth-century
dictionary presented friendship as a mixture of passionate attachment
and practical service. For Furetière the point of friendship lay in effective assistance; a friend was someone "who has affection for some
person, and who procures or wishes for him all sorts of advantages.
There are friendly peoples and friendly *maisons,* which have the same
interests." Yet Furetière combined this stress on utilitarian friendship
with a view of friendship as a passion. Affection he defined as a "passion of the soul which makes us wish someone well. . . . One speaks
thus of both love and friendship." Furetière's language juxtaposes passion and interest and emphasizes the place of action in friendship.
Friendship, he suggested, is an urge to advance another, a wish that
the other receive "every sort of advantage." It is thus bound up with
calculations of interest. Yet he also defined friendship as a passion,
which in Cartesian fashion he understood to begin with the senses:
passion, he wrote, is one of "the different agitations of the soul following the various objects that appear to our senses." Though its aims
were calculating, in other words, friendship's origins, like those of
love, lay in a physical inner agitation. Hence it is not surprising that
for Furetière true friends, intimate friends, are *amis de jeunesse*; he
linked friendship to a youthful capacity for receiving external impres-
sions and responding passionately to them.[31] In this view he followed

29. Charles Sorel, *Histoire comique de Francion,* ed. Yves Guiraud (Paris, 1979),
81, 327.
30. Pierre Marivaux, *Le paysan parvenu* (Paris, 1965), 302.
31. Antoine Furetière, *Dictionnaire universel,* 3 vols. (The Hague, 1690; repr.
Geneva, 1970), s.vv. *ami, amitié, affection, passion.*

Aristotle, who believed that purely utilitarian friendships occurred most commonly among the old, because the old are readier to pursue self-interest than emotion.[32] Even within Furetière's vision of friendship as serving usefulness, there remained the assumption that friendship was essentially a passion.

Because of friendship's basis in the passions, it was not limited to masculine relations; in seventeenth-century opinion, at least some women could have friendships as well. A pamphlet described Madame de la Vallière, Louis XIV's first mistress: "[S]he is sincere and faithful, far from any coquettishness, and more capable than anyone in the world of great attachments; she loves her friends with an unbelievable warmth."[33] Arnauld d'Andilly numbered two women among the four great friends of his life.[34]

If seventeenth-century friendship began in physical attraction, however, it developed also from strongly felt needs for intimacy and service. In the seventeenth century, these needs were not so separate as might be supposed; to be able to exchange confidences with a friend figured as an important practical need in the unsettled, disguised world of court society. "The thorniest problem" that a newcomer to court encounters, counselled Nicolas Faret, "is to know how to choose a faithful, wise, and experienced friend, who can supply *les bonnes adresses* and give us an idea of the customs that are followed, of the powers that reign, of the cabals and parties that are in favor, of the men who are admired, the women who are honored, of the morals and fashions that prevail, and in general of everything that can only be learned through being there."[35]

Faret presented friendship as an instrument to success, but also as a source of sincerity in an otherwise unknown, potentially hostile setting. In this view, friendship acquired its importance partly from the ill-defined social relations within which the courtier moved; the need for friendship rose with the uncertainty and anonymity of other relations. For Faret, the concept of friendship combined calculating self-interest, self-revealing intimacy, and physical attraction. With "our particular friends," he wrote, "our souls feel free of that constraint

32. Aristotle, *Ethics*, trans. J. A. K. Thomson (London, 1953), 238.
33. "Le Palais-Royal ou les amours de Mme de la Vallière," in *Histoire amoureuse des Gaules par Bussy Rabutin*, ed. Boiteau, 2: 35.
34. Arnauld d'Andilly, *Mémoires*, 34: 102–3.
35. Faret, *L'honnête homme*, 39–40.

that other people cause us, and we allow free expression to all its natural movements, with a nonchalance that often renders us almost entirely different from what we seem in public."[36]

Faret was not alone in these thoughts. When Bussy-Rabutin described his friendship with the duc de Candale, he made the revelation of secrets its defining element: "[T]his friendship lasted until his death, and reached the point that he scarcely had a secret that he did not confide in me."[37] Arnauld d'Andilly claimed of a friend that "the friendship between two brothers could not be stronger than that between us, and . . . thus I knew the secrets of his heart as well as I knew my own."[38] From Corneille's early comedies onward, friendships gave structure to seventeenth-century drama; both men and women in the plays require friends in whom they can confide their inner thoughts. "Have I ever concealed from you my heart and my desires?" asks Orestes of his friend at the outset of *Andromaque*.[39] "Friend, what dare I say? You who have known my heart since first I drew breath," asks Hippolyte of *his* friend at the outset of *Phèdre*;[40] and the latter drama points throughout to the contrast between the confidences of friendship and the ferocity of familial bonds, which ultimately destroy Hippolyte. *Britannicus* too opens with an exchange between the hero and his confidant, in which Britannicus describes false friends revealing to Nero "the secrets of my soul, . . . the movements . . . of my heart."[41] We may recognize such stage friendships as a convenient dramatic device, allowing rapid exposition of the characters' situations and hopes. But the dramatists, who were much concerned with realism, nonetheless presented intimacy as a normal need: to expose one's heart to a friend was at least an important cultural model, and the need was especially strong at court, where sincerity was not otherwise to be found.

Partly because of its origins in the passions, friendship was also dangerous. One might reveal oneself to inappropriate people, to false friends; one might misunderstand the social realities that governed friendship and pay insufficient attention to the insincerities of the so-

36. Ibid., 57.
37. Bussy-Rabutin, *Mémoires*, 1: 404.
38. Arnauld d'Andilly, *Mémoires*, 34: 103.
39. *Andromaque*, Act I, Scene 1, in Jean Racine, *Oeuvres complètes*. Vol. 1: *Théâtre-poésies*, ed. Raymond Picard (Paris, Pléiade, 1950), 247.
40. *Phèdre*, Act I, Scene 1, ibid., 751.
41. *Britannicus*, Act I, Scene 4, ibid., 403.

cial world. These ideas received extreme elaboration in the eighteenth century. Marivaux sets false friendship at the center of *La double inconstance:* "You, Arlequin, whatever happens, you can always look upon me as a friend who would like to help you," promises the paid seductress Flaminia, and misleading promises of friendship pass back and forth throughout. "[N]ow I can laugh at the trick that our friendship has played on us," says Arlequin to conclude the play.[42]

The plot of Laclos's *Les liaisons dangereuses* likewise moves forward mainly because of a series of false friendships. Like Kant's individual, Laclos's characters need to confide in others whom they suppose to be like themselves; they fail to perceive their fundamental isolation. The seducer Valmont thus writes to his fellow-conspirator the marquise de Merteuil, "Finally I know him [Danceny] completely, this fine romantic hero! He has no more secrets from me. . . . [H]e found in me ways of thinking so like his own that, in his enchantment at my candor, he told me everything and swore friendship without reserve."[43] In this case, Laclos ascribes the quixotic urge to imagine real life as a novel to the specific context of friendship; self-revelation rather than great deeds is the absurd dream. In parallel, the innocent Cécille Volanges continually reveals herself to another false friend, using the most flowery terms of friendship.[44] Danceny and Cécille believe themselves to be no longer alone, in Kant's phrase, but in fact they are more isolated and vulnerable than ever. (But in the end it is the self-revealing Danceny who kills Valmont, and by this point the urge to self-disclosure has shifted; Valmont brings to the fatal duel the packet of letters that explicates his actions and reveals his thoughts.)

Though not in such elaborated form, the theme of false friendship already troubled seventeenth-century writers. "Around me I see only perjured friends, all of them assiduous spies, bought by Nero for this repulsive trade, trafficking in the secrets of my soul"—thus the unfortunate Britannicus, complaining to the false friend who is in fact Nero's spy.[45] Yet the convolutions of the exchange go beyond simple irony. There is no equality between Britannicus and his putative

---

42. Pierre Marivaux, *La double inconstance*, Act I, Scene 11, in *Théâtre complet*, ed. Marcel Arland (Paris, Pléiade, 1949), 216.
43. Choderlos de Laclos, *Les liaisons dangereuses*, 57, in *Oeuvres complètes*, ed. Laurent Versini (Paris, Pléiade, 1979), 115 (letter 57).
44. Ibid., 58 (letter 27).
45. *Britannicus*, Act I, Scene 4, in Racine, *Oeuvres complètes*, 403.

friend, the one a royal heir, the other a freed slave; part of Britannicus's folly lies in his belief that he could share the "secrets of my soul" with one who is an equal neither in birth nor in circumstances.

Saint-Evremond's "On Friendship" argued the point explicitly: social inequality stood in the way of friendship. Thus no real friendship with a prince was possible, because of the distance between prince and courtier; the insincere and calculating courtier, he argued, had far better chances of preserving the prince's affection, for he was less likely to intrude on the prince's goodwill. Social inequalities did more than restrict intimacy; they virtually demanded the creation of false relations. But this was only one instance of the larger opposition that Saint-Evremond perceived between the functioning of civil society and friendship. Thus he contrasted friendship with two other qualities, justice and prudence. These stand at the base of civic life, the former "established for maintaining human society," the latter "to help us acquire property." But neither is in fact compatible with friendship. The essay opens with praise of a Spartan king who overturned civil rules in order to help a friend, and it argues that justice by itself is "wilder than the men she brought together." As for prudence, "the deep reflections of a wisdom that holds us back when inclination pulls us toward another" are in fact the enemies of friendship.[46]

Saint-Evremond here offers a vision of friendship as in some senses the enemy of society itself, and he presents the contrast as one between nature and culture. Justice is "the achievement of men; friendship is the achievement of nature."[47] This is a paradoxical conclusion that we will encounter in other areas of aristocratic culture. "The achievement of nature" here supplies the most genuine content of social relations; the political is not only the artificial but the asocial, the *sauvage*. Saint-Evremond's emphasis on the polarity between friendship and civic life is the more striking because of his belief in the importance of reason and the dangers of excessively passionate friendship.

With Saint-Evremond's distinction between civic engagement and personal friendship, the problematic qualities of seventeenth-century friendship received their most elaborate statement. Friendship was not

---

46. Charles de Marguetel, seigneur de Saint-Evremond, *Oeuvres en prose*, ed. René Ternois, 3 vols. (Paris, 1962–66), 3: 307–10, 311, 314.
47. Ibid., 310.

the ally of civic relations (as in Ciceronian tradition) but their enemy; it was not a constituent of political life but a shelter from political deceptions, struggles, and disappointments; its relations to morality were essentially hostile. Though men needed social rules and political bonds, Saint-Evremond suggested, these had less reality than the amoral, "natural" relations of friendship.

Both the intensity of seventeenth-century friendships and their origins in physical attraction posed a further ethical problem: friendship easily shaded into sexual feeling and activity.[48] Anxiety about homosexuality formed an ongoing theme in courtly literature from the reign of Henri III through that of Louis XIV.[49] Henri III and Louis XIII, of course, were famous for the intensity of their feelings for their favorites,[50] but well-informed gossips such as Bussy-Rabutin and Tallemant des Réaux attributed comparable feelings to a wide range of courtiers. "From the beginning monsieur le prince has been accused of this vice," wrote Tallemant of the Grand Condé's father.[51] The Grand Condé himself was likewise widely reported to have had extensive homosexual relations and to have taken little trouble to conceal them.[52] Tallemant presented Richelieu's companion Boisrobert boasting of his sexual relations with the pages around him, and he quoted Mademoiselle de Gournay: "[O]ne day when someone asked her whether pederasty was not a crime, 'Please God,' she replied, 'that I not condemn what Socrates practiced.'" Tallemant quoted popular

---

48. Cf. the similar findings of Alan Bray, "Homosexuality and the Signs of Male Friendship in Elizabethan England," *History Workshop* 29 (Spring 1990): 1–19, and for nineteenth-century America, Estelle Freedman and John D'Emilio, "Problems Encountered in Writing the History of Sexuality: Sources, Theory and Interpretation," *Journal of Sex Research* 27, 4 (November 1990): 481–95.

49. For strong emphasis on the frequency of homosexuality in seventeenth-century society, see Maurice Lever, *Les bûchers de Sodome* (Paris, 1985); conversely, Chartier, ed., *History of Private Life*, gives very little attention to the subject. Anxiety, rather than the absence of homosexual behavior, appears to explain the nearly complete absence of French artistic portrayals of homosexual themes, in contrast to the frequency of such subject matter in fifteenth- and sixteenth-century Italy (James M. Saslow, *Ganymede in the Renaissance: Homosexuality in Art and Society* [New Haven, 1986], 7, 179–85).

50. Jacqueline Boucher, *La cour de Henri III* (Rennes, 1986), argues that Henri was not homosexual; Moote, *Louis XIII, the Just*, and Marvick, *Louis XIII*, agree that Louis had strong homoerotic desires, but hesitate as to whether he acted on them.

51. Tallemant des Réaux, *Historiettes*, 1: 417.

52. Georges Mongrédien, *Le Grand Condé: L'homme et son oeuvre* (Paris, 1959), 60; Lever, *Les bûchers de Sodome*.

songs attributing similar feelings to the maréchal de Grammont ("Monseigneur prenez courage, / il vous reste encore un page") and retailed stories of the group surrounding the notoriously homosexual Théophile de Viau.[53]

Even the most sober observers offered similar assessments of the seventeenth-century court. Ezéchiel Spanheim, the scholarly envoy of the elector of Brandenburg, noted that Louis XIV "has vigorously spoken out against the crying vices in which the youth of the court and his own blood have unfortunately involved themselves, and he has not hesitated to punish or correct those who were suspected or convicted of [these vices]"—including Louis's brother, his illegitimate son the duc de Vermandois, and the prince de Conti. At a later point Spanheim noted that the cardinal de Bouillon had "the reputation of being touched by the same disgusting vice that was spreading among the leading *jeunesse* of the court."[54]

Homosexuality frightened early modern Europeans as a violation of nature. It was traditionally believed also to be associated with heretical views of all kinds—an association that seventeenth-century libertines did nothing to dispel.[55] But the practice also overlapped with forms of friendship that constituted the normal fabric of nobles' careers and political lives. Nobles perceived the civic world in which they moved as a web of such friendships, but these relationships existed at the margins of what could be considered natural behavior. Bussy-Rabutin suggested the uncertain boundary between sexual relations and the more acceptable relations of friendship. His *Histoire amoureuse des Gaules* included the story of the comte de Guiche and his intimate friend Manicamp. Invited to make love with the beautiful Madame d'Olonne, Guiche finds himself impotent. To "repair his fault," he takes special precautions before a second rendezvous: "I . . . went to bed without Manicamp. I was so determined to repair my fault that I fled my friends like the plague."[56] Men frequently slept

53. Tallemant des Réaux, *Historiettes*, 1: 413–14, 379–80, 528.

54. Ezéchiel Spanheim, *Relation de la cour de France en 1690*, ed. Charles Schefer (Paris, 1882), 6, 58, 92, 127. See also the discussion of these circles in Nancy Nichols Barker, *Brother to the Sun King: Philippe Duke of Orleans* (Baltimore, 1989).

55. Judith Brown, *Immodest Acts: The Life of a Lesbian Nun in Renaissance Italy* (Oxford, 1986), 13; cf. Richard Popkin, *The History of Skepticism from Erasmus to Descartes*, rev. ed. (New York, 1968), for a more purely intellectual view of seventeenth-century libertinism.

56. *Histoire amoureuse des Gaules*, ed. Boiteau, 1: 127.

together in the sixteenth and seventeenth centuries; Bussy's story made clear the anxieties this situation might produce.

His comments also make it clear that in the seventeenth century homosexuality remained chiefly a definition of acts rather than of persons.[57] Guiche could be both one of the leading gallants of the court and a man rumored to enjoy physical intimacies with his friend. The same was true of Condé and his *petits maîtres,* notorious for both homosexual and heterosexual debauches. Despite recent arguments,[58] it seems mistaken to view such figures as participants in a homosexual subculture. Rather, their experiences reflected the ease with which members of courtly society moved from fully acceptable to dangerous modes of behavior.

Further complicating assumptions about homosexuality were the connections contemporaries drew between sexuality and the vagaries of courtly power. Bussy-Rabutin, we have seen, ascribed his failure with Condé to the latter's preference for a beautiful young follower, and Condé was assumed to be surrounded by libertine, sexually ambiguous young men. Henri de Campion used vague but similar terms to describe the duc de Vendôme: "I knew that he was controlled by young valets, who, according to common opinion, maintained themselves in his favor by shameful and infamous means. I had always detested them in France without this ever disturbing the duc; since I was not his domestic, he made no effort to subject me as he did his own people [*les siens*]. But I thought that if I attached myself to him in places where he had no need to restrain himself, he would wish me to enter into relations with his favorites, so as to sanction his mode of living; or, if I couldn't bring myself to do so, I would fall out with him and would receive nothing for my efforts. I reflected that all his gentlemen . . . had formed friendships with his *mignons* to maintain their positions."[59] In his delicate language, Campion conveyed another side of the sexualized and unequal nature of *fidélités* with a prince. Power allowed sexual relations; those who criticized such relations could expect to suffer, since connectedness to the prince required at

---

57. This is the position developed by John Boswell, *Christianity, Social Tolerance, and Homosexuality: Gay People in Western Europe from the Beginning of the Christian Era to the Fourteenth Century* (Chicago, 1980), and Michel Foucault, *The History of Sexuality.* Volume 1: *An Introduction,* trans. Robert Hurley (New York, 1978).

58. Lever, *Les bûchers de Sodome.*

59. Henri de Campion, *Mémoires,* ed. Marc Fumaroli (Paris, 1967), 175.

least good relations with his *mignons*. Homosexuality symbolized power on one side, submission and weakness on the other.

Passionate friendship provided one alternative to familial relations during the seventeenth century. Heterosexual love might have supplied another such alternative, but for most men and women it apparently failed to do so. They spoke often of feeling intense, even overwhelming love, but they also stressed the likelihood that love would eventually fail. The failure raises important questions about seventeenth-century culture and practices: given the emotional needs that, I am claiming, dominated polite society, why was love so rarely successful?

Historians have of course proposed answers to this question. Political and financial calculations surrounded early modern marriage arrangements, often leaving husband and wife hopelessly ill-matched. There was little chance in these circumstances that stable relations between men and women would develop, and those that occurred often came about outside marriage.[60] This was recognized even at the time. Tallemant des Réaux quoted one noblewoman notorious for her adulteries: "If they'd married me as I wanted, I wouldn't behave as I do."[61] Traditional European misogyny further limited hope of successful relations between men and women, by suggesting that women were unworthy objects of male affections. Montaigne argued that women could not equal the depth of male feelings and hence were incapable of real friendship.[62] From an early age, finally, aristocratic young men were encouraged in a predatory form of sexuality; military metaphors permeated even courtly love poetry, offering images of women as fortresses to be captured and celebrating love as male power.[63]

All of these interpretations reasonably characterize male views of women and of relationships with them during the sixteenth and seventeenth centuries. But they are also clearly insufficient, for they fail to convey the complexity either of seventeenth-century men's feelings or

---

60. Stone, *The Family, Sex, and Marriage.*
61. Tallemant des Réaux, *Historiettes*, 2: 110 (the comtesse de Suze).
62. Montaigne, *Oeuvres complètes*, 185; cf. Brown, *Immodest Acts*, 6ff.
63. Marvick, *Louis XIII*, 40ff.; Marguerite de Navarre, *The Heptameron*, trans. P. A. Chilton (London, 1984), 214–19; A. Jordan, "L'esthétique de Malherbe," *XVIIe Siècle* 104 (1974): 3–28.

of the position these accorded to women. They fail, in the first place, to give a place to the seriousness with which contemporaries talked about love, and even about married love. That talk of love permeated late-seventeenth-century drama was a truism of contemporary criticism; audiences now demanded *beaucoup d'amour,* as Fontenelle observed in explaining the declining popularity of his uncle Corneille, and indeed all of Racine's principal characters are violently in love.[64] Capacity for love formed part of what contemporaries expected of an elegant man. "One cannot be a true gentleman [*honnête homme*]," wrote Bussy-Rabutin, "without being always in love."[65] For Bussy himself this chiefly meant adulterous love, but he was not the less serious for that reason. When his mistress abandoned him after his arrest, "I was in despair at her inconstancy; I almost died of it, but time consoled me, and in the end I arrived at the blessed state of indifference that she had long merited."[66] Bussy contrasted this love with mere sexual feeling. "Gallantry does have its limits," he counselled. "There is an age at which it is ridiculous, and if there remains enough heat at that advanced age that one cannot do without women, one should meet them in private, rather than parading the perfect love publicly."[67] For the old, love might be a matter of mere bodily heat and hence something to be kept private; but for others it was more substantial and more important.

Nor was the ideal of intense marital love absent from seventeenth-century high society, however unusual the reality might be. Jean de Mergey described the mid-sixteenth-century comte de La Rochefoucauld, who on learning of his wife's death "locked himself away in the abbey of Saint-Victor to sigh away his regrets," until his friends finally drew him out (and into a rapid remarriage).[68] Tallemant's friend Madame Pitou, an acute observer of mid-seventeenth-century high society, told him that "as long as they're not outrageous, she strongly approves of love matches [*les mariages par amour*]"—suggesting that such matches occurred often enough to stimulate contemporary

64. Fontenelle, "Vie de Corneille," in Pierre Corneille, *Oeuvres complètes,* ed. André Stegman (Paris, 1963), 24; for a theoretical exploration of seventeenth-century love, see Nicolas Luhman, *Love as Passion: The Codification of Intimacy,* trans. Jeremy Gaines and Doris L. Jones (Oxford, 1986).
65. Quoted in C. Rouben, *Bussy-Rabutin épistolier* (Paris, 1974), 196.
66. Bussy-Rabutin, *Mémoires,* 2: 264.
67. Ibid., 2: 203.
68. Jean de Mergey, *Mémoires,* 561.

debate.[69] Antoine Arnauld ascribed his failure to marry to his insistence on a love match, though he believed himself unusual in preferring love to money: "[Y]oung though I was, I could never understand how someone could decide to marry without love."[70]

A few years later, the comte de Souvigny recalled the love that had in fact marked his own marriage. When his wife accidentally discovered that Souvigny had soon to return to the army, "her heart was so stricken with grief that she spent the whole day without drinking or eating."[71] Underlying love was intimate companionship. "It often happened," he remembered after his wife's death, "that after having strolled for three or four hours in the great hall at Souvigny and they told us that dinner was served and the soup turning cold, we said to each other, '[W]e'll take one more turn'; and then we would spend several hours without realizing it, unable to end our talk [*nos discours*]. This was not of domestic matters, fifteen minutes a day sufficing for our family, nor news of the neighborhood, nor of the fashionable world, for we spoke little of others. Such conversations can only be imagined by those who love each other faithfully and sincerely, as we did."[72] Souvigny believed that his brother had enjoyed a similar marriage: his brother's wife was so upset at the young man's death that she refused all nourishment and died in childbirth two weeks later.[73] Clearly there existed marriages that were successful in modern terms, marriages that combined intense attachment with intimate companionship.

Contemporaries might seek to present even failed marriages in these terms. By the early 1630s Louis XIII and Anne of Austria had lived for a decade on terms of indifference or outright hostility; yet for public consumption the newly formed *Gazette* presented their marriage as idyllically happy. "The affection their majesties have for one another is such that they can bear to be separated only when the king goes to make foreign conquests," reported one article. "They bear such affection for one another that they could not put up with being

69. Tallemant des Réaux, *Historiettes*, 2: 174; cf. Stone's discussion of these issues in mid-seventeenth-century England, *The Family, Sex, and Marriage*, chap. 5.

70. L'abbé Arnauld, *Mémoires*, 34: 170.

71. Comte de Souvigny, *Mémoires*, 2: 110.

72. Ibid., 2: 333.

73. Ibid., 2: 274.

housed apart," reported another.[74] These were outrageous fictions, but fictions that mattered to the reading public; a happy marriage formed part of what the public expected of its king.[75]

Contemporary fears, like contemporary fictions, testified to the strength that was seen in some marriages. Montmorency-Damville fell so in love with his second wife, a woman far below him in standing, "that they say she'd made a pact with the devil."[76] Montmorency's successor as constable, the duc de Lesdiguières, was so in love with *his* wife that contemporaries believed she too must have used sorcery to snare him.[77] Madame de Lafayette's prince de Clèves claimed to have concealed most of his passion for his wife, "for fear of importuning you, or losing some of your esteem with manners unsuited to a husband."[78]

Indeed, it was precisely the overlap between ideals of romance and ideals of married love that disturbed pious contemporaries. Pierre Nicole, for instance, had to address the nature of marriage as he sought to evaluate the culture around him by rigorous Christian standards. Nicole thought plays, poetry, and novels dangerous because they stimulated love: "Since the passion of love is the strongest trace that sin has left on our souls," he wrote, "there is nothing more dangerous than to excite it, nourish it, and destroy what holds it in check. . . . Now, nothing serves this purpose better than the horror of love that custom and a good education establish; and nothing more diminishes that horror than theater and novels, for that passion appears there with honor, in ways that, far from making it seem horrible, make it lovable. It appears there without shame or infamy; the characters boast of being touched by it. . . . It does not justify novels and comedies, to say that only legitimate passions appear there, passions that end in marriage. For even though marriage turns sinful desire to good use, desire in itself is always bad and uncontrolled. . . .

74. Quoted in Ruth Kleinman, *Anne of Austria, Queen of France* (Columbus, Ohio, 1985), 90.

75. It is worth noting that Louis XIV presented his relations with his mistresses as stable, long-term intimacies, and that Racine converts the king's flirtation with Mancini into the tragedy of *Bérénice*, illustrating the sacrifice of personal fulfillment in favor of public responsibilities.

76. Tallemant des Réaux, *Historiettes*, 1: 66.

77. Ibid., 1: 52.

78. Madame de Lafayette, *La princesse de Clèves*, in *Romans et nouvelles*, ed. Emile Magne (Paris, 1961), 374.

Representations of legitimate and of sinful loves have almost the same effect and excite the same feelings. . . . Indeed, portrayal of love covered by this veil of honor is the more dangerous, for the observer watches less warily."[79]

Nicole believed that images of passionate love were all about. He thought them dangerous because they appealed so powerfully to his contemporaries and because they were legitimated by images of marriage based on love. Nicole was clearly right at least about the frequency of such images. Starting with *L'Astrée,* at the turn of the century, readers and theatergoers were surrounded by depictions of romantic love. Even if few had the experience of happy marriage, most would have seen its image on the stage and in novels. Nicole feared that fascination with love might spread beyond marriage and encourage adulterous relations. But he also believed that romantic marriage itself posed dangers, for the ideal encouraged Christians to attach excessive importance to sex and romance, at the expense of the love that they owed God. His contemporaries disturbed Nicole, not because they expected too little of marriage, but because they expected too much.

Love thus mattered enormously to seventeenth-century polite society. But other aspects of seventeenth-century thought and practice worked to make love seem especially difficult. One problem to which contemporaries returned again and again was that of women's independence: women were expected to spend much of their time apart from their husbands and to have separate interests and friendships. Pressure for women's independence came from a variety of sources. Montesquieu argued that all monarchical societies required sexual freedom for women. Female society was one of the lures by which kings could draw powerful men to their courts, and hence it served as a mechanism of political control. Thus Montesquieu believed that such virtual republics as Holland and England controlled women closely, whereas courtly societies accorded them enormous freedom.[80] Others saw women's freedom as a custom specific to France. "I am not surprised,"

79. Nicole, *Oeuvres philosophiques et morales,* 438–39.

80. Charles-Louis de Secondat, baron de Montesquieu, *The Spirit of the Laws,* ed. David Wallace Carrithers (Berkeley, 1977), 168. Cf. the similar observations of Marc Fumaroli, "Le 'langage de cour' en France: Problèmes et points de repère," in August Buck et al., eds., *Europäische Hofkultur im 16. und 17. Jahrhundert* (Hamburg, 1981), 2: 23–32.

wrote Tallemant des Réaux of the opinion that French women were especially difficult and demanding, "for practically everywhere else they are virtually imprisoned and cannot practice gallantry, since they see no men."[81] Men who failed to allow their wives freedom could expect mockery from polite society.[82]

Expectations of women's independence took concrete form in seventeenth-century architecture that accorded wives separate apartments within the aristocratic household. Marivaux's Jacob noted of the first Parisian household in which he served that "the master and mistress each had a private suite, from which they dispatched somebody every morning to inquire how the other was"; and household manuals made it clear that this was the standard to which all aristocratic families should aspire.[83] As important, seventeenth-century comedy regularly presented women as independent, indeed, as far more independent than was typically the case in daily life.

Both Corneille and Molière presented women living and making romantic choices in almost complete independence from familial influences. Thus Corneille's heroine Mélite has a mother, to whom she owes "everything, and with any other lover I would wish to subordinate everything to her command."[84] But for her beloved she is ready to ignore her mother's wishes, and in fact the mother's powers remain invisible; she never appears in the drama, and the potential conflicts between old and young, love and family interest, never emerge. Mélite foreshadows the still more extreme instance of Célimène of Molière's *Misanthrope*. Célimène too makes no reference to family in making her romantic choices, and she too appears to live by herself; to all intents and purposes she is a free actor, receiving men as she chooses and in the end setting terms for an eventual marriage. Corneille's *La suivante* offers a different reading of women's place, with a father very much present and a sister whose marriage is entirely arranged for her, in effect as an exchange for her brother's advantage. Yet in this play as well Corneille raises the possibility of a daughter's resistance to her father's dictates; and the *suivante* herself offers again an image of women's explosive power. She is a female figure whose only attachments are

81. Tallemant des Réaux, *Historiettes*, 1: 66.
82. Carolyn Lougee, *Le Paradis des Femmes: Women, Salons, and Social Stratification in Seventeenth-Century France* (Princeton, 1976).
83. Marivaux, *Le paysan parvenu*, 52; Norbert Elias, *The Court Society*, trans. Edmund Jephcott (New York, 1983), 49–51.
84. *Mélite*, lines 713–14, in Corneille, *Oeuvres complètes*, 38.

social, with no family mentioned at all; and she is the source of re-peated disruptions and uncertainties in the plot—an image of women as at once independent of organic connections (though occupying a subject social position) and dangerous.

These should not be taken as images of contemporary behavior, though they may suggest the range of possible behavior in the early seventeenth century. This was, rather, a chosen image of women's place and potential powers within society.[85] Comedy, architecture, and the expectations of courtly life itself offered intensified visions of women's independence and potential powers precisely during years when women's legal independence was probably deteriorating, and in a society that remained heavily dominated by male authority, the threat of male violence, and anxieties about dynastic continuity and purity.[86]

Women were expected to be independent during these years, but within settings that—as Nicole feared and Montesquieu claimed to observe—continually stimulated erotic impulses and made romantic love a constant preoccupation. Dance, music, novels, poetry, and plays were all thought to stimulate erotic feelings and hence to lead both men and women into dissatisfactions and adventures (as will be seen in more detail below). Romance and romantic freedom were essential components of courtly culture; the court was not a scene of height-ened self-control only, but also one of continuous ruptures of self-control. At court, as Madame de Lafayette observed, love and ambi-tion went together.[87]

This combination of ideas—romantic visions of love, belief in women's freedom, incorporation of erotic longings into the official culture of the court—accorded ill with the ideology of lineage. Seventeenth-century society prized dynastic purity and sought to ex-plain personal qualities by dynastic inheritance. One might expect such ideas to have produced close control of women and the careful channeling of illicit male sexuality toward social inferiors, so as to

85. Cf. Greek tragedy, in which powerful, dangerous women illustrate contempo-rary male fears rather than practices.

86. On the increasing control exercised over women in these years, see Sarah Han-ley, "Engendering the State: Family Formation and State Building in Early Modern France," *French Historical Studies* 16, 4 (Spring 1989). Cf. Lougee, *Le Paradis des Femmes*, for the argument that autonomy and "feminism" were a distinctly robe vision during the seventeenth century.

87. Madame de Lafayette, *Romans et nouvelles*, 252, discussed above, Chapter 1.

avoid troubling questions about the purity of lineages. But if anything the reverse occurred. Courtly sexuality undercut the solidity of the family as a *race,* an eternal chain of blood and biological qualities. Seventeenth-century visions of adultery made high-born women proper objects of sexual pursuit by their social equals and repeatedly stressed the interest such women might have in sexual relations with inferiors.

Early in the century Malherbe emphasized these troubling implications of sexual freedom for serious belief in dynastic purity: "He used to say often to Racan . . . that it was a folly to boast that one came from the old nobility; that the older it was, the more doubtful it was; and that it needed only one lascivious woman to pervert the blood of Charlemagne and Saint Louis; that someone who thought himself descended from those great heroes perhaps descended from a valet or violin player."[88] (Malherbe, it is worth noting, associated music with dangerous sexuality.) That noble ladies would find their servants attractive was a long-standing theme in French literature. " 'Ah! Madame, if you only knew,' " says one of the men in Marguerite de Navarre's *Heptameron,* " 'what a great difference there is between a gentleman who spends his whole life in armour on active service and a well-fed servant who never budges from home, you'd excuse the poor widow in this story' " for making love with her servant.[89] The ideology of *race* implied direct correspondence between social and natural order, by presenting the aristocracy as a collection of lineages, whose political rights and allegiances flowed from biological continuity. Courtly culture persistently contradicted this ideology and rendered uncertain the individual's place within the biological patterns it offered.

And indeed a series of noteworthy scandals suggested that these concerns were not mere literary imaginings. At the end of the sixteenth century there was the widely followed case of the princesse de Condé: strongly suspected of having become pregnant by a servant and of having poisoned her husband, she was incarcerated for seven years. The male Condé line survived only because of this pregnancy, and a decade after the event rumors about it continued to circulate.[90]

88. Tallemant des Réaux, *Historiettes,* 1: 113–14.
89. Marguerite de Navarre, *The Heptameron,* 232.
90. M. le duc d'Aumale, *Histoire des princes de Condé pendant les XVIe et XVIIe siècles,* 6 vols. (Paris, 1885), 2: 222ff., 246.

After the Fronde the Grand Condé publicly accused *his* wife of sexual relations with her servants and relegated her to a country house; the ambassador of the duc de Savoie wrote to his master that "for a long time that princess had *commerces infâmes* with her valets; that's why her husband had for a long time not wanted to see her."[91] All of these episodes had public dimensions; contemporaries followed them in pamphlets and satirical poetry and discussed them abroad. Malherbe's snickers at aristocratic lineage and his belief in servants' sexual allure expressed common beliefs about social reality—a widespread sense that women threatened the purity of the lineage.

Fear for the authenticity of a lineage arose still more easily within the aristocracy itself. In the mid-seventeenth century the duc de Candale accused his wife of sleeping with one of his followers, and a few years later came the notorious lawsuit over the Rohan inheritance, a case that turned on Madame de Rohan's well-known infidelities with Candale himself.[92] Madame de Lafayette focused the conclusion of her novella *La comtesse de Tende* on the problem of illegitimacy. As she died, the comtesse "had the consolation of seeing her child born alive, but of being assured that he couldn't live and that she was not giving her husband an illegitimate heir."[93]

Fear of illegitimacy was one reason that illicit sexual relations were no mere game to seventeenth-century high society. Madame de Lafayette's fictional comte de Tende "thought only of killing his wife" on learning of her adultery.[94] Lafayette's *Princesse de Clèves* turns on a similar assumption: the mistaken belief that his wife had committed adultery effectively destroys the prince de Clèves, leaving him in a despair so absolute that he "could not resist his overwhelming grief. Fever took him that very night," and he died a few days later.[95] Even in the eighteenth century, adulterous sexuality might have terrible consequences for women: the three *inséparables* of *Les liaisons dangereuses*, like the présidente de Tourvel and Cécille Volanges, all find themselves confined to convents once their seductions become public knowledge. In the sixteenth and seventeenth centuries, such episodes

---

91. Quoted in Mongrédien, *Le Grand Condé*, 181–82.

92. Tallemant des Réaux, *Historiettes*, 1: 640–48.

93. Madame de Lafayette, *Histoire de madame Henriette d'Angleterre, la princesse de Montpensier, la comtesse de Tende*, ed. Claudinne Hermann (Paris, 1979), 124.

94. Ibid., 122.

95. Madame de Lafayette, *Romans et nouvelles*, 373.

might lead to bloodshed for men; the duc de Mayenne twice arranged assassinations in defense of his family's honor.[96]

Courtly preoccupation with love created a central contradiction within seventeenth-century aristocratic society. The ideology of the lineage required rigid control of women and careful channeling of male sexuality, if not exclusively into marriage, then in socially harmless directions; the court, on the contrary, required sexual freedom for both men and women, and many of its entertainments encouraged thought about love. Seventeenth-century scandals display contemporaries' uneasy awareness of this clash of principles, a clash that might still easily lead to violence.

If contemporaries nonetheless persisted in their pursuit of love, this reflected a vision of personality that accorded an extraordinary place to the passions. "It is on the passions alone that all the good and evil of this life depends"—the writer is no gallant, but René Descartes, opening the final section of his treatise on *The Passions of the Soul*.[97] Descartes confirmed this emphasis by according an extraordinary range to the passions, which he presented as much more significant and wider in scope than animal drives. Among the passions that his treatise lists are hope and anxiety, generosity, vanity and humility, pity, cheerfulness, wonder, and friendship. With regard to the passions, as with so much else, Descartes claimed absolute originality, on the grounds that the ancients had produced nothing useful on the subject.[98] But in fact ancient rhetorical tradition implied a comparable vision of passion as both larger than physical needs and ethically positive. To touch passions in this sense, after all, was the rhetorician's purpose; passion had a respectable place even within public life.[99]

96. Tallemant des Réaux, *Historiettes*, 1: 33, 703, nn. 2, 4, 5.

97. *The Philosophical Writings of René Descartes*, trans. John Cottingham, Robert Stoothoff, and Dugald Murdoch, 2 vols. (Cambridge, 1985), 1: 404; elsewhere, of course, Descartes could use rather different language, suggesting that real felicity lies in the soul, which can stay detached from the passions (1: 345ff.).

98. Ibid., 1: 328. For stress on the radicalism of Descartes's evaluation of the passions, see Charles Taylor, *Sources of the Self: The Making of Modern Identity* (Cambridge, Mass., 1989), 147–58.

99. Aristotle, *On Rhetoric*, ed. George A. Kennedy (Oxford, 1991), book 2, chapters 1–17, presents an analysis of passions and personality types, as a basis for effective argument; see also Paul Griscelli, "Un aspect de la crise de la rhétorique à la fin du XVIIe siècle: Le problème des passions," *XVIIe Siècle* 143 (April–June 1984): 141–46; and Marc Fumaroli, *L'âge de l'éloquence: Rhétorique et "res literaria" de la Renaissance au seuil de l'époque classique* (Geneva, 1980), passim.

Yet emotions remained dangerous, for reason and will could never fully govern them. Seventeenth-century writers took trouble to emphasize both the extent of this autonomy of the passions and its ethical implications. Beyond control, the passions stood also beyond moral censure. Though actions resulting from them might indeed be condemned, the realm of feelings admitted no such judgment. In a defense of *La princesse de Clèves*, thus, the abbé de Charnes argued that "since we cannot master all the movements of our passions, we do not rule as we wish their birth or duration; . . . all we can do is not to allow ourselves to be carried away by their violence, and to modulate them by our reflections."[100] This was more or less the view that Madame de Lafayette herself had taken: the princesse, grieving at her failure to love her husband properly, "told herself it was a crime to have no passion for him, as if it had been something in her power."[101] The princesse illustrated in extreme form both the possibilities and the limits that late-seventeenth-century high society attributed to self-control. She can neither prevent herself from loving the duc de Nemours nor make herself love her husband; in her world affections cannot be learned or acquired through habit. She can only make herself act with perfect propriety.

*La princesse de Clèves* ends, of course, with still darker reflections on human emotional capacities. Widowed, at full liberty to marry her beloved Nemours, the princesse nonetheless refuses him, not on grounds of propriety but because of her view of love itself: "Do men preserve passion in these eternal bonds [of marriage]? Am I to hope for a miracle in my case, and can I place myself in the position of assuredly seeing die that passion that would be my entire happiness? M. de Clèves was perhaps the only man in the world able to preserve love in marriage. My destiny determined that I could not benefit from this good fortune; and perhaps his passion survived only because he found none in me. But I would not have this means to preserve yours."[102]

This was a vision of love as ultimately hopeless, necessarily failing because of the inconstancy of human (or at least male) sentiments.

100. J.-A. de Charnes, *Conversations sur la critique de la princesse de Clèves* (Paris, 1679; repr. Tours, 1973), 219.

101. Madame de Lafayette, *La princesse de Clèves*, in *Romans et nouvelles*, 377–78. Here and below I emphasize the novel's pessimism more than does Nancy K. Miller, *Subject to Change: Reading Feminist Writing* (New York, 1988), 25 ff.

102. Madame de Lafayette, *La princesse de Clèves*, in *Romans et nouvelles*, 377–78.

Passion arose from obstacles, even in the case of the adoring prince de Clèves, and would disappear with them. The result was a fundamental disconnectedness between individuals. Equality of love could not exist, because the one partner's indifference or inaccessibility sustained the other's passion. The princesse spoke of male infidelity, but others applied the same terms to women. "The heart is blind, hence all our errors," concluded Saint-Evremond. "[I]t prefers a fool to an *honnête homme* . . . gives itself to the ugly and deformed and refuses the handsomest. . . . It disconcerts the most restrained women, steals prudes from virtue . . . faithless to husbands, uncertain to lovers . . . it gives and withdraws its affections without reason."[103]

Her choosing to avoid these tumults leads the princesse de Clèves to a famous impasse. Though she has avoided unhappiness, her effort to control passion leads to the destruction of all other feeling. Having given up love, "the other things of the world seemed so indifferent that she renounced it forever."[104] She can turn only to religion and retreat from the world, and even then she survives only a short while. If passion brings misery, in this view, refusal of passion constricts human relations and eventually destroys human life.

For both the princesse de Clèves and the moral theorists around her, there could be no real control of emotion, only its channeling into the forms of social propriety. Hence some of the intensity with which seventeenth-century nobles addressed the problem of civility, the forms of behavior and self-control that the well-born ought to exhibit. Numerous books taught newcomers how they ought to behave in polite society and at court; salon members discussed standards of elegance; and, so historians have suggested, standards of behavior actually changed; men and women became less violent, less impulsive, and cleaner.[105] Interest in civility reflected attitudes toward both the self and others. As historians have pointed out, to follow the rules of the civility manuals was in some degree to view the self as malleable, as a

---

103. Saint-Evremond, *Oeuvres en prose*, 12: 289–90.
104. Madame de Lafayette, *La princesse de Clèves*, in *Romans et nouvelles*, 394.
105. Among scholars who have explored these changes, see, for example, Elias, *The Court Society*; Jean-Louis Flandrin, *Familles: Parenté, maison, sexualité dans l'ancienne France* (Paris, 1976); Orest Ranum, "Courtesy, Absolutism, and the Rise of the French State," *Journal of Modern History* 52 (September 1980): 426–51; Georges Vigarello, *Le propre et le sale* (Paris, 1985); Jean-François Solnon, *La cour de France* (Paris, 1988).

construct that could be reshaped by the exercise of thought and will. But to practice civility was also to accord great importance to other people, for civility's purpose was to win affections. Polished behavior thus represented another response to the need for others that, I have argued, permeated seventeenth-century high society. Bussy-Rabutin, as we have seen, made "being in love" part of being an *honnête homme,* a gentleman; Faret's handbook of civility gave a central place to friendship, as the first thing that a newcomer to court would need.

The most extensive discussion of the overlap between civility and friendship came from the Jansenist Pierre Nicole. Civility originated, Nicole argued, in those complex needs for affection that he believed dominated human personality: "Since we so need the love of others, we are led naturally to seek it and obtain it. And as we know . . . that we love those who love us, either we love others or we pretend to do so. This is the foundation of human civility, which is only a sort of commerce of self-love, in which one attempts to attract the love of others by expressing affection for them." Civility, Nicole concluded, was *un langage d'affection* that men and women offered in place of real feelings.[106] It expressed the asymmetry of the human condition, which mixed an intense need to be loved with a very limited capacity to love others. Yet Nicole sought to preserve the value of such civility even within his system of high ethical demands. The pious Christian, he wrote, cannot hope to attract others to his ways if his piety "is wild, uncivil, crude, and if it does not seek to show men that it loves them, wants to serve them, and is full of warm feelings for them. . . . We must try thus to purify civility, not to banish it."[107] Acceptance of civility reflected an acceptance of human nature, with all its imperfections. Even the pious had an obligation to enter into what Nicole called the "infinite number of tiny human bonds . . . which consist of esteem and affection."[108] Hence his concern with developing the basic lines of a "Christian civility." The group surrounding the Hôtel de Rambouillet, the Parisian center of refined thought and manners, likewise sought to ally elegance of behavior with elevated morality.[109]

106. Nicole, *Oeuvres philosophiques et morales,* 268.
107. Ibid., 276.
108. Ibid., 275.
109. David Maland, *Culture and Society in Seventeenth-Century France* (New York, 1970).

Others had less confidence that a mixture of ethics and civility could be achieved. Instead they argued that concern with civility and manners necessarily contradicted Christian morals. Many of the leaders of the move to more refined behavior during the seventeenth century were in fact well-known libertines, lax in morals and often freethinkers in religion as well. During the late sixteenth and early seventeenth centuries, Queen Marguerite's household was far more important than the royal court as a center of cultivation, despite Marguerite's famous love affairs.[110] The groups around Gaston d'Orléans, Condé, and Philippe d'Orléans were notoriously irreligious; even in the more repressive moral atmosphere of Louis XIV's later reign, the courtesan Ninon de L'Enclos's home remained a center both of elegant behavior and of discreet freethinking; though the court never received Ninon, polite society accorded her a large role in defining elegant behavior.[111]

But the association of civility with libertinism involved more than individual personalities and choices. At the center of much courtly refinement stood direct challenges to Christian views. "*Honnête homme* and morals don't go together," went one contemporary aphorism; "the first quality of an *honneste homme*" is "scorn for religion," went another.[112] Such comments partly reflected the materialist orientation of much elegant behavior in the seventeenth century, its preoccupation with the physical world and its pleasures. Saint-Evremond made the point explicitly: "[T]he enjoyment of pleasure, *volupté* in a word, is the true purpose to which all our actions tend."[113]

In keeping with these materialist views, gastronomy became something of a mania in seventeenth-century Paris, leading to instances of extreme eccentricity. "He was a handsome man, and clean," wrote Tallemant of M. de Bernay, a member of a famous robe family, "but he was so fanatical in his vision of keeping the best table in Paris that he was ridiculous. They called him the satin cook; for he went into his kitchen, where they put an apron on him and he meddled with

---

110. Jean-H. Mariéjol, *La vie de Marguerite de Valois, reine de Navarre et de France (1553–1615)* (Paris, 1928; repr. Geneva, 1970), 248–49, 343ff., 359.

111. Roger Duchêne, *Ninon de L'Enclos: La courtisane du grand siècle* (Paris, 1984).

112. Quoted in René Pintard, *Le libertinage érudit dans la première moitié du XVIIe siècle*, 2 vols. (Paris, 1943), 1: 15.

113. Antoine Adam, ed., *Les libertins au XVIIe siècle* (Paris, 1964), 231.

everything. . . . He was, so to speak, a pedant of good eating, for he was a slave to the proper ordering of his dishes."[114]

Bernay was eccentric but not unique, for gastronomy formed a central part of the new standards of elegance that characterized mid-seventeenth-century Paris. Good food became a subject for books and for boasting in polite society. The marquise de Sablé, reported Tallemant, "claims that there is no one with such delicate taste as she, and that she has no use for those who do not appreciate fine things. She is always inventing some new foolishness."[115] Regnard included mockery of gastronomic excess in his comedy *Le Joueur,* suggesting how widespread the theme had become in the late seventeenth century: "So it's this magistrate, . . . this Doctor of Suppers, who dozes in court but pronounces sentence on the stew; who judges without appeal on wines of Champagne—is it from Rheims, the Clos, or the Montagne? who, never encumbered with books of law, carries cookbook and ground pepper in his pocket."[116] Boisrobert made fun of the exigent delicacy of a group known as the *côteaux,* about whom a fellow epicure complained "that in France there are not four hillsides whose wine they approve of. . . . He criticized two rather sharply, that is, Sablé and Saint-Evremond, as people who found nothing good, and who in their lives hadn't given a glass of water to anyone."[117] Elegant gastronomic discriminations, these examples suggested, involved an anti-Christian concern with the physical world, a failure of civic duties, and a more fundamental failure of charity, a mocking, critical view of those who did not meet the new standards of behavior. Its essence was critical distance from others.

Still more disturbing to moralists, of course, was the fact that elegance was so often associated with illicit sexuality. "At that time," remembered the duc de Bouillon of the 1550s and 1560s, "there was a custom that it was inappropriate for a young man of good *maison* not to have a mistress. They were not chosen by the young men them-

---

114. Tallemant des Réaux, *Historiettes,* 2: 252–53.

115. Ibid., 1: 516.

116. Jean-François Regnard, *Le Joueur,* ed. John Dunkley (Geneva, 1986), 181.

117. Tallemant des Réaux, *Historiettes,* 1: 412–13. Late in the century, it is worth noting, Boileau turned his satire not against exaggerated delicacy but against a host who pretended to elegance but served stringy chicken, Auvergnat wine disguised as Hermitage, and "pour comble de disgrace, / Par le chaud qu'il faisait nous n'avions point de glace" (Satire 3, in Nicolas Boileau, *Oeuvres complètes,* ed. Françoise Escal [Paris, 1966], 21–22).

selves, still less because of affection, but, rather, were either given by some relative or superior or themselves chose the young men by whom they wished to be served." His own mistress "became very careful for me, correcting everything that I did that seemed to her inappropriate, indiscreet, or uncivil. . . . No other person helped so much to introduce me to the world and to give me the manners of the court."[118] A century later, Ninon de L'Enclos claimed to perform a similar role, introducing young men to elegant manners and thought.[119] Women were essential to the court, attracting men to it and shaping their behavior; erotic relations readily followed.

Moralists pointed to other ways in which elegance stimulated the senses. Late in life, with the enthusiasm of the reformed sinner, Bussy-Rabutin urged that court dancing be prohibited: "[I]n those places, . . . the beautiful objects, the lights, the violins, and the excitement of the dance would enflame a hermit. . . . I hold that one must not go to a ball if one is a Christian."[120] Elegant entertainments, so Bussy's complaint ran, did not produce self-control; on the contrary, they risked producing dangerous freedom.

The fashion of masked balls early in Louis XIV's personal reign expressed as well the liberating implications of elegance. Contemporaries saw this liberation clearly and found it highly pleasurable. "It's a new style of ball, and quite agreeable," reported the duc d'Enghien to an absent friend. "[E]veryone at court comes disguised . . . so that one is not at all known, and one dances sometimes for an hour without recognizing anyone whom one sees. . . . [S]ometimes rather amusing adventures occur."[121] A year later the fashion continued, and Enghien

---

118. Henri, duc de Bouillon, *Mémoires*, in Michaud and Poujolat, eds., *Nouvelle collection des mémoires relatifs à l'histoire de France . . .*, 11 (Paris, 1854), 5.

119. Duchêne, *Ninon de L'Enclos*.

120. Bussy-Rabutin, *Mémoires*, 2: 299. Cf. Sorel's *Francion*, 340, for the impact of music, dancing, and decorations: "That tune that the musicians took up on their lutes . . . ravished all those present; there was a rhythm so humorous and so lascivious, that together with the words—themselves sufficiently so—it invited everyone to the pleasures of love. Everything in the room sighed for the charms of pleasure, even the candles—agitated by I know not what wind—seemed to breathe like men and to be possessed by some passionate desire. A sweet madness having taken hold of their souls, they struck up sarabands, which most danced in, mixing confusedly in sweet and immodest postures. A few ladies who until then had kept their modesty . . . allowed it now to escape, so that they did not return as chaste as they had come."

121. Emile Magne, ed., *Le Grand Condé et le duc d'Enghien: Lettres inédites à Marie-Louise de Gonzague, reine de Pologne, sur la cour de Louis XIV (1660–1667)* (Paris, 1920), 4 (22 February 1664).

emphasized its social implications: "[S]ince masked balls have been invented, no one can endure any others; nothing approaches them; there is a liberty without disorder, one places oneself where one wishes, speaks to whom one wishes, and one acts as if everyone were equal."[122] The ball was not only a scene of heightened eroticism but a setting of deliberately created anonymity. For both reasons, it was a site of freedom.

Music by itself was thought to have the same unsettling effects, and it too was a constant presence in seventeenth-century polite society. Madame de Lafayette described the pleasures of life around the king's sister-in-law: "[A]fter supper, all the men of the court appeared there, and the evening passed amid the pleasures of comedies, gambling, and violins—in brief, with all the pleasure imaginable and with no mix of sorrow."[123] Gourville described his escape from Paris after Fouquet's arrest, in his carriage "with all my domestics, who were composed of a cook, a butler who played the bass, an *officier* who served also as valet de chambre, and two lackeys. All three played the violin; it was the fashion then."[124] Bussy-Rabutin described a famous debauch with several of the court's most notorious figures: "[A] little later we sent to Paris to have four of the king's violinists" to liven up the party.[125] Violins thus provided the normal background both to private life and to the morally uncertain world of libertine banquets. At least until the mid-seventeenth century, these courtly pleasures were seen to carry clear moral dangers. "At the end of three months," wrote Tallemant as a mark of a widow's immorality, "she entered houses where there were violins and comedy."[126]

The attempt to end this ambiguity, to bring courtly pleasure within the sphere of morally appropriate behavior, concerned Madame de Maintenon in her establishment of Saint-Cyr: "[A]ttentive to everything that might provide the young ladies of Saint-Cyr with an education appropriate to their birth, [she] complained of the danger that one ran in teaching them to sing and recite verses, because of the na-

122. Ibid., 131 (23 January 1664).

123. Madame de Lafayette, *Histoire de madame Henriette d'Angleterre*, 46.

124. Jean Hérauld, sieur de Gourville, *Mémoires*, ed. Léon Lecestre, 2 vols. (Paris, 1894), 1: 192–93.

125. Bussy-Rabutin, *Mémoires*, 2: 90.

126. Tallemant des Réaux, *Historiettes*, 1: 504.

ture of our best verses and most beautiful tunes."[127] She turned to Racine in the hope of finding morally suitable verses for her young ladies; Racine was sympathetic, for he had given up writing profane poetry because of religious scruples.

Like Pierre Nicole, then, Madame de Maintenon sought to reconcile the demands of contemporary civility with Christian morality, by creating a Christian poetry—an effort akin to Nicole's call for a Christian civility. But by and large contemporaries found the contradictions between Christianity and elegant behavior more striking than their potential integration. Maintenon and Nicole found themselves having to reject or modify much that was at the center of polite culture: not only gastronomy, but also novels, theater, music, and dancing. If preoccupation with civility reflected need for others, then, it also reflected a degree of indifference to religious authority. Even Nicole, in the course of his argument for a Christian civility, concluded that "we must deal with men as men, and not as if they were angels."[128]

Just as it limited the hold of religious authority on contemporary life, so also concern with civility led seventeenth-century polite culture to reject the authority of the past. In this realm at least, seventeenth-century men and women expressed an overwhelming sense of the distance between their own era and earlier generations. In the sixteenth century, aristocratic rhetoric had emphasized decline, the inferiority of the present to even the recent past; seventeenth-century writers spoke instead of progress and viewed the past as primitive in nearly all domains.

One element in this vision of progress was a readiness to see the sixteenth and early seventeenth centuries as an era almost entirely without self-control. Thus the brutishness of high society through the reign of Louis XIII forms a unifying theme in Tallemant des Réaux's *Historiettes* from that period; though Tallemant wrote only about fifteen years after Louis's death, his tales convey a sense of amazed historical distance, as he surveys an era of wildly different behavior. He stressed the violence that prevailed in the highest social circles: "The

127. "Mémoires sur la vie et les ouvrages de Jean Racine," in Racine, *Oeuvres complètes,* 1: 69.
128. Nicole, *Oeuvres philosophiques et morales,* 275.

king did not want his first valets de chambre to be gentlemen," reported Tallemant of Louis XIII, "for he used to say that he wanted to be able to beat them, and he did not think he could beat a gentleman without losing his dignity."[129] Tallemant presented beatings as the normal fate of all early-seventeenth-century dependents, not just of servants. He reported having been told, "[B]ut I wouldn't want to guarantee it, that Bullion [Richelieu's *surintendant des finances*] died from chagrin at being kicked by the cardinal de Richelieu." Tallemant had other reports that Richelieu "had a tendency to beat his men" and that the victims included the captain of his guards and the chancellor Séguier.[130] Tallemant ascribed a different form of brutality to the duc d'Angoulême, the bastard son of Charles IX who survived into the mid-seventeenth century. Angoulême refused to pay his servants; when they complained, he urged them to rob those who passed by his Parisian mansion. "It's for you to take care of yourselves," he told them. "[F]our streets end at the hotel d'Angoulême; you're in a fine location; take advantage of it if you wish."[131]

But violence was only one of the forms of vulgarity that impressed mid-seventeenth-century writers about earlier generations. Tallemant retailed a long series of stories about the loose sexual morality of the years before the Fronde. His point was not that sexual behavior was purer in his own time, but, rather, the animal quality of sexual behavior in earlier years; his contrast was not between misbehavior and virtue, but between the free rein of animal impulses and cultivated refinement. Thus François de Montmorency, who died in 1614: "[H]e was accused of being very brutal; he barely knew how to read." Tallemant doubted rumors that Montmorency had deflowered his daughters, "but as for his aunts, his sisters, his cousins, his nieces, he had no scruples. . . . They lived in complete license."[132] The duc de Sully presented only a slightly more respectable picture. Tallemant described his nightly dancing, as a collection of dependents and prostitutes watched, and his nearly incestuous relations with his daughter, the future Madame de Rohan.[133]

129. Tallemant des Réaux, *Historiettes*, 1: 343.
130. Ibid., 1: 265, 304.
131. Ibid., 1: 96.
132. Ibid., 1: 65.
133. Ibid., 1: 49, 622. David Buisseret, *Sully and the Growth of Centralized Government in France, 1598–1610* (London, 1968), describes Sully's habits.

These were stories about the gap between nature and culture. Early in his century, as Tallemant presented it, civility posed few checks on violent or sexual impulses. Other forms of disorder were likewise to be seen in the houses of the great. "One day," reported Tallemant, "[Gaston d'Orléans] saw a servant sleeping with his mouth open; he went over and farted into it. The page, half asleep, cried 'Bugger, I'll shit in your mouth.'"[134] Another of Gaston's dependents, the comte de Louvigny, was famous for his miserable clothing: "[T]hey used to say that he would have done better to do without his pants."[135] Richelieu's own household was not exempt from these kinds of vulgarity: "Once when the Cardinal wanted some clavichord music, Boisrobert [Richelieu's companion] said, 'M. de Bullion [the financier and dependent of Richelieu] pissed in it.' He pissed everywhere."[136] Into the era of Louis XIV there survived the complicated example of the Grand Condé: devoted to elegance in cuisine and the beautification of his estate at Chantilly, but someone whom Mademoiselle described as "the dirtiest man in the world"; Madame de Sévigné thought his having himself shaved and combed for his nephew's wedding so extraordinary that she described the transformation for her daughter.[137] Around Condé too there persisted rumors of incest, with his sister Madame de Longueville.[138] As Tallemant and others presented the period, the sixteenth and early seventeenth centuries formed an age with strikingly few checks on natural impulses. They described the age as a realm of nature, of brutality and disorder; they saw the culmination of this disorder in the incestuous or nearly incestuous households of Montmorency and Sully. Early in the seventeenth century, so these stories sought to show, even the most basic checks on natural impulses had been lacking—even among the loftiest families, even at court.

But in these respects Condé seemed a survival from another era, for alongside these stories Tallemant presented others that suggested at least hesitant progress in manners and cultivation—and that made clear the overwhelming superiority of his own times. Thus Antoine Arnauld "passed for eloquent in a time when scarcely anything was known about eloquence"—that is, in the late sixteenth and early

134. Tallemant des Réaux, *Historiettes*, 1: 359.
135. Ibid., 1: 534.
136. Ibid., 2: 194.
137. Quoted in Mongrédien, *Le Grand Condé*, 72, 175.
138. Ibid., 59–60.

seventeenth centuries.[139] Madame des Loges, in about 1600, was "the first person of her sex to write reasonable letters. . . . Her letters are not very impressive; they were fine for that time."[140] The duc de Nemours was "the first who applied himself to writing gallantries in verse and who taught himself to design ballets and parades."[141] Of Viète, Tallemant wrote. "[B]efore him, there was no one in France who concerned himself" with mathematics;[142] of the comte de Cramail, that he "lived in a time when it didn't take much to seem a wit."[143]

Such claims for progress formed part of a recognizable rhetoric in the mid-seventeenth century, a rhetoric that was especially congenial to mid-seventeenth-century poets and essayists: they readily presented themselves as having achieved something new, without guidance from the past. Thus Descartes, in his famous (and exaggerated) insistence on his complete rejection of previous authority.[144] Thus Boileau, in his claim that "I advanced bravely, guided by myself alone, aided on the journey by my own genius only."[145] Corneille expressed a delicate modesty about his achievements, but he too emphasized the taste for cultural innovation among his contemporaries and the novelty of his own works. He said of *L'illusion comique,* "Let them call it bizarre or extravagant as much as they like, it's new";[146] in 1660, reflecting on the success of his first play, *Mélite,* he argued that "the novelty of this kind of comedy, of which there is not a single example in any language," partly accounted for its success.[147] The seventeenth-century cultural world included strong pressures for innovation and a confident sense that real advances had been achieved.

Corneille's assertions rested not only on notions of personal invention but also on a claim to have redrawn the relationship between social class and drama. *Mélite*'s success, he wrote thirty years after the event, reflected its "depiction of the conversation of *honnêtes gens.* . . . Never before had a comedy drawn laughter without ridicu-

139. Tallemant des Réaux, *Historiettes,* 1: 504–5.
140. Ibid., 1: 606, 607.
141. Ibid., 1: 89.
142. Ibid., 1: 191.
143. Ibid., 1: 232.
144. On Descartes's originality, see above, n. 98.
145. Boileau, *Oeuvres complètes,* Epistle 10.
146. Dedication to *L'illusion comique,* in Corneille, *Oeuvres complètes,* 193.
147. Ibid., "Examen," *Oeuvres complètes,* 28.

lous characters, the comic servants, the hangers-on, the captains, the doctors, and all the rest. Mine achieved its effect with the delicate humor of people of a higher standing than those seen in the comedies of Plautus and Terence, who were mere merchants."[148] Corneille thus described his originality as lying in the new relationship he had created between aristocratic society and artistic representation. Comedy shifted from representing the distant, the stock comic figures of older dramatic tradition, the peasants, servants, boastful soldiers, to representing the like, the substantial figures of the court and the city. This meant a sharpening of social boundaries; the lower classes were not to be present even in the theatrical self-representations of the wealthy. Like elegant manners, drama became a mechanism of social distinction.

As it sought to represent a narrower band of social types, drama also became more delicate in its selection of subject matter. Sex and some forms of violence disappeared from public representation; in their place came extended treatments of the feelings. The public, wrote Fontenelle of Corneille's later years, found distasteful "the very idea of the peril of prostitution" in the play *Théodore;* "and if the public had become so delicate, whom should Corneille have blamed but himself? Before him, rape succeeded in the plays of Hardy."[149] Racine took delicacy still further, boasting that in *Phèdre* the mere thought of sin sufficed to pull down punishment. For this reason, Racine hoped, it might avoid the censures that moralists applied to the contemporary theater.[150] Racine's drama—that which drew audiences in the later seventeenth century and to which Corneille could never entirely adapt—was a drama of inner emotions. With this in mind, theorists had steadily less patience for dramatic action itself. Excessive action, so mid-seventeenth-century theorists believed, signified vulgarity and superficiality, and an excessive concern with plea-

---

148. *Oeuvres complètes,* 28. It is all the more striking that Corneille here exaggerated his innovations. Others had already written comedies using the language and situations of polite society and avoiding the stock characters of Roman comedy (Antoine Adam, *La littérature française: L'âge classique,* 4 vols. [Paris, 1968], 1: 176); the claim to originality clearly had value in itself. Cf. Ian Watt, *The Rise of the Novel: Studies in Defoe, Richardson and Fielding* (Berkeley, 1962), 14: "It is significant that the trend in favour of originality found its first powerful expression in England, and in the eighteenth century."

149. Fontenelle, "Vie," in Corneille, *Oeuvres complètes,* 23.

150. Racine, *Oeuvres complètes,* 39.

sure in drama.[151] The new drama advanced by parallel exclusions, of lowly social types and of improper behavior.

As drama became steadily more refined over the seventeenth century, so its theorists asserted, it became both more socially exclusive and more inward-turning; it portrayed ever less violence and ever more shades of feeling, and it presented these in increasingly courtly milieux. These changes testify to some of the changing meanings of civility, for (as the theorists suggested) drama functioned as both a reflection and a teacher of upper-class tastes.[152] Like Pierre Nicole, the dramatists sought to link exploration of the emotions with refinement of manners; developing civility accompanied a developing preoccupation with relations of friendship and love.

But in both drama and life, concern with civility ultimately led its aristocratic practitioners into contradictions: first, between pursuit of affection and pursuit of distinction; second, between different forms of distinction. Seventeenth-century civility expressed urges for attachment to others. Through elegance and graces, so the seventeenth century believed, men and women could attract others and secure their love; the language of friendship, love, and even familial relations used the notion of "merit" to explain why individuals received more or less love from those around them. Yet civility also offered means for setting oneself apart from others. This meant partly the sharper social discriminations seen in seventeenth-century drama, the growing distance from popular social types and amusements. But more fundamentally, concern with elegance encouraged constant evaluation and criticism of others' performances even within polite society. Such leaders in elegant behavior as Bussy-Rabutin and Saint-Evremond had the reputation of being cool toward others, difficult to please, and vain about their own accomplishments. Madame de Lafayette described the comte de Guiche as "the handsomest young man of the court and the best-proportioned, appealing [*aimable de sa personne*], gallant, hardy, brave, high-minded: the vanity that so many fine qualities gave him and a scornful air visible in all his actions somewhat tarnished all this merit; but one must admit that no man at court had as much as

151. Adam, *La littérature française*, 1: 164–73.
152. A point suggested by Orest Ranum, *Paris in the Age of Absolutism: An Essay* (New York, 1968).

he."[153] Such men as Guiche, Saint-Evremond, and Bussy-Rabutin were viewed as *médisants,* who delighted in criticism and mockery; and eventually each was punished for the failing, Bussy with imprisonment, Guiche and Saint-Evremond with exile. If civility began with the urge to please others, it seemed to lead quickly to detachment and criticism.[154]

This was the first of civility's contradictions. The second lay in its awkward place within a social hierarchy based on bloodlines and family traditions. Virtually all seventeenth-century nobles believed in the superiority of noble birth and thought that specific family traditions had an important effect on individual personalities. But ideals of elegant behavior suggested a rather different, and in some measure contradictory, understanding of social distinction. These ideals belittled the relevance of the past for contemporary practice and stressed the need for individuals to train themselves to meet new standards. Tradition could have little significance in such circumstances, for even the recent past seemed to seventeenth-century men and women an age of brutish behavior and limited ability. Religious tradition had still less relevance: much in seventeenth-century civility called into question basic Christian values. Though it did not so explicitly contradict ideas of familial inheritance, the practice of civility did require seventeenth-century men and women to view themselves as in some degree newly created, following new forms of behavior and carefully shaping their gestures and expressions.

Especially during the sixteenth century, much of the need for this kind of self-control came from the royal court, "a land," as the comte de Souvigny advised his children, "where it is permitted to watch and listen, but forbidden to speak save with very good reason, on pain of prompt penitence."[155] Contemporaries spoke often of this self-control that life at court demanded, and they noted also the manners and even the special language that developed around the court. Yet to stress the role of Crown and court in creating elegant manners is to overlook the degree to which elegance developed at the margins of court life,

---

153. Madame de Lafayette, *Histoire de madame Henriette d'Angleterre,* 43.

154. Cf. historians' stress on the concern for physical separation that much seventeenth- and eighteenth-century civility showed: for instance, Elias, *The Court Society;* Vigarello, *Le propre et le sale;* Orest Ranum, "The Refuges of Intimacy," in Chartier, ed., *History of Private Life,* 207–63.

155. Comte de Souvigny, *Mémoires,* 3: 68.

around such figures as Queen Marguerite, Ninon de L'Enclos, Saint-Evremond, Bussy-Rabutin, La Rochefoucauld.[156] All of these inspired some degree of active dislike at court and suffered varying forms of exile from it; all seemed to violate established moralities. Yet such figures played the dominant role in defining what courtliness meant, and their role became more important over the seventeenth century. The grim Versailles of Louis XIV's last years offered few pleasures to compare with those of the great aristocracy's Parisian houses.

Numerous accidental factors help to explain this divergence between the court and the leading exponents of civility, but ultimately it testified to the problems that civility posed for a society based on family and religious traditions. The Crown itself sought to embody these traditions, enforcing Christian and familial discipline, presenting itself as defender of order, hierarchy, and inheritance. As a result, it could never fully endorse the ethic of civility. Patterns of elegance could be modulated so as to fit Christian and dynastic social ideals, as Madame de Maintenon and Pierre Nicole sought to do. But the accord could never be perfect. More often, the pursuit of elegance placed serious strains on the society of orders, by implicitly proposing a social order oriented to progress and to worldly pleasures, dismissive of both religion and the past.[157] Models of civility could not enjoy an entirely easy relationship with the monarchy.

French nobles, so runs a principal argument of this chapter, felt a larger discomfort about the social order they inhabited, a discomfort that came from their growing sense of the disjuncture between personal and civic life. Both classical and medieval traditions taught that the civic and the personal world overlapped. In these traditions, friendship was a constituent element of public life, a form of emotional attachment that allowed familial and political groups to function more effectively; friendship rested on virtue, that is, on publicly shared evaluations of personal qualities. Many of these beliefs remained vigorous in the seventeenth century, but alongside them had arisen quite different views of personal connectedness. These situated friendship among the passions, explained its origins by immediate personal, often physical, attraction, and saw its function as providing a private shelter from public life.

---

156. In this my interpretation differs from those who have stressed the political functions of civility, cited above, n. 105.

157. A point emphasized by Paul Bénichou, *Morales du grand siècle* (Paris, 1948).

Seventeenth-century thought also stressed the difference between the self that one presented to a friend and the self that emerged in society. These ideas too had troubling implications for a society of orders, for they presented the social self as an artificial construct, in contrast to the authentic being that one revealed to a friend. Implicitly more upsetting, real attachment to others required likeness, for the friend had to be another self, whose inner life one could share; there could be no real attachment between unequals, for instance between patron and client. Seventeenth-century writers continued to describe as friendship the mutual confidence between leader and follower, but by the time of Racine the problems of friendship between unequals seemed very great. Deference and fidelity lay increasingly in the realm of the social and inauthentic, and at an increasing distance from personal emotion.

The force of such emotion during the seventeenth century is the final point to be emphasized here. Seventeenth-century nobles believed that a variety of dangers surrounded both friendship and love, and they believed both likely to fail, as feelings shifted. But they also attached large and apparently increasing importance to love and friendship. Seventeenth-century moralists complained not of lack of feeling in those around them but of excess. It was this strength of feeling that made the collision between personal and social realms so painful.

# 5

# Money and the Problem of Power

Even in modern societies, monetary exchanges provoke discomfort. Exchange undermines certainty, as participants confront one another's differing evaluations of their goods and the infinity of their own desires. Use of money demands calculation and the reduction of warm feelings to cold numbers. It defines limits, setting sharp boundaries to what one can have and do; and it destroys community, by requiring that individuals treat one another as radically distinct actors, to be argued with and possibly deceived. The spread of monetary exchanges inevitably troubles relations between individuals and the community in which they live.[1]

The aristocratic and Catholic society of seventeenth-century France experienced further problems when it confronted money. The Catholic church taught that certain monetary dealings were entirely illegitimate, and it raised questions about the propriety of many others. Pursuit of gain threatened the individual Christian's spiritual health, and it destroyed bonds of charity uniting the larger Christian community.[2] Money might be equally corrosive of the values of an aristocratic social order. By its nature it softened certain social contrasts. As sumptuary laws complained, anyone with money might buy the external trappings of high status; with the development of venal office-holding during the sixteenth and seventeenth centuries, it seemed that money could buy public power as well. Aristocratic ideology proclaimed a generous indifference to monetary calculation, and theorists of the

---

1. For examples of these anxieties in the early modern period, see Joyce Appleby, *Economic Thought and Ideology in Seventeenth-Century England* (Princeton, 1978); William Reddy, *The Rise of Market Culture: The Textile Trade and French Society, 1750–1900* (Cambridge, 1984); and Jean-Christophe Agnew, *Worlds Apart: The Market and the Theater in Anglo-American Thought, 1550–1750* (Cambridge, 1986). Parts of this chapter appear in "The Ruling Class in the Marketplace: Nobles and Money in Early Modern France," in Thomas Haskell and Richard Teichgraeber, eds., *The Culture of the Market*, Cambridge, forthcoming.

2. Benjamin Nelson, *The Problem of Usury, from Tribal Brotherhood to Universal Otherhood* (Princeton, 1949).

landed estate urged avoidance of the marketplace whenever possible. To the extent that they could, estate owners were to supply themselves from their own lands, and so avoid the extravagances and indebtedness that the marketplace seemed inevitably to bring with it.[3]

For all the problems it raised, money also became a steadily more pervasive fact in seventeenth-century high society. As the century advanced, monetary exchanges took place more frequently and touched more areas of life. Conspicuous display seemed far more common, and fortunes seemed both larger and more unstable than in earlier years. Conflicting so visibly with ideals that all French nobles held, these changes produced predictable cultural disturbances and irritated protests. But they also led to more surprising responses, for the nobles did not find in the spread of monetary relations only challenges to their vision of themselves. Seventeenth-century nobles encountered money, so I argue here, in a variety of contexts, only some of them directly connected to the market economy. Money was as likely to be an element of political power and social deference as of economic exchange. As such, money participated in the discomforts that, this book argues, characterized relations within the society of orders. In venal office-holding, lending relations, and other spheres, money functioned less as a challenge to established patterns of power and subordination than as a newly effective implement for their exercise. Such encounters with money, so runs a further element in this chapter's argument, help to explain the striking pleasure with which seventeenth-century nobles turned to monetary exchanges of a different kind, exchanges that embodied or mimicked the experience of the free market itself. Nobles turned eagerly to certain forms of market or market-like activity as a release from the constraints of the society of orders. The market seemed less a threat than a pleasurable alternative to long-standing forms of social control.

For most French nobles, the mid-seventeenth century was a period of booming economic possibilities. The brightest chances lay before

3. For emphasis on the European nobilities' commitment to such views, see, for instance, George Huppert, *Les Bourgeois Gentilshommes: An Essay on the Definition of Elites in Renaissance France* (Chicago, 1977); E. P. Thompson, *Whigs and Hunters: The Origins of the Black Act* (New York, 1975); Jonathan Dewald, *Pont-St-Pierre, 1398–1789: Lordship, Community, and Capitalism in Early Modern France* (Berkeley, 1987), 49ff., for nobles' interest in self-sufficiency; Ralph Albanese, "The Dynamics of Money in Post-Molièresque Comedy," *Stanford French Review* 7, 1 (Spring 1983).

those who enjoyed connections with the state; for them, contemporaries believed, the mid-seventeenth century saw both a new scale of wealth and a new speed in its accumulation. At the head of the government, Richelieu, Mazarin, and their teams set previously undreamed-of standards of rapacity; after losing his wealth during the Fronde, Mazarin managed in less than a decade to accumulate the largest private fortune that the Old Regime would ever see.[4] Such possibilities beckoned even at the bottom of the social scale. Gourville had been the La Rochefoucaulds' servant, but his place in the financial system allowed him to make a fortune, and then to make others after he lost the first. Late in his life, it seems, he secretly married the duc de La Rochefoucauld's daughter.[5] Tallemant had no doubt that all of this was new. He compared Bullion, Richelieu's leading financier, with "today's finance ministers. In their hospitality, their pleasures, their houses, these spend more in six years than Bullion left at his death" twenty years before.[6]

The royal finances offered one avenue to rapid wealth, but so also did the royal armies. "They didn't pay the troops regularly," recalled a biographer of Saint-Evremond. "[I]nstead they gave officers rights on the cities and towns, and everyone took what he could. Clever in taking advantage of situations and supported by Monsieur Fouquet, who knew him well, Monsieur de Saint-Evremond did not do badly in Guyenne. He admitted it himself, and used often to joke that in two and a half years he had made 50,000 livres profit."[7] This was a common pattern. Nobles might display greater or lesser degrees of greed, but acceptable standards encompassed extraordinarily grasping behavior. In the 1670s, the marquis de Roncherolles served as military governor of a frontier town in Flanders. He was accused of using this position to make money in the most undignified ways: he sold part of the firewood that had been allotted to his guards, forced villagers to

---

4. Daniel Dessert, *Argent, pouvoir et société au Grand Siècle* (Paris, 1984), and *Fouquet* (Paris, 1987); Joseph Bergin, *Cardinal Richelieu: Power and the Pursuit of Wealth* (New Haven, 1985); Françoise Bayard, *Le monde des financiers au XVIIe siècle* (Paris, 1988).

5. Jean Hérauld, sieur de Gourville, *Mémoires*, ed. Léon Lecestre, 2 vols. (Paris, 1894). For a provincial example, see James Collins, "Geographic and Social Mobility in Early Modern France," *Journal of Social History* 24, 3 (1989): 563–77.

6. Gédéon Tallemant des Réaux, *Historiettes*, ed. Antoine Adam, 2 vols. (Paris, Pléiade, 1960–61), 1: 303.

7. Charles de Marguetel, seigneur de Saint-Evremond, *Oeuvres en prose*, ed. René Ternois, 3 vols. (Paris, 1962–66), 1: xxvii.

fatten his lifestock for the market, became the tenant farmer for church and municipal lands in the region, and refused to pay his rents.[8] Military values provided only feeble inhibitions against minute monetary calculations. The seventeenth-century economy was one in which inside information, position, and social relations could produce rapid fortunes.

Landowning offered no such rapid accumulation, yet these were good years for aristocratic landowners also. Nobles who controlled seigneurial rents suffered, for inflation cut away most of the value of permanently fixed dues. But most nobles held substantial amounts of land as well as dues, and in the long run they could scarcely help being economic winners in these years. They controlled resources of food and fuel for which the society had an increasingly desperate need, and an increasingly efficient commerce gave monetary value to properties that had previously been virtually worthless. Forests had supplied little revenue in the Middle Ages, but they quickly became valuable in the sixteenth century, as a rapidly growing population bought wood for heating and construction. Food prices rose faster than any others in the sixteenth-century price revolution, and leases rose correspondingly.[9]

The seventeenth century offered even better times for landowners: tenant farmers competed to lease their domains, and periods of food shortage offered windfall gains. Improving commercial networks and the development of an enormous Parisian market helped as well. Goods that once could be consumed only in "rustic hospitality at home"[10] (Adam Smith's phrase) could now be sold; Smith saw the spread of consumer goods as inevitably corroding the economy of the feudal household, turning landowners from paternalists to self-interested economic actors. For French landowners, circumstances soured only after 1660, when prices and leases both declined, to revive only in the mid-eighteenth century.[11] Until the 1660s, the nobles became richer, controlling more land and drawing more from what they did control. Individual families might fail, but the group as a whole prospered.

8. Dewald, *Pont-St-Pierre*, 179–80.
9. Emmanuel Le Roy Ladurie, Hugues Neveux, and Jean Jacquart, *Histoire de la France rurale*, vol. 2 (Paris, 1975).
10. Adam Smith, *Wealth of Nations*, ed. Andrew Skinner (London, 1982), 508–12, 335.
11. Le Roy Ladurie, Neveux, Jacquart, *Histoire de la France rurale*.

With prosperity came a readiness to spend. Money was highly visible in seventeenth-century society, and it made itself conspicuous in the most important symbol of aristocratic society, the aristocratic house. A violent building mania gripped seventeenth-century polite society. It reflected both the quantities of money circulating in high society and some of its unsettling effects. Building allowed new people to affirm a place within society. Tallemant described the financier Bordier spending a million livres on his house at Les Raincys, "one of the greatest follies that one could possibly commit," and noted what this meant for Bordier's sense of his family: "After having built Les Raincys . . . was I to say to the queen: 'Madame, I am marrying my son to Anne Margonne?' " (the daughter of another financier).[12] But fully established families too were drawn into excited building, far beyond any reasonable needs. "One gives oneself to building as to gambling; a house comes to be like a mistress," wrote Fénelon at the end of the seventeenth century.[13] Gourville watched in amazement as the Condé family managed to spend 200,000 livres yearly in beautifying Chantilly, but then described how he himself "fell into the trouble of all those who wish to fix up houses": instead of the 240,000 livres he had planned to spend, he finished by spending nearly 400,000.[14] The chancellor Le Tellier worried about his son's building expenses, and Gourville sought to comfort him by arguing that "I was persuaded that there always were times when mental maladies circulated . . . by the follies I had seen many people undertake in building and gardens."[15] Building combined the follies of love with an assertion of self and lineage and with the urge to make oneself known within polite society.

This was only one of many ways in which money was especially visible in seventeenth-century social life. There was no effort to hide financial details of dowries, office prices, and other such matters; instead, social practice accentuated the presence of money. There were the expenditures of fashionable dress and elegant dining. There was the cost of gallantry: "Excessive expenditures are inseparable from love," opined Bussy-Rabutin during his old age.[16] Gambling was yet

12. Tallemant des Réaux, *Historiettes*, 2: 181.

13. François de Salignac de La Mothe-Fénelon, *Oeuvres spirituelles*, ed. François Varillon, S.J. (Paris, 1954), 319.

14. Gourville, *Mémoires*, 1: 51, 2: 66–67.

15. Ibid., 2: 159.

16. Roger de Bussy-Rabutin, *Mémoires*, ed. Ludovic Lalanne, 2 vols. (Paris, 1857; repr. Westmead, 1972), 2: 303.

another occasion for spending. Henri de Campion, an advocate of stoical morality who came from a provincial family, nonetheless found
his camp life troubled only "by my misfortunes at dice, which I loved
so passionately that they kept me in continual poverty."[17] Gourville,
who was unusually successful at gambling, described winning 18,000
livres in one session, and in another 55,000 livres "in seven
minutes."[18] In keeping with the high visibility of money itself, mon-
eyed men moved easily into seventeenth-century high society. Men
newly enriched by the royal finances found ready acceptance in aristocratic social circles, and their children advanced quickly in more
dignified careers, as magistrates and military officers.[19]

It is relatively easy to identify these patterns. It is more difficult to
untangle the attitudes that underlay economic realities. For a long
time nobles had thought hard about money and had displayed care
in manipulating it, so that some forms of economic reasoning had
long histories by the seventeenth century. In upper Normandy, land
was bought and sold about as frequently in the fifteenth century
as in the eighteenth, and purchases substantially outnumbered land
transfers through inheritance.[20] Late medieval nobles kept impressive
account books, far more orderly than those of their sixteenth- and
seventeenth-century successors.[21]

As a more explicit statement of late medieval attitudes to money,
we may take Jean Froissart's description of his visit to Gaston de Foix,
in southwestern France, at the end of the fourteenth century. Gaston
was not a typical nobleman, but Froissart offered him as something
better, a pattern of what a nobleman ought to be. Gaston's economic
behavior contributed to this role: "He always disliked excessive ex-
travagance and required an account of his wealth once every month.
He chose twelve prominent men from his country to receive his rents
and administer his retainers. For each period of two months, two of

17. Henri de Campion, *Mémoires*, ed. Marc Fumaroli (Paris, 1967), 96.
18. Gourville, *Mémoires*, 1: 171.
19. See Bayard, *Le monde des financiers*, 421–49.
20. Dewald, *Pont-St-Pierre*, 51–52.
21. A point discussed by Guy Bois, in *Crise du féodalisme: Economie rurale et démographie en Normandie orientale* (Paris, 1976). For other examples of declining accounting practices in the sixteenth century, see André Plaisse, *La baronnie du Neubourg: Essai d'histoire agraire, économique, et sociale* (Paris, 1961); Jonathan Dewald,
*The Formation of a Provincial Nobility: The Magistrates of the Parlement of Rouen,
1499–1610* (Princeton, 1980), 190–97.

them worked in his receiving-office and at the end of that time they were changed and two others took their place. . . . The comptroller brought his accounts to his master on rolls or books, and left them for the Count to look over. He had a number of chests in his private room and from time to time, but not every day, he had money taken from them to give to some lord, knight or squire who had come to visit him, for no man ever left him without receiving a present. He was always increasing his wealth, as a precaution against the hazards of fortune, which he feared. He was approachable and agreeable to everyone, speaking to them kindly and amiably."[22]

Gaston, so Froissart's description suggests, had at his disposal a full range of economic techniques and assumptions. He kept close records, controlled his expenditures, and assumed that his wealth would grow. He and Froissart both believed that wealth was money, rather than lands or retainers, and Gaston, at least, assumed that only his money would shelter him against unfriendly developments in the future. Neither he nor Froissart perceived contradictions between gentility and hard economic calculation. Record-keeping, mistrust of economic agents, and constant accumulation allied easily with hospitality and affability, in fact were their preconditions; abundance and calculation went together.

Gaston, to repeat, offers an ideal type rather than a representative case, and perhaps Froissart thought him interesting because unusual. But his example raises complexities when we seek to define a specifically seventeenth-century stance toward money, for, clearly, instrumental rationality toward money and calculations of profit had long histories by then. Gaston seems not to fit any of Max Weber's categories of economic action. If he lacked the self-restraining, acquisitive ethic that Weber saw in Benjamin Franklin, he also seems far from "the capitalistic adventurer" whom Weber contrasted with Franklin and whose "activities were predominantly of an irrational and speculative character"; and he seems still farther from Weber's traditional social actor, who wishes "simply to live as he is accustomed to live and to earn as much as is necessary for that purpose."[23] Neither unrestricted greed nor traditional norms governed his monetary dealings.

22. Jean Froissart, *Chronicles*, selected, ed., and trans. Geoffrey Brereton (London, 1968), 264–65.

23. Max Weber, *The Protestant Ethic and the Spirit of Capitalism*, trans. Talcott Parsons (New York, 1958), 20, 60.

Gaston gave generously to his followers, but his giving reflected careful political thought; and his generosity made him all the more intent on accumulating and controlling his wealth.

Some of Gaston's attitudes survived into the seventeenth century. Early in the century, there was the prince de Condé (1588–1646). In Tallemant's words, Condé "had the soul of a manager of a great house; no man ever kept his papers in better order." Condé paid his debts on time, followed his lawsuits carefully, and dramatically expanded his family's wealth.[24] He transformed what had been a small and unstable patrimony into one of the country's greatest fortunes.[25] Philippe d'Orléans showed similar qualities in the second half of the century: he was careful with his money, vigorous in pursuit of new sources of wealth, and, above all, successful.[26]

But the careful control that Condé and Philippe d'Orléans exercised over their money was unusual in the seventeenth century; it coexisted uneasily with the century's demand that money be displayed. More typical was Condé's son, the Grand Condé. Twenty years after his father's death, the Grand Condé had debts of 8 million livres, at a time when leading provincial nobles enjoyed yearly revenues of about 15,000 livres; his servants had received no money for five years, and he himself could barely leave his rooms for fear of the waiting throng of creditors. Condé lived in nearly complete financial confusion. Despite his unpaid creditors, he continued buying land in the 1660s; he and his son the duc d'Enghien were spending about 200,000 livres yearly in beautifying Chantilly; and amid the wreckage the duc d'Enghien "wished only to reserve for himself 100,000 livres for his clothes and small pleasures" (in the words of a financial adviser).[27]

Condé was in many ways the greatest nobleman of his age, the paradigm on whom others modeled their behavior and who appeared, thinly disguised, in contemporary fiction by Mademoiselle de Scudéry

24. Tallemant des Réaux, *Historiettes*, 1: 420ff.
25. See M. le duc d'Aumale, *Histoire des princes de Condé pendant les XVIe et XVIIe siècles*, 6 vols. (Paris, 1885), 3: 136–48, 250–51; and, more generally, Jean-Pierre Labatut, *Les ducs et pairs de France au XVIIe siècle: Etude sociale* (Paris, 1972), 244–45. Daniel Roche, "Aperçus sur la fortune et les revenus des princes de Condé à l'aube du 18e siècle," *Revue d'Histoire Moderne et Contemporaine* 14 (July–September 1967): 217–43, though mainly concerned with later developments, describes the family's development over the seventeenth century.
26. Nancy Nichols Barker, *Brother to the Sun King: Philippe Duke of Orleans* (Baltimore, 1989), 166–98.
27. Gourville, *Mémoires*, 2: 34–53.

and Pierre Corneille. His example had more than personal impact, and indeed aristocratic spendthrifts were common figures in the mid-seventeenth century. Such a one was Georges de Brancas, duc de Villars and governor of Normandy. Though he inherited the enormous wealth that his brother had accumulated by a well-timed settlement with Henri IV, "there has never been such a poor man. He and his wife have consumed 800,000 écus in cash and 60,000 livres in landed rents; there remain only 17,000 livres in rents that have been entailed."[28] Retz described the duc d'Elbeuf as "the first prince whom poverty had degraded [*avili*]."[29] In contrast to Gaston de Foix's world, to the seventeenth century expenditure was glorious. As Montesquieu presented the argument: "For the preservation therefore of a monarchical state, luxury ought continually to increase and to grow more extensive . . . ; otherwise the nation will be undone."[30] In this view, luxury was both the mechanism by which social differences were maintained and displayed and the mechanism by which those lower in society, who supported its unequal arrangements, could receive back some of what they paid to their superiors; luxury in some degree mitigated the injustices of inequality. The refusal of luxury could only be a vice—a refusal to enter into the exchanges on which society was based, a form of misanthropy.

Figures like Condé moved in an economic world that was heavily influenced by political power; contemporaries knew that economic and political realms overlapped, and they discussed the overlap often. All nobles confronted this situation, but it especially affected those who wished to participate in public life. There were expenses associated with specific political moments and maneuvers. When the Grand Condé entertained the king and court at Chantilly, the cost came to 180,000 livres.[31] There were also the expenses associated with maintaining a visible position, necessary if one was to be taken seriously. The mid-seventeenth-century Provençal political operator Oppède left debts of more than half a million livres at his death, most of this the result of expenses to maintain his influence at court and in the

28. Tallemant des Réaux, *Historiettes*, 1: 83.

29. Cardinal de Retz, *Mémoires*, ed. Maurice Allem and Edith Thomas (Paris, Pléiade, 1956), 156.

30. Charles-Louis de Secondat, baron de Montesquieu, *The Spirit of the Laws*, ed. David Wallace Carrithers (Berkeley, 1977), 166.

31. Gourville, *Mémoires*, 2: 37–40.

province.[32] Nearly penniless in his Roman exile, Retz nonetheless felt obliged to spend freely. "Had I listened only to myself," he wrote, "I would have cut back to two valets. But necessity carried the day. I recognized clearly that I would be scorned if I did not maintain myself in splendor. I sought a palace to live in; I assembled my entire household, which was very large . . . ; I maintained a lavish table."[33] A political role required visible expense.

All of these were incidental expenses, however. Most nobles encountered the association between politics and money in the more systematic form of venality of office: they needed to pay to enter any form of public life. This had been true since the early sixteenth century for judicial and administrative offices; by the early seventeenth century, the practice had become fully systematized, with clear rules for inheritance and sale to third parties. By the mid-seventeenth century, venality no longer touched the judicial nobility alone. Military positions, governorships of both whole provinces and small towns, honorific positions at court: all of these required money. The system included highly sensitive positions, such as that of the comte de Saint-Aignan, who spoke daily with Louis XIV and controlled the flow of petitioners to him, and it involved enormous sums: shortly before the Fronde, 50,000 livres for a cavalry company, 90,000 écus for a position as "mestre de camp général de la cavalerie legère," 60,000 écus for the government of the Nivernais; in the generation after the Fronde, 120,000 livres for the governorship of a small city; and several hundred thousand livres for more important positions.[34] The Saint-Aignans still owed 200,000 livres of what they had borrowed to purchase their position twenty years later.[35] Nearly twenty years after the death of Marillac, his heirs were still seeking to recover the 50,000 écus that the family had lost when the Crown confiscated his office as lieutenant of the king.[36]

Aristocratic participation in public life now required a substantial investment, usually comparable to the cost of an estate and to several

---

32. Sharon Kettering, *Patrons, Brokers, and Clients* (New York, 1986), 49.

33. Retz, *Mémoires*, 848.

34. Bussy-Rabutin, *Mémoires*, 1: 207; Dewald, *Pont-St-Pierre*, 179; for some other examples, see Robert Harding, *The Anatomy of a Power Elite: The Provincial Governors of Early Modern France* (New Haven, 1978), 124–26.

35. Tallemant des Réaux, *Historiettes*, 2: 193.

36. Retz, *Mémoires*, 1067, n. 2, quoting Madame de Motteville.

years of most nobles' annual income.[37] Venality thus placed money—but not the market—at the center of public life, and this created significant ethical problems. Intellectuals could justify purchasing an office in terms of Aristotelian ethical tradition, which presented liberal expenditure as a fundamental demand on a public man, and could note the importance of associating power with property; venality ensured that the wealthy would occupy important positions and (it was claimed) protected against the greed that poorer men might feel.[38] The practice was so widespread, in any case, that denunciation could be only be antisocial, indeed misanthropic. But even defenders, among them Richelieu, agreed that the practice corrupted government functions and ought eventually to be eradicated from a reformed France.[39] Venality demonstrated the fallen nature of political life.

Historians have not given much attention to the venality of military offices, but it seems to have differed from the venality of civil offices chiefly in its looseness of organization. Seventeenth-century civil officials collectively defended their financial interests in office and succeeded in institutionalizing the trade. Soldiers and courtiers seem to have been less successful, and their experience of venality was substantially more risk-filled and insecure. There was no Paulette, the system of taxation that regularized inheritance of civil office, and the Crown intervened much more frequently in the process of transmission. The Crown might prohibit sales for political reasons or merely to assist a favorite; it might forbid individuals to sell offices or might force them to do so. Richelieu refused Henri de Campion the right to sell his office, on the ground that he was planning to join the comte de Soissons's conspiracy, whereas the prince de Condé forced Bussy-Rabutin to sell his to a favorite.[40]

Clearly, nobles who participated in public life needed from the outset to think in the calculating terms of monetary exchange and competition. Aristocratic rhetoric might contrast the world of public life

37. For examples, see *Mémoires de Roger de Rabutin,* 1: 207, 312, 313; Tallemant des Réaux, *Historiettes,* 2: 193.

38. Aristotle, *Ethics,* trans. J. A. K. Thomson (London, 1953), 111, 118; Bernard de La Roche Flavin, *Treze livres des Parlemens de France* (Bordeaux, 1617), 349–50; Montesquieu, *Spirit of the Laws,* 149–50.

39. Cardinal de Richelieu, *Testament Politique,* ed. Louis André (Paris, 1947), 230–43; but he too offered conventional defenses of venality, as a barrier to intrigue, the excessive patronage of the great, and the presence of the low-born in high positions.

40. Campion, *Mémoires,* 135; Bussy-Rabutin, *Mémoires,* 1: 207, and see 1: 159.

with the world of money, but the contrast was not between monetary and nonmonetary domains; rather, it was between the world of the household—economy in its original sense—and the intensely monetary world of public life. But venality brought nobles into a monetary system of public life without establishing absolute property rights, bringing the need to calculate without clear rules for doing so. In this instance, money entered the nobles' lives independently of the market, indeed in ways that contradicted important assumptions of a market economy.

To attain a public role in the army or at court, further, nearly always required borrowing, for no family could raise the immense sums that military or court office required. This in turn placed nobles within a complicated set of exchanges with those whose cash they used. Before the Fronde, Condé forced Bussy-Rabutin to sell his captaincy but, according to Bussy, in recompense, "if I wished to buy some position at court or as lieutenant of the king in Burgundy, he offered me his credit and his purse." After the Fronde, still according to Bussy, such credit relations centered on Fouquet: "One was his pensioner, his spy, as soon as one wished, and the shame of this trade did not repel most of the great lords of the court from being on his payroll; those who bought high positions had his purse at their disposal, provided that they bound themselves up with him."[41] The advent of money in public life thus strengthened rather than weakened bonds of patronage, because political actors had greater need of patronage support. To that extent there was no contradiction between the monetarization of public life and traditional forms of dependence. But the dependence that money brought had an uncomfortable character, for it so firmly subordinated the client to his financial patron. Withdrawal or change of allegiance was extremely difficult, given such commitments of financial resources.

It is not surprising in these circumstances that "credit" became a central metaphor of seventeenth-century public life. Contemporaries typically described the standing of leading figures in terms of the "credit" they enjoyed. Intendants were asked to describe " 'magistrates of the cities, their reputations, talents, credit, and properties.' "[42] In the mid-1680s Furetière defined the word in terms

41. Ibid., 1: 207, 2: 49.
42. François Bluche, *Louis XIV* (Paris, 1986), 751–52.

of the overlap between money and power: credit, he wrote, is the "confidence [*croyance*] and esteem that one acquires in the public by one's virtue, probity, good faith, and merit; . . . [and] the power, authority, and wealth that one acquires by means of that reputation. . . . [For instance,] this minister has acquired a great credit at court over the mind of the prince; this président has gained credit in his company by his knowledge. . . . ['Credit'] is more ordinarily used in commerce, to describe that mutual lending of money and merchandise, on the reputation of probity and solvency of the businessman."[43] For Furetière, the word retained its commercial overtones even when used in political contexts; political credit was not yet a dead metaphor.

Money thus permeated seventeenth-century public life, as both a practical reality and an organizing metaphor. To avoid the exchange relationship, however uncomfortable it might be, meant to avoid public life altogether. In effect, this was the choice of the miser and the misanthrope, both risible because of their refusal to endure the discomforts of exchange. But at the same time, property itself depended heavily on politics, for it required constant defense against litigation and against direct political interference. Historians have shown how quickly fortunes could collapse in moments of special political strain. Despite the fantastic wealth that Richelieu had accumulated and his eagerness that it pass intact to his heirs, his death brought immediate financial uncertainty: thirty-five-year-old debts and purchases came under litigious questioning; the Crown demanded the restoration of its gifts and refused to honor financial commitments; and family members feuded among themselves.[44] The Grands Jours d'Auvergne, during which the government sent its commissioners to investigate aristocratic abuses in a backward area, produced comparable effects. Long-standing financial arrangements came under question, and levels of litigation rose dramatically.[45]

But these were only extreme examples of a general situation, for all property was vulnerable to litigious assault. Landowners could expect to be involved in dozens of lawsuits. In July 1585 the duchesse

---

43. Antoine Furetière, *Dictionnaire universel* (The Hague, 1690; repr. Geneva, 1970), s.v. "crédit." See also Arlette Jouanna, *Le devoir de révolte: La noblesse française et la gestation de l'Etat moderne, 1559–1661* (Paris, 1989), 65ff.

44. Bergin, *Cardinal Richelieu*, 264–92.

45. James Lowth Goldsmith, *Les Salers et les d'Escorailles: Seigneurs de Haute Auvergne, 1500–1789* (Clermont-Ferrand, 1984).

de La Trémoille had nine lawsuits ready to be decided at the jurisdiction of Poitiers, only one of several jurisdictions that might affect
the family's properties.[46] She did not leave these matters to the lawyers, but received constant reports about the state of her cases—in
September and October 1589, she received fifteen letters from just one
of her lawyers. "Since I've been here," he wrote, "I've done nothing
but write about the lawsuits you wrote to me about and specially
recommended."[47]

Madame's intervention was needed because success in litigation depended on political considerations: litigants were expected to mobilize whatever influence they could to "solicit" their cases. They and
their friends were to visit the judges, argue the merits of their cases,
perhaps offer bribes, and certainly offer future goodwill and service.
Tallemant des Réaux described a widely followed lawsuit at Nantes,
in the course of which a group of noble ladies "formed such a cabal
with the wives of the councillors and présidents [of the Parlement], for
whom they performed every imaginable service, that the girl not only
won her case, but afterward was placed on a sort of chariot, crowned
with laurel, and paraded thus through the whole city."[48] Bussy-
Rabutin wrote to a Parisian judge in 1677: "[M]y daughter has . . .
just learned, monsieur, that you are to be the principal judge [*rappor-
teur*] in a matter that she has before the council; if you knew the joy
that she and I have had, you would judge what confidence we have in
your ability and your friendship. She has asked that I beg Madame de
Sévigné to speak with you on her behalf, but, though I do not dispute
her influence with you, I believe that I have enough to act on my
own."[49] Even expressions of delicacy in such matters testified to the
pervasive role of politics in property matters. In 1607, so his wife reported to her sister, the duc de Bouillon's council in Paris thought one
of his lawsuits "of such importance that they have urged him to go do
the soliciting himself," but he "has contented himself with writing to
each of the judges and with hoping that his right will protect him."[50]

Few displayed such reluctance, though; most threw themselves eagerly into the process of visiting and arguing with their judges. "I have

46. AN 1 AP 286, Rouhet to Madame, 30 July 1585.
47. Ibid.
48. Tallemant des Réaux, *Historiettes*, 1: 193.
49. Quoted in C. Rouben, *Bussy-Rabutin épistolier* (Paris, 1974), 43.
50. AN 1 AP 333, 78, 2 July 1607.

two or three lawsuits pending ready to be judged, which have me running from morning to night," wrote the marquis de la Moussaye to the duchesse de La Trémoille.[51] For this reason Paris represented, as one of the duchesse de La Trémoille's correspondents put it, *le rendez-vous des playdeuses.*[52] Anyone with land had to participate in these efforts, and those with other forms of revenue had still more constant need of them: no one could expect government pensions or salaries to be paid without the constant help of well-placed intermediaries. Again, the interconnectedness of money and public life gave central importance to relations of patronage and friendship.

The importance of friendships and manipulations in the workings of property led contemporaries to reflections on the role of chance in human affairs and to social humiliations, for the property owner was invariably a petitioner before those who held even the meanest forms of judicial authority. "What is a gentleman?" asks the rascally petty judge of Racine's *Plaideurs.* "A pillar in the waiting room [*pilier d'antichambre*]. How many of them have you seen—I mean the richest of them—warming their hands in my courtyard."[53] In 1624 the duchesse de La Trémoille found herself indeed forced to wait for hours outside a minister's door, in hopes of securing payment of a pension promised to her son. When finally admitted, she realized that "he was listening to her very casually and that he barely wished to stop [his previous business]; she took him by the arm and said to him, monsieur, one should not treat in this manner persons of my standing." Madame retained a sense of her family's potential power, and she told the minister that "some day, you'll have more need of him [her son] than he now has of you," but the interview reduced her to public tears.[54] In view of the political pressures that surrounded litigation, it is not surprising that contemporaries turned to metaphors of chance to describe their experiences. "Whatever hopes the situation and the moment may promise," counselled the La Trémoilles' lawyer in 1589, "nonetheless one must always guard oneself against the hazards of fortune, which has great authority over human affairs."[55]

51. AN 1 AP 436, 31, 29 March 1653.
52. AN 1 AP 649, Judith de Chavigny to Madame, n.d., letter no. 4.
53. Jean Racine, *Oeuvres complètes.* Volume 1: *Théâtre-poésies,* ed. Raymond Picard (Paris, Pléiade, 1950), 316 (Act I, Scene 5).
54. AN 1 AP 648, Chateauneuf to Monseigneur, 19 February 1624.
55. AN 1 AP 286, Rouhet to Madame, 11 September 1589. My emphasis here diverges from that of Jouanna, who stresses the firm basis that property offered for noble political action: *Le devoir de révolte,* 29–39.

Large property enjoyed no immunity from such risks; in fact its very size and complexity made it especially vulnerable. "If the lawsuits to preserve your rights were decided before a single jurisdiction or province," wrote a lawyer to Madame de La Trémoille in 1584, "it would be easier to receive justice; but since that cannot be done, both because of the varied levels of jurisdiction and because of the multitude of properties that you own, no sooner have those in charge of your affairs put them in order in one place, than they are called to another."[56] Constantly distracted from their tasks, the La Trémoille lawyers could not match the effectiveness of lesser litigants, who could concentrate their energies on the case at hand. Even the most elementary aspects of litigation could pose problems. There was, for instance, the problem of making documents available where they were needed: in 1585 the La Trémoilles' lawyer explained that one set had proved too large for the ordinary messenger service between Poitiers and Paris and thus had to be shipped in barrels, by cart.[57]

Vulnerabilities of this kind help to explain the nervousness that seventeenth-century men and women sometimes expressed about property ownership. In the late seventeenth century, at the end of an adventurous life, Gourville congratulated himself that "my fortunate star has so well led me that I find myself enjoying abundance without owning either lands or houses that might cause me some minor pain in the midst of my pleasure."[58] Already by the mid-seventeenth century, Gourville's view had acquired a certain currency. Land retained its powerful attractions, but some important fortunes included little or none of it. Mazarin after the Fronde held the Old Regime's largest private fortune, but land amounted to less than 20 percent of his assets; the Fouquet family had virtually none before the 1650s.[59]

A century later, these attitudes typified Parisian high society. "I am beginning to think like all the rich people of Paris," wrote one nobleman in 1736. "There is not one of them who wants land. Most of them have only shares or *rentes* on the *Hôtel de Ville*."[60] By the end of the Old Regime, the same outlook could be found in at least some

56. AN 1 AP 286, Rouhet to Madame, 9 September 1584.

57. Ibid., Rouhet to Madame, 30 July 1585. Cf. Roche, "Aperçus sur la fortune," for analysis of other vulnerabilities of large property.

58. Gourville, *Mémoires*, 2: 149.

59. Dessert, *Fouquet*, 206–25, 45–46.

60. Quoted by Robert Forster, "The Nobility During the French Revolution," *Past and Present* 37 (July 1967): n. 40.

provincial settings as well: in one upper Norman village during the last generation of the Old Regime, nobles sold 227,778 livres of land and bought 26,000 livres.[61] By this time Paris had a booming stock market as an alternative focus for investment. But already in the later seventeenth century, Daniel Dessert has shown, nobles had begun investing heavily in the French tax farms, using bourgeois financiers as front men.[62] In the early eighteenth century John Law's system of shares seemed to offer still greater opportunities for profiting from the state, and Montesquieu indignantly described the eagerness with which contemporaries sold real property in order to profit from the high returns the system promised.[63] Such alternatives seemed especially tempting in the face of the declining agricultural prices and rents of the century after 1660.

In France as throughout western Europe, seventeenth- and eighteenth-century landowners thus had a growing array of alternative investments, many of which brought substantially higher returns than land. Yet the retreat from landowning remains an extraordinary fact, for during these same years the French aristocracy became increasingly preoccupied with its feudal origins and with setting itself apart from the bourgeoisie and new nobility.[64] Landowning, as a symbol of family continuity and distinctively aristocratic modes of life, might be expected to have contributed to these efforts. This in fact happened in England, where the country house became the subject of a celebratory poetic genre and the gentry held so tenaciously to its estates that almost none appeared on the market.[65] Specific conditions partially explain why this did not happen in France. Above all there were the lures of Paris and the French court, which dimmed the attractiveness of rural life even for those who had no real place with the king. But these years also showed the dangers of turning away from

61. Dewald, *Pont-St-Pierre*, 68–70.

62. George Taylor, "The Paris Bourse on the Eve of the Revolution," *American Historical Review* 67 (July 1962): 951–77; Dessert, *Argent, pouvoir et société au Grand Siècle*.

63. Charles-Louis de Secondat, baron de Montesquieu, *Persian Letters*, trans. J. Robert Loy (Cleveland, 1961), 237–38, 246–48, 282.

64. For recent discussion of eighteenth-century aristocratic ideologies, see Harold A. Ellis, *Boulainvilliers and the French Monarchy: Aristocratic Politics in Early Eighteenth-Century France* (Ithaca, 1988).

65. See, for instance, Don E. Wayne, *Penshurst: The Semiotics of Place and the Poetics of History* (Madison, Wis., 1984); Lawrence Stone and Jeanne Fawtier Stone, *An Open Elite?* (New York, 1987).

land: the Law system collapse in 1720 ruined both shareholders in Law's companies and creditors throughout French society, as debtors used worthless bank notes to pay off their loans. Purely practical calculations do not explain nobles' long-term imperviousness to shocks of this kind. Rather, their choice seems to have expressed discomfort at the political uncertainties of landowning and a larger fascination with more fluid exchange relations. In high French society landed property failed to acquire the symbolic functions that it had long had in England because the realm of property could not be seen as beyond the reach of political constraint, as a source of independent identity. Even for its ruling groups, it appears, traditional forms of economic practice imposed burdensome anxieties and restraints.

This did not mean that French nobles turned away from land altogether, or that they lost interest in their country houses. We have seen the enthusiasm for building that touched old and new families alike in the seventeenth century. The Condés, we saw, spent a fortune beautifying their palace at Chantilly, and numerous other families behaved in similar ways. Political careers as well as family finances suffered from this devotion to country homes. Louis XIV accused his finance minister Fouquet of spending too much money on his country house, and his foreign minister Arnauld de Pomponne of spending too much time at his, to the neglect of his official duties.[66] This view of the country house, however, implied a special view of the countryside: as a focus for consumption, amusement, and expense, a retreat from activity, rather than as a center of production, income, and power.

Thus far I have sought to develop two arguments. First, models of economic rationality and self-control already existed among the fourteenth-century nobility, and they probably became more difficult to live up to as the early modern period advanced. Second, much of seventeenth-century nobles' experience of money was intertwined with their experience of political power. Landowning demanded the constant use of political influence, and public careers of all kinds required nobles to mobilize large sums of money. Such experiences of money in political life doubtless encouraged attitudes of calculation and selfishness that may be thought of as characteristic of market

66. Dessert, *Fouquet*, 155–57; Bluche, *Louis XIV*, 151–56; Madame de Sévigné, *Lettres*, ed. Roger Gailly, 3 vols. (Paris, Pléiade, 1955), 2: 508ff.

economies. However, these experiences came not from outside the traditional social and political order but from within it. Money was a means by which kings and other powerful figures secured obedience and deference, a new mechanism for obtaining the old ends of a feudal society. Far from breaking down, feudal relations (loosely understood) were acquiring a newly burdensome strength in the seventeenth century. It is partly in terms of these burdens that we can understand the nobles' retreat from landownership after about 1650—though numerous practical calculations contributed to the process as well.

I want to suggest that we understand a last facet of the nobles' dealings with money in similar terms, as a form of flight from the discomforts of traditional dependency and subordination. This was seventeenth-century nobles' increasing readiness to play with money, to gamble. Contemporaries believed that an unprecedented gambling mania held seventeenth-century courtly society. Although a long-standing pastime, one especially favored among soldiers, it had acquired a new appeal to polite society in the seventeenth century. By the 1690s it had become a stock theme in Parisian comedy and a normal part of aristocratic behavior.[67]

Given this rising enthusiasm for gambling, it is striking that none of it seems to have taken place in settings that might have emphasized gentry community, social hierarchy, or separation from other social groups. I have encountered no horse-racing or other such contests, which became central to nineteenth-century aristocratic life in both England and France. We can easily imagine the appeal of such sports to landed nobles. They display both property and bloodlines, thus replicating in play deeply held social ideals; and they establish clear gender boundaries, visible both in the events themselves and in the social forms surrounding them. All of these functions emerged in such events as the nineteenth-century horse race. But seventeenth-century nobles chose instead to gamble in contests and settings that emphasized impersonal social exchange, a relative equality of both class and gender. Both men and women gambled, and they gambled on the numerical abstractions represented by cards and dice. Seventeenth-century gambling was a world of skill and fortune, rather than one of bloodlines, breeding, property, and male strength.

67. See Jean-François Regnard, *Le Joueur*, ed. John Dunkley (Geneva, 1986); Georges Jamati, *La querelle du Joueur: Regnard et Dufresny* (Paris, 1936); Gourville, *Mémoires*, 1: 167ff.

This was also a world open to all social classes. Indeed, the combination of social promiscuity with numerical abstraction was one of the principal reasons that gambling disturbed contemporary moralists. Thus La Bruyère: "Everyone says of gambling that it equalizes conditions ... in a word, it's a reversal of all propriety."[68] "Lansquenet [among the most popular of seventeenth-century games]," offered another late-seventeenth-century writer, "is a sort of badly policed republic, where everyone becomes equal; there is no more subordination; and the last among men, with money in his hands, takes whatever rank his card gives him, and finds himself above a duke and peer."[69] Comedy might present the same view in a more positive light: "Gaming assembles all: it brings to one place / The peaceful bourgeois, the marquis turbulent by race. / The banker's wife ... / ... defeats the ... duchess / ... / And though a jealous fate has concealed our worth / Thus can one avenge the injustices of birth."[70]

Conversely, gaming offered separation from social obligations, existence as a free individual, another principal reason that it upset moralists. Georges de La Tour presented the prodigal son as an aristocratic gambler, and in Regnard's *Le Joueur* the gambler has similarly cut himself off from his father and lives in rented rooms; in his excitement at success he forgets as well about his fiancée. Charles Perrault included gaming as one of the forms that a wife's disobedience might take, another disturbing liberation that the gaming table seemed to promise.[71] La Bruyère summarized these images of social atomization in picturing the gamblers assembled: "[I]mplacable toward one another, and irreconcilable enemies while the session lasts, they no longer recognize friendships [*liaisons*], connection [*alliance*], birth, or distinctions."[72]

To play cards, so ran the argument, was to experience republican equality, freedom from the constraints of both natural and social position. Gaming encouraged wives and sons to disobey patriarchal authority, and it turned social connectedness into hostile individualism.

68. Jean de La Bruyère, *Oeuvres complètes*, ed. Julien Benda (Paris, Pléiade, 1951), 195 ("Des biens de la fortune," no. 71).
69. Quoted by Dunkley in Regnard, *Le Joueur*, 15.
70. Regnard, *Le Joueur*, 152.
71. Charles Perrault, *Contes*, ed. Jean-Pierre Collinet (Paris, 1981), 62.
72. La Bruyère, *Oeuvres*, 196 ("Des biens de la fortune," no. 72).

Obviously the moralists and comedians overstated their case, for much gaming took place within highly restrictive settings, among men and women who knew each other well. Yet the practical workings of card-playing in fact conformed to the moralists' vision of it, for gambling was widely seen as a way for outsiders to enter society, even the relatively closed society of the royal court: "There is nothing that brings a man more suddenly into fashion, or attracts so much attention to him, as playing for high stakes."[73] La Bruyère meant to be sarcastic, and so did Regnard's play *Le Joueur*, which included a "marquis *de hasard,* created by lansquenet / . . . / Who, it is said, gains much by his play, / And before a marquis, was once a valet."[74] But others made the same point in positive terms. "By gambling," Tallemant des Réaux claimed, "young people who have scarcely any property introduce themselves everywhere and find a means of living."[75] Nicolas Faret's best-selling *Honnête homme* presented gaming as one of the skills that a young man needed to learn, "because thus he can sometimes mix familiarly" in good company.[76] Excessive gaming might be a dangerous vice, but within limits it represented one of the normal ways by which a young man or woman entered society. Gaming was a means of social mobility, a mechanism by which outsiders broke through social distinctions.

Gaming thus offered experiences of competition, calculation, and freedom from ascribed social roles, experiences in which value rested entirely on the cards that one held and in which activity was directed toward acquisition. Moralists correctly saw these as ways in which gaming undermined the ideals of a society whose distinctions were clear, permanent, and founded on birth. To be sure, gaming had other dimensions. The gaming table offered chances to display wealth and demonstrate indifference to its loss, indeed, to show oneself above mercantile calculations. It allowed for the display of competitive toughness, hence presumably its early appeal to military men; and it was a way of coping with the boredom of both military camp and court. One need not deny the significance of these impulses to emphasize instead the structural patterns of seventeenth-century gambling.

73. Ibid., 393 ("De la mode," no. 7).
74. *Le Joueur*, 94.
75. Tallemant des Réaux, *Historiettes*, 2: 264.
76. Nicolas Faret, *L'honnête homme, ou l'art de plaire à la cour,* ed. Maurice Magendie (Paris, 1925; repr. Geneva, 1970), 17.

As the seventeenth century practiced it, gaming was strikingly detached from the world of landed property, and indeed from the countryside altogether; it infringed boundaries of gender and status; and it centered on the pursuit of money. It represented, I am suggesting, a voluntary withdrawal from aristocratic society, a deliberately sought experience of competitive, anonymous social relations.

As such, I think, it should be attached to other forms of seventeenth-century sociability that pointed in the same directions. In the salon as at the gambling table, gender distinctions were blurred.[77] Masked balls, at which participants interacted anonymously, without knowledge of one another's standing, were another such form, and we have seen that they acquired enormous popularity in the later seventeenth century as an occasion for "liberty without disorder," an occasion to act "as if everyone were equal."[78] Like gambling, the masked ball represented a deliberate experiment in doing without social distinctions. At a greater remove, but with important parallels, there was the growing readiness of noble women and men to write for publication and to encourage others to set their personal lives before the anonymous public that printing implied, in the form of *romans à clef* and written portraits of well-known persons.[79] The urge to exchange and the acceptance of anonymous terms of exchange that gaming implied found echoes elsewhere in aristocratic culture.

Contemporaries thought about money, I am suggesting, by playing with it, by insisting on its visible presence in their society. At least some contemporaries also thought more directly about money, and they might praise the social relations that it produced. Thus even so conservative a writer as the Jansenist Pierre Nicole might be led to praise money. Nicole's vision of the social uses of greed resembled Adam Smith's: "[M]en having no charity, because of the disorder of sin, nonetheless are full of wants and depend on one another for an infinite number of things. Greed has thus replaced charity to fill these needs, and it has done so in a way too little admired, and which

---

* 77. For emphasis on the relative egalitarianism of the seventeenth-century salon, see Carolyn Lougee, *Le Paradis des Femmes: Women, Salons, and Social Stratification in Seventeenth-Century France* (Princeton, 1976).

78. Emile Magne, ed., *Le Grand Condé et le duc d'Enghien: Lettres inédites à Marie-Louise de Gonzague, reine de Pologne, sur la cour de Louis XIV (1660–1667)* (Paris, 1920), 131.

79. Discussed below, Chapter 6.

ordinary charity cannot match." Nicole offered the example of rural innkeepers, always ready to serve their fellows and carry out their orders: "What would be more admirable than these people, if they were moved by the spirit of charity? It's greed that makes them act. . . . There is nothing from which we derive greater services than the greed of men."[80] A century before Smith, then, Nicole attributed public benefits to private interests. So long as police powers restricted the forms of greed to proper economic limits, it could effectively replace charity in a fallen world.

Like Smith, moreover, Nicole could express a dazzled sense of the advantages that even ordinary inhabitants of his society enjoyed, thanks to the workings of properly regulated greed. Civil society (what he called *l'ordre politique*), he wrote, "is thus a wonderful invention that men have found to provide everyone with commodities that the greatest kings could not enjoy, no matter how many officials they had or how much wealth, if this society [*ordre*] did not exist. Without this invention, how much wealth, how many servants would a man need merely to enjoy the advantages that a Parisian bourgeois enjoys with 4,000 livres income?" Following a long list of the products and services that his society offered, Nicole concluded: "[A] simple bourgeois has all this, and he has it without effort, disputes, or anxieties. . . . He can truthfully say that he has a million men working for him in the kingdom. He can count as his servants all the artisans of France, and even those of neighboring states, since they are all ready to serve him and he need only command them, adding an agreed-on recompense. . . . Who can sufficiently admire these advantages that make the condition of individuals equal to that of great kings and that, dispensing them from the anxieties of wealth, provide them all the benefits?"[81] Nicole's Parisian bourgeois, like Smith's ordinary Englishman, could live better than the most powerful primitive ruler, because of the economic networks that a money economy created and made available to everyone. A monetary economy was infinitely more effective than one based on command or private services. Even the most elaborate patriarchal authority could not produce the well-being that the contemporary market offered ordinary bourgeois.

80. Pierre Nicole, *Oeuvres philosophiques et morales*, ed. C. Jourdain (Paris, 1845; repr. Hildesheim, 1970), 397–98 ("De la grandeur").
81. Ibid., 399–400.

Such reflections represented a decisive break with Aristotelian traditions of economic reasoning. Aristotle had divided economic activity between natural and cultural spheres. On the one hand, there were genuinely productive activities, those that contributed to meeting the real needs of a good life; on the other, there were activities detached from real human needs, those directed only to making money. Aristotle emphasized the moral qualities inhering in each form of activity: "Hence we seek to define wealth and money-making in different ways . . . for they *are* different; on the one hand [there is] true wealth, in accordance with nature, belonging to household management, productive; on the other money-making, with no place in nature, belonging to trade and not productive of goods in the full sense."[82]

Nicole reversed these evaluations. Not only did he celebrate commerce and money, those forms of economic life that seemed most unnatural to Aristotle. More fundamentally, he removed the household from the center of economic life, by contrasting its ineffectiveness with the power of the national economic network; not even the most elaborate household, he argued, could supply what the market offered— and the household offered its meager supply of goods at the cost of continual oversight and anxiety. Nicole could take this stance because he viewed all human society as in some ways a realm of the unnatural. Because humanity's fallen nature made real charity impossible, there could be no realm of natural and proper exchanges. Aristotle had set the division between ethically positive and negative economic activities at the limits of the household; in Nicole's fallen world all domains were equally distant from genuine good—and hence all were good in their limited ways.

Among these limited goods, Nicole placed a surprising value on material comfort. His comments do not suggest that the bourgeois of Paris would do better to limit his consumption, and he dwells lovingly on what this might include: cloths, medicines, "curiosities" and "works" from "distant peoples," news and facilities for travel.[83] The bourgeois's comforts, in other words, derive from his access to products and information from all over the world. Where the great were concerned, Nicole was still more emphatic about the ethical value of wealth. He wrote: "The splendor that goes with the position of the

82. Aristotle, *The Politics*, trans. T. A. Sinclair (London, 1962), 43.
83. Nicole, *Oeuvres philosophiques et morales*, 399.

great is not what in fact makes them worthy of honor, but it is what makes them honored by most people. And since it is good that they be honored, it is just that grandeur be allied to external magnificence. . . . [I]t is by their wealth that [the great] preserve the proprieties necessary to their condition, without which it would be useless to men."[84] Nicole set his argument against those (he cited Tertullian) who believed that genuine Christianity required imitation of Christ's poverty. Even for the *dévot* of the seventeenth century, material grandeur had important ethical functions. It assured that political order would be respected.

Nicole did not for that reason accept all the frivolous uses to which contemporaries might put their wealth, any more than did Smith or Franklin. Indeed, his moral vision of wealth encouraged a highly critical look at some of its contemporary uses. The issue emerges unexpectedly in his essay on learning ("De la manière d'étudier chrétiennement"), something to be undertaken, Nicole argues, with great care and self-control, so that "the time we employ may not be lost. For it is not permitted uselessly to dissipate one's wealth, and it is a great sin to lose a considerable sum of money by gambling or on some other unnecessary thing, for temporal goods have been given us by God, to be used in good works, not in silly amusements. If this is true, it is even less permitted uselessly to consume our time, which has been given us to seek our salvation and whose loss is more irreparable than that of any other temporal good."[85] Wealth for Nicole had religious functions, and therefore its use must be a subject for self-control. Like time, it must not be wasted; both are to be used purposively. Nicole did not argue the equivalence of time and money, but he had already taken the step of seeing them as natural metaphors for each other; and it is striking that he speaks specifically of money, rather than limiting himself to *biens temporels* more broadly. Pierre Nicole had no sympathy for gambling, but like the gambler he welcomed much in the market society around him. Within the limits of mankind's fallen nature, the market offered comforts and justice; it replaced charity and did so more effectively than the patriarchal household ever could. Nicole gave his blessing to the splendor of aristocratic society, but he de-

84. Ibid., 393.
85. Ibid., 424.

tached aristocracy from visions of a patriarchal household and rooted it instead in the practices and values of a market economy.

Molière's misanthrope proposed retreat from the corruptions of city and court to a rural property. The retreat would have been appealing but implausible to contemporaries, for they experienced rural property itself as part of a public world of exchanges and fortune. As a final image of this world, we may return to the prince de Condé and his debts in the later seventeenth century. With their affairs in chaos, the family turned to the financier Gourville for help, and he managed to set things right with surprising speed—at least, by his own, self-interested account. Gourville himself was a highly successful gambler, but his reflections on the Condés' finances echo the Weberian Benjamin Franklin. The first step in restoring the family's situation involved knowledge and writing. Gourville drew up memoranda of the family's normal expenses and of its income and debts—following his own practice, which was "every morning to examine in detail what I spent the previous day, as I've always done since I've been able." After this acquisition of written knowledge came a second step, a regularization of credit relations. Gourville arranged for regular, bi-weekly payments of the Condés' creditors, to replace the earlier clamor in the antechamber; having made his first payment on time, "this gave me a great deal of credit and ease with the others," so that new money could flow in and judicial seizures could be lifted. Gourville described his achievement as the creation of order, as "giving a form to the business affairs of Monsieur le Prince."[86]

We may note both the resemblance to and the distance from Gaston de Foix, two and a half centuries earlier. Like Gaston, Gourville proposed an order based on knowledge, counting, and writing, but Gourville's order rested also on credit, and in this it was new. Unlike Gaston, Gourville viewed money as a relationship rather than a thing. Its essence was the confidence of lenders and suppliers, hence the borrower's public image. With that established, the Condés could resume their amazing train of life. If Gourville was the heir to Gaston's vision

---

86. Gourville, *Mémoires*, 2: 144, 37, 45. Clearly Gourville sought to emphasize his own probity and successes at the expense of others who had managed the Condé finances; but Daniel Roche, "Aperçus sur la fortune," 218–21, largely accepts Gourville's claims.

of accounting and self-control, the heir to his notion of money's nature was Molière's miser, with his *chère cassette* of coins.

I have argued here that the contrast between Gaston de Foix and Gourville cannot be understood as the rise of self-interest or of economic rationality. What had changed between the fourteenth century and the seventeenth was the rise of credit and the need for economic interdependence. The market became more important in the lives of French nobles and less tangible, but, I have argued, nobles often encountered money and had monetary calculation forced upon them because of developments quite removed from the market as historians have usually understood it. Money formed part of the monarchical order's functioning in the mid-seventeenth century. It was a political tool, attaching individuals to the Crown and to great men, who could supply the immense sums that entering public life required. As in Gaston's world, money did not necessarily threaten hierarchy. Monetary exchanges too need to be seen in their historical specificity, not as an abstract force with an unvarying psychological impact.[87]

In fact seventeenth-century discomfort with money seems to have resulted as much from the hierarchies and dependencies that attended its use as from the freedoms and individualism it promoted. Nobles disliked the credit relations of venality, which forced them to depend on wealthier figures for offices, and they intensely disliked the humiliations that other property ownership entailed, the need to "solicit" legal support from both superiors and inferiors. Such dislikes help us to understand nobles' readiness to play with money and with the roles that an unascribed society might offer them, as at the gaming table or the masquerade. "Play" need not suggest only comfort. We can imagine nobles trying out social roles in play situations precisely because they felt uncertain or uncomfortable about them. But they nonetheless sought out these situations as sources of pleasure.

This returns us to perspectives that have emerged in considering other aspects of seventeenth-century culture. Tradition in such domains as the family and the polity offered seventeenth-century nobles surprisingly little comfort. Though in many ways they followed the roles that tradition assigned them, they found them oppressive and turned readily to alternatives. In similar ways, they turned readily to

87. A point suggested in somewhat different terms by Joyce Appleby, in her review of Agnew, *Worlds Apart*, *Albion* 19, 1 (Spring 1987).

the alternative economic patterns that monetary exchange offered. The nobles' inherited economic world, the world of privileges, feudal property, and landed household, was one they found uncomfortable, despite the benefits they drew from it. It inflicted uncertainties and humiliations, and the nobles stepped out of it with corresponding readiness, selling land and playing with an alternative set of roles, those of gambling. I have also argued that some forms of modern economic calculation were already to be found among the fourteenth-century landed aristocracy. With Adam Smith, then, we may stress both the oppressiveness of the old economic regime and the cultural means the nobles had for responding to alternative possibilities. But we have also seen the complicated ways in which these alternatives arrived. For the nobles, there was no mere "penetration" of traditional arrangements by market forces. On the contrary, one of the most important forces working to monetize social relations was the monarchy itself—and it used money to strengthen bonds of dependence. Money had no inherently liberating effects, nor did the nobles' economic calculations necessarily become more effective as the period advanced. Not their advancing economic rationality but their eagerness to escape the old economic order supplies the principal theme in this account. Against the discomforts of monetary exchange and social fluidity we need to set the discomforts of power and subordination.

# 6

# The Meanings of Writing

The written word played a large role in seventeenth-century aristocratic culture. Nobles turned to writing in a variety of surprising circumstances, as a part of both public and intimate life. They wrote political reflections and love letters; many began assessing their lives in written form, producing memoirs for their own amusement or the instruction of their families. They closely followed contemporary poetry, and they participated intently in contemporary discussions of linguistic purity. Most striking, in the course of the seventeenth century good writing came to be closely associated with nobility itself. The courtly style became the model of good prose, and contemporaries contrasted its elegance with the plodding style of scholars and lawyers. Good writing seemed to exemplify specifically aristocratic qualities: confident ease of manner, grace, lack of pompous learning.

Practical needs fail adequately to explain this enthusiasm for giving written form to experience, feeling, and thought. To be sure, there were such needs, and many of them were important. Seventeenth-century nobles needed to draw up accounts, legal documents, and letters; church and state both encouraged a substantial degree of learning; even seventeenth-century military practice, as we have seen, encouraged eloquence and the careful use of documents. But practical needs do not fully account for the excitement with which nobles took up writing in the seventeenth century. Nobles turned to writing in situations where it served no practical ends, and in some situations where it was actually dangerous. They did so, I want to suggest, because writing encouraged a certain vision of their lives. When they wrote, nobles separated themselves from their surroundings, establishing themselves as individuals and freeing themselves from a variety of constraints.[1] At the same time, with writing they entered a new

1. See Michel de Certeau, *L'invention du quotidien*. Volume 1: *Arts de faire* (Paris, 1980), 233–38, for a vision of writing as a paradigmatic activity of modern so-

kind of relationship with the society around them, for written words inevitably escaped the limited circles of family, friendship, and court; despite efforts to control their circulation, written words reached unexpected and unwanted readers. Like money, thus, writing drew nobles into forms of exchange that were often anonymous and unpredictable. The circulation of writing, like that of money, challenged the principles of a hierarchical society. Like their experiences with money, the nobles' encounters with this aspect of writing gave them both pleasure and anxiety.

Concern with writing, finally, paralleled concern with civility and, indeed, preoccupied many of the same individuals. Like good manners, writing created boundaries: between an elegant present and a crude past, between city and country, between high society and other groups. Yet, also like the rise of civility, good writing seemed to have unsettling moral consequences. It was believed to stimulate passions and undercut ethical beliefs, and it visibly disrupted boundaries between men and women. Though it brought certain forms of order, writing also brought important forms of disorder to seventeenth-century high society. It offers yet another example of contradiction within aristocratic culture.

Seventeenth-century nobles spoke often of their fascination with writing, and they made clear that they found it a pleasure rather than a mere task. "My greatest pleasure at that time," wrote Hortense Mancini, duchesse de Mazarin, about her childhood, "was to lock myself up alone to write down everything that occurred to me."[2] Other seventeenth-century women shared this sense of pleasure in writing, and it easily became a shared enterprise. "She had the fantasy," wrote Tallemant des Réaux of an important noblewoman, the wife of the maréchal de La Meilleraye, "that there is nothing so beautiful as to write well; and that without this one is only a beast; she persuaded three other sensible women of this; and all four of them practice good

---

cieties: in writing, the individual acts alone, in apparently complete freedom; the writing process embodies order, the step-by-step production of a finished product from neutral raw materials; and writing allows accumulation, paralleling money's capacity to store up past activity. For a broad view of the connections between writing and individualism in early modern Europe, see Roger Chartier, ed., *A History of Private Life*, vol. 3, trans. Arthur Goldhammer (Cambridge, Mass., 1989), 111–59.

2. Charles de Marguetel, seigneur de Saint-Evremond, *Mémoires*, in *Oeuvres mêlées*, ed. Charles Giraud, 3 vols. (Paris, 1867), 2: 102.

writing, often in the four corners of a room, each with a table, writing sweet nothings to each other."[3] Men too spoke of writing as a source of pleasure and escape. Bussy-Rabutin described undertaking his memoirs "with no other aim than my own amusement," and he too traced the habit of writing to his youth: "From my very earliest youth I have written down everything that I have done," he claimed.[4] At about the same time, the retired soldier Antoine Arnauld began his memoirs without "any objective but to amuse myself in the solitude in which I spend most of my time."[5]

A source of private pleasure, writing also permeated seventeenth-century personal relations. Following one of their numerous quarrels, Louis XIII and Cinq-Mars sought to fix the terms of their friendship in written form, using writing to supply the stability that daily relations lacked. "We, the undersigned," so their accord began, "are most satisfied and contented the one with the other and . . . we have never been in such perfect mutual understanding as we are at present."[6] Love letters of course circulated in large and apparently increasing numbers. Retz, in his attempt to seduce Madame de Longueville, "every day wrote three or four notes, and received as many."[7] Bussy-Rabutin advised anyone interested in love to work at his writing: "A lover without his writing desk," he counselled, "is in a bad way; he's a man out for glory who goes to combat without his weapons."[8] Love letters were expected even in the pursuit of temporary liaisons with social inferiors. Charles de Sévigné, in the course of a disorderly youth, had affairs with both the famous courtesan Ninon de L'Enclos and the actress Marie de La Champmeslé, and each affair, despite the women's inferior social standing, involved extensive correspondence.[9] In keeping with these expectations, nobles were set early to learn letter-writing. In 1608 the duchesse de Bouillon wrote to her sister the

3. Gédéon Tallemant des Réaux, *Historiettes,* ed. Antoine Adam, 2 vols. (Paris, Pléiade, 1960–61), 1: 330–31.

4. Roger de Bussy-Rabutin, *Mémoires,* ed. Ludovic Lalanne, 2 vols. (Paris, 1857: repr. Westmead, 1972), 1: 3, 4.

5. L'abbé Arnauld, *Mémoires,* in M. Petitot, ed., *Collection des mémoires relatifs à l'histoire de France,* 33–34 (Paris, 1824), 34: 119–20.

6. Quoted in Philippe Erlanger, *Richelieu and the Affair of Cinq-Mars,* trans. Gilles Cremonesi and Heather Cremonesi (London, 1971), 52.

7. Cardinal de Retz, *Mémoires,* ed. Maurice Allem and Edith Thomas (Paris, Pléiade, 1956), 134.

8. Quoted in C. Rouben, *Bussy-Rabutin épistolier* (Paris, 1974), 80, n. 17.

9. Madame de Sévigné, *Selected Letters,* trans. Leonard Tancock (London, 1982), 86–91.

duchesse de La Trémoille praising her "admirable child": "[H]is love letter was read at the table, to everyone's complete astonishment; we assured them that it proceeded entirely from his [own] thought and style."[10] The child was nine, and his parents were among the leaders of French Protestantism; but already at this age, educational practice established connections between love and written words and expected from him a personal writing style for dealing with adult subjects.

Such fascination with writing led to the appearance of a new social type in seventeenth-century Paris, the young man of good family whose love of poetry had drawn him out of respectability and into a literary career. The Jansenist moralist Pierre Nicole observed with despondency that no era had been so enthusiastic about poetry and drama as his own;[11] and even Descartes described himself as having been "in love with poetry" during his youth.[12] Jean Racine's *passion démesurée pour les vers* distressed his family,[13] but his determination to establish himself as a poet typified the ambitions and enthusiasms that centered on writing in these years, for Paris swarmed with men of letters trying to make their way. Tallemant des Réaux described their difficult lives, eccentricities, and occasional successes. Conrart provided a typical example. His father, a well-to-do bourgeois of Valenciennes, "did not want his son to study" and raged as well against his efforts at noble style: "[H]e was an austere bourgeois who did not allow his son to wear garters or decorations on his shoes, and made him cut his hair above the ears. . . . The desire to be a wit and the passion for books overtook [Conrart] all at once."[14] Because he had money, he could establish himself at the center of literary life, eventually coming to dominate the Academy.

Conrart's case illustrates not only the *passion des livres* that might touch young men in the seventeenth century but also the connection between literary enthusiasm and aristocratic stylishness; Conrart's rebellion meant both dressing like a nobleman and taking up

10. AN 1 AP 333, no. 99, 22 September 1608.

11. Pierre Nicole, *Oeuvres philosophiques et morales*, ed. C. Jourdain (Paris, 1845; repr. Hildesheim, 1970), 436.

12. René Descartes, *Discourse on Method*, trans. F. E. Sutcliffe (London, 1968), 31.

13. Quoted by Louis Racine, "Mémoires . . . sur la vie et les ouvrages de Jean Racine," in Jean Racine, *Oeuvres complètes*. Volume 1: *Théâtre-poésies*, ed. Raymond Picard (Paris, Pléiade, 1950), 15.

14. Tallemant des Réaux, *Historiettes*, 1: 577–78.

literature. The same conflicts persisted through the reign of Louis XIV. Just after the king's death, a distraught father wrote to the président de Nicolay complaining that the regent had recalled his son "from exile, which for me has been much less distressing than this much too rapid return; this will finish off the young man, drunk with the success of his poetry and with the praises and welcome that *les grands* have given him."[15]

All of this excitement is especially significant because in the seventeenth century, written words attracted, but they also raised serious ethical and social doubts. Many of these derived from writing's connections with love and seduction, for contemporaries viewed writing (like music and dance) as a stimulus to passion. The Jansenist Nicole developed these fears at length. "A novelist and dramatist," he argued, "is a public poisoner, not of bodies, but of souls. He should regard himself as guilty of an infinite number of spiritual homicides, which he either has actually caused or might have caused."[16] He caused these deaths by teaching his listeners to think of love, to idealize passionate impulses, and to lose their taste for ordinary life; poets and novelists taught "the language of the passions."[17] Nicole's fears implied views both of human needs and of the power of language. Our need for love is such that even mild stimuli can excite it; and apparently innocuous words themselves have mysterious powers, lying "long hidden in the heart, without any visible effect," then bursting forth to produce action, whether for good or ill.[18] In such circumstances, words required careful control; they were dangerous.

Others agreed. The comte de Souvigny was no Jansenist, but he shared these suspicions and urged his daughter to preserve her chastity by "never going to the theater or to other suspect places."[19] The mid-seventeenth-century preacher Père André sought to dissuade the women who listened to him from reading novels, but he complained that they returned to them as soon as his back was turned.[20] Seventeenth-century teachers assumed that novels would indeed over-

15. AN 3 AP 26, 32 C 128, Le Rouet to Nicolay, 25 October 1716.
16. Racine, *Oeuvres complètes*, 1: 24.
17. Nicole, *Oeuvres philosophiques et morales*, 436ff., 443 ("De la comédie").
18. Ibid., 441.
19. Comte de Souvigny, *Mémoires*, ed. Ludovic de Contenson, 3 vols. (Paris, 1906–09), 3: 80.
20. Tallemant des Réaux, *Historiettes*, 2: 161.

whelm their readers with romantic images; thus Racine's teachers at Port Royal twice confiscated his copies of the Greek novelist Heliodorus, until finally he memorized a third copy and himself presented it to his teachers for destruction.[21] Eventually Racine's own doubts about the morality of poetry culminated in his famous renunciation of the genre. Racine had sought to purify drama; in *Phèdre*, as his son described it, even the idea of sin brought forth punishment, and he had enjoyed a unique degree of favor from the Crown—but this had not sufficed to render his writing morally acceptable. Once he had given up writing profane drama, his son claimed, "he never attended a play, or spoke before his children of either comedy or profane tragedy."[22]

Corneille shared these doubts about poetry. "Agitated by some anxieties about his plays," he repeatedly sought reassurance from the church, and, like Racine, he tried his hand at religious drama.[23] But in other moods he simply accepted poetry's unsettled moral position. His treatise on tragedy stressed the genre's capacity for exciting emotions but attacked Aristotle's idea that the experience could be purging or tranquilizing—in other words, socially useful: "I am indeed afraid," he wrote, "that Aristotle's reasoning on this point may be only a lovely idea, which has never functioned in reality."[24] In this view, the poet was indeed a dangerous figure, who brought emotions to the surface but offered no help in resolving them; and Corneille offered a starkly amoral vision of his function, as simply that of "pleasing within the rules of his art."[25] The libertine Saint-Evremond took the same view: tragedy might awaken emotions, but how they might be purged remained entirely mysterious.[26] Discussions of comedy pointed in similar directions. An anonymous, mid-seventeenth-century discussion of comedy described its functions as "either to be useful or to please" but emphasized the morally problematic methods at its disposal: "[S]erious words not being suited to elicit laughter, of necessity one must have recourse to the language of folly, of malice [*médisance*], or of

21. Racine, *Oeuvres complètes*, 1: 12.

22. Ibid., 65.

23. Ibid., 62; see also Fontenelle's "Vie de Corneille," in Pierre Corneille, *Oeuvres complètes*, ed. André Stegman (Paris, 1963), 25.

24. "De la tragédie," in Corneille, *Oeuvres complètes*, 831.

25. Ibid., 840.

26. Saint-Evremond, "De la tragédie ancienne et moderne," in *Oeuvres mêlées*, ed. Luigi de Nardis (Rome, 1966), 284–93, 289.

love."[27] It was not only the pious who saw poetry as morally problematic. Corneille, Saint-Evremond, and this anonymous writer all stressed poetry's capacity to unsettle; it gave pleasure and little else.

Seventeenth-century thought about prose extended the scope of these fears, for even the mildest literary genres might, like poetry, produce physical effects on their readers. A contemporary wrote of Guez de Balzac that his prose had the power of poetry, "that secret power . . . , which acts on its listeners . . . a harmony that touches the passions, that goes straight to the soul, moving the inner man and capable of the same effects that are told of the ancient lyre, which with its different tones could render Alexander furious or calm."[28] Such beliefs derived from a long tradition of rhetorical theory, which stressed the speaker's ability to move his listeners. For the seventeenth century, music, poetry, and prose occupied points along a single continuum of emotional power. All had the capacity to excite passion, because all exerted physical effects on those who listened or read.

As moralists saw the situation, the power words exercised was especially dangerous because skilled writers failed to use them responsibly. Rhetoricians were notoriously ready to use their skills for any end, without regard for truth or social utility. Poets did the same. "I find that many poets are blameworthy," wrote the theologian Antoine Arnauld to Racine, "for putting all their ingenuity into making their characters speak so well on behalf of their cause that one is moved rather to approve or excuse the worst actions than to hate them."[29] Poetry thus shared the moral ambiguity of its civic cousin rhetoric; both were skills that might be used for immoral ends.

In these cases, writing threatened morals because of the potential physical effects of words themselves: it was the power he exercised that made the writer dangerous. But still other doubts might attend less obviously troubling genres. By the late seventeenth century, memoir-writing had become a normal pursuit for retired gentlemen and ladies, but moral reservations surrounded their efforts. There was the danger of excessive self-regard: Antoine Arnauld reported, "I've seen some who disapproved of the memoirs of Monsieur de Pontis,

27. AN 1 AP 397, La Trémoille, anonymous "Prologue de comédie en prose," copied into La Trémoille letter book of the 1630s–1640s, 61.

28. Quoted in Marc Fumaroli, *L'âge de l'éloquence: Rhétorique et "res literaria" de la Renaissance au seuil de l'époque classique* (Geneva, 1980), 701.

29. Racine, *Oeuvres complètes*, 1: 77.

which recently appeared. 'He speaks only of himself,' they say, 'and what do we care about his preoccupations?' "[30] There was the more serious danger that the memoir writer would criticize those whom she or he had known. Saint-Simon felt obliged to begin his memoirs with the question, "Can a Christian . . . write and read history?"[31] Memoirs and history involved deliberate violation of Christian charity, because they required detailing wicked acts and criticizing those who had performed them. After lengthy argument, Saint-Simon refuted these objections and proceeded with his project, but clearly he felt that they had to be taken seriously.[32]

Writers' behavior did little to calm doubts about the moral value of what they produced, for the ambitious young writers who filled seventeenth-century Paris proved startlingly indifferent to social and moral conventions. Daily they strained the expectations of an ordered society. Vincent Voiture, wrote Tallemant, "was sometimes so casual [*familier*], that he has been seen, in the presence of madame la princesse, taking off his clogs to warm his feet. It was bad enough [*assez de familiarité*] to be wearing clogs in the first place, but that's truly the way to gain the esteem of the great nobles, to treat them like that! . . . [H]e always spoke to them unreservedly [*assez familièrement*]."[33] Malherbe was famous for the "scorn that he expressed for everything that was most esteemed in the world,"[34] while the poet Vauquelin des Yveteaux showed eccentricities of every sort: he associated with courtesans, was accused of homosexuality, and in his garden acted out scenes from pastoral novels.[35]

Such behavior reflected more than individual eccentricity or the irritations of literary low life. It also reflected a developing literary ideology. The writers extravagantly asserted their indifference to every distinction save merit, and they acted on this conviction. "They exhorted him," wrote Louis Racine of Boileau, "not to attack Chapelain, since (as they told him) he is protected by Monsieur de Montausier, and sometimes receives visits from Monsieur de Colbert. 'And if the Pope,' he answered, 'paid him visits, would his verses be any

30. L'abbé Arnauld, *Mémoires*, 119.
31. Louis de Rouvroy, duc de Saint-Simon, *Mémoires*, ed. Gonzague Truc, 8 vols. (Paris, Pléiade, 1953–61), 1: 5.
32. Ibid., 1: 5ff.
33. Tallemant des Réaux, *Historiettes*, 1: 489.
34. Ibid., 1: 113.
35. Ibid., 1: 142–43, 825 n. 5.

better?' "[36] Despite the power the state came to exercise over it, the Académie Française continued to illustrate this stance. From the outset it disregarded distinctions of birth, mixing together poor professionals with figures of high birth, all of them devoted to assessing excellence and criticizing shortcomings.[37] The claim to critical professionalism challenged ethical as well as social ideals, for it defined the writer as uncharitable to others, difficult to please, always ready to find fault—precisely the qualities that troubled contemporaries about concern with elegant behavior.[38]

The poets' behavior must have seemed especially upsetting because it came not from the fringes of polite society but from somewhere near its center. Racan was noble; Malherbe and Vauquelin at least claimed nobility and certainly came from solid robe families; Voiture came from the provincial bourgeoisie but had acquired an ennobling office. All four had important attachments at court and were well received by the great. Yet they could be a troubling presence: quite ready (as Boileau's remark suggests) to assert the claims of ability against those of status and patronage, hostile to restraints of every kind. Their conspicuous presence only strengthened moralists' concerns about the dangers of contemporary writing as a powerful tool in irresponsible hands.[39]

Writing was dangerous on moral grounds, because of the powers latent in all words and because of the moral dangers that excessive preoccupation with language seemed to threaten. By their nature, written words posed more specific dangers as well: unlike speech, writing might readily move beyond its author's intended audience and hence beyond her or his ability to control its interpretation. Almost inevitably, writing escaped the bounds of personal communication. The process of escape posed troubling questions of propriety and political order.

Nobles rarely sought to publish what they wrote, and indeed much of it remained in manuscript until the eighteenth century. Publication subjected thought to commerce, an upsetting prospect to nobles and

36. Racine, *Oeuvres complètes*, 1: 19.
37. Valentin Conrart, *Mémoires*, ed. J. N. Monmerqué (Paris, 1826; repr. Geneva, 1971), 12–13; this was pointed out to me by Orest Ranum.
38. Above, Chapter 4.
39. Cf. Peter Burke, *The Italian Renaissance: Culture and Society in Italy*, 2d ed. (Cambridge, 1987), 83–87, for a comparable process of professionalization of writing.

professional writers alike: to publish a play, wrote Corneille, was "to debase it."[40] A mid-eighteenth-century publisher of Henri de Rohan's *Le parfait capitaine* made the same point. "If there are some who think it strange," he wrote in his preface to the work, "to see books come from a man of this birth and profession, I have already said at the outset that his intention was not to work for the public, nor to expose to the world his observations and thoughts about the military art."[41] Writing for the public demeaned anyone of high birth.

Mademoiselle de Scudéry expressed these doubts still more generally and more bitterly; even without publication, writing for others in itself reduced the author's standing. By writing well enough "to be able to produce books," one of her female characters says, "one loses half of one's nobility . . . , and one ceases to be equal to another who, though from the same house and blood, stays away from writing. They treat you differently, and they say that you're destined only to amuse others . . . for in the end nearly all the young people of the court treat those who get involved with writing as they treat the artisans."[42] To write for others' pleasure reduced the noble to the status of other producers, who likewise depended on customers' judgments. To write for the public was to risk becoming its servant.

Rather than publish for a mass audience, nobles typically circulated their letters, memoirs, and personal reflections among a range of acquaintances, and occasionally beyond. Poets and playwrights typically read their pieces aloud to aristocratic patrons and integrated others' suggestions into their work. "Much in the comedy *Les plaideurs* was the fruit of those meals," wrote Racine's son of his father's dinners with fellow writers; "everyone sought to furnish examples to the author."[43] In the 1670s, Condé assembled writers at his palace at Chantilly and commented vigorously on their works.[44] Bussy-Rabutin read his *Maximes d'amour* and then his *Histoire amoureuse des Gaules* aloud to small groups of courtiers; the works became matter for scandal only when they began to circulate more widely.[45]

40. Corneille, *Oeuvres complètes*, 27 (preface to *Mélite*).
41. Henri de Rohan, *Le parfait capitaine ou abrégé des guerres des Commentaires de César*, new ed., expanded (n.p., 1757), preface.
42. Quoted in Nicole Aronson, *Mademoiselle de Scudéry, ou le voyage au pays de Tendre* (Paris, 1986), 43.
43. Racine, *Oeuvres complètes*, 28.
44. Ibid., 38.
45. Bussy-Rabutin, *Mémoires*, 2: 160ff.

Nobles sought to make writing an act at once personal and social. It was to take place in a middle ground between public and private, between an anonymous world of invisible readers and the purely personal world of immediate, oral communication.

Yet such private writing readily escaped these boundaries and found its way to wider publics. The seventeenth-century public avidly followed news and novelties, and to meet its demand the printing industry constantly sought new material and paid substantial sums for it. Corneille and Mademoiselle de Scudéry both published for the money, despite their reservations about the process. Conversely, Saint-Evremond claimed that his works had been drawn into commercial circulation against his will. He had written hastily to a friend (he wrote later, in defending himself against charges of malicious criticism) giving his immediate responses to Racine's *Alexandre*. "It turns out," he later complained, "that she has shown [the letter] to everyone, and it has placed me in the embarrassing situation that you describe." Another friend had now arranged for the letters to be printed. "It is better," Saint-Evremond concluded, "that they be printed as you have arranged, and as correctly as possible, than in the disorder in which they pass from hand to hand until they reach those of a printer."[46] He reported a similar experience to his friend about three years later: "I have never been so surprised as to see on sale here [in Holland] three little books that are said to be by me, and published in Amsterdam. About twenty years ago I wrote some little comments [*discours*] on the maxims in these books; I don't know who could have had them."[47] At the end of the path of manuscript circulation stood the devouring figure of the printer, ready to convert personal communication into a mass-market consumer good. Written words inevitably escaped from their authors' control; for a time they might circulate along known social networks, from hand to hand, but in the end they risked being drawn into the more anonymous mechanism of printing.

But printing was only an extreme instance of a larger problem. Even unpublished writing had disruptive qualities, since audience and interpretation could not be controlled. When they touched on political or social standing, privately circulated written words might seem

46. Saint-Evremond, *Oeuvres mêlées*, ed. Giraud, 3: 75–76.
47. Ibid., 2: 88.

terribly threatening, far more so than mere court gossip. Bussy-Rabutin learned this to his cost: he spent thirteen months in the Bastille "for having written as an amusement and without intending that it become public the details of the gallantries of two ladies that everyone already knew."[48] His manuscript had circulated more widely than he had intended, and consequently it had provoked both the figures it mocked and the king. In this case writing was dangerous because it gave new force to what "everyone already knew."

Private letters too might escape their intended audiences, with upsetting social consequences. Seventeenth-century enthusiasm for love letters led to a long series of tragicomic discoveries and scandals, making obvious to all the latent contradictions between romantic sensibility and a dynastic organization of society. Caskets of compromising love letters figured regularly in the exiles and arrests that marked seventeenth-century court life. After Cinq-Mars' arrest, Marie de Gonzague found herself "very embarrassed, for Monsieur le Grand had a vast quantity of her letters. . . . They say," adds Tallemant, "that when des Yveteaux, intendant of the Roussillon army, went to open Monsieur le Grand's coffers, a servant warned that he would find things he had not sought—letters from his wife."[49] Love letters were discovered at balls, leading to embarrassment and conflict both at the highest levels of aristocratic society and among petty provincials.[50]

Writing thus created new forms of vulnerability by exposing the personal to public scrutiny. The tense circumstances of Parisian polite society increased the pressure for such exposure, by encouraging men and women to reveal others' secrets. Self-assertion provided one stimulus to revelation. Thus the seducer La Tour Roquelaure boasted of his successes but was asked, " 'Who would believe you . . . you haven't a single letter.' 'You're right,' he answered, 'I'm a fool. From now on I won't sleep with one of them unless she has previously written.' "[51]

The hope of establishing new intimacies through shared secrets offered other encouragement to circulate private letters; revelation

48. Bussy-Rabutin, *Mémoires*, 2: 288.
49. Tallemant des Réaux, *Historiettes*, 1: 585.
50. Emile Magne, ed., *Le Grand Condé et le duc d'Enghien: Lettres inédites à Marie-Louise de Gonzague, reine de Pologne, sur la cour de Louis XIV (1660–1667)* (Paris, 1920), 150, 27 February 1665; AN 1 AP 333, no. 98, 8 September 1608.
51. Tallemant des Réaux, *Historiettes*, 2: 383.

served as a demonstration of sincerity. In the novella *La princesse ou les amours de Madame,* the duc de Manicamp, wildly in love, finds himself subjected to a series of tests. The most serious—to assure the lady "that you are entirely mine" and overcome her doubts—requires that he reveal the secrets of a court scandal; and this he is able to do "because he had in his pocket copies of all the letters that concerned the story."[52] Madame de Sévigné described her son Charles's similar troubles with Ninon de L'Enclos. Ninon had insisted that Charles give her the letters his former mistress had written him: "[S]he was jealous," reported Madame de Sévigné, "and wanted to give them to a lover of this grand lady, so as to deal her a few little jabs. . . . I told him it was infamous to have dealt such a blow to this poor little thing because she had loved him, that she had not sacrificed his letters, as he had been given to believe . . . but had freely given them back to him."[53] If accidental discoveries testified to the dangers of writing, such deliberate exposures made the point more clearly still. Writing changed intimacy to vulnerability.

Such misadventures, and the anxieties that attended them, were sufficiently predictable that they recur in comedy. Molière's *Misanthrope* presents two misplaced letters; one of them upsetting because its addressee is unclear, so that its real significance cannot be understood; the other upsetting for the opposite reason, that its excessive clarity reveals truths the author wanted to keep secret.[54] Corneille's *Mélite* turns on fraudulent love letters, but these likewise illustrate the power of written words when they escape from face-to-face contexts. Like La Tour Roquelaure, Corneille's characters expect to use love letters as public proofs of amorous success. "Such trivial favors dupe only the credulous; have you nothing but this?" the hero Tircis is asked after he has recounted the sighs and loving glances he has shared with his beloved. "At least some letters would confirm her claim to love you."[55] Letters in fact appear, purporting to come from the beautiful Mélite, and on receiving them the flighty Philandre promptly abandons his lover and boasts publicly of a new triumph;

52. Roger de Bussy-Rabutin, *Histoire amoureuse des Gaules,* ed. Charles-Augustin Sainte-Beuve, 2 vols. (Paris, 1868), 1: 336–37.

53. Madame de Sévigné, *Selected Letters,* 91.

54. *The Misanthrope,* Act IV, Scene 3; Act V, Scene 4.

55. *Mélite,* lines 808ff., in Corneille, *Oeuvres complètes,* 39.

long in love with Mélite, Tircis despairs and threatens suicide. Neither consults with Mélite herself (indeed, the letters forbid visits and insist that the text be the only vehicle of the relationship); neither questions the letters' authenticity, and the truth emerges only after a series of accidents. Years after the play's success, Corneille himself wondered at audiences' indulgence of such implausibly instant acceptance of the written word.[56] But we may read *Mélite,* not as reflecting real behavior, but as an exploration of the anxieties that accompanied written communication of personal emotion. *Mélite* starts from the fact that writing cannot be fully controlled. It will reach unintended audiences, and it will give rise to divergent interpretations. Seventeenth-century men and women experienced at first hand the impenetrability of authorial intentions, and they found the experience disquieting.

Writing posed moral and social dangers, but during the seventeenth century aristocratic men and women paid steadily less heed to them. They wrote enormous amounts, and they proved increasingly ready to record personal experience in writing, exposing details about their lives to the potential audience that writing created. They did so partly because long-standing social values offered encouragement for, as well as anxiety about, writing. Thus careful household management had long called for written records, and these shaded easily into accounts of daily existence. Gilles de Gouberville, for instance, read rarely and his tastes were traditional, tending to the chivalric romances that already had an old-fashioned ring in the mid-sixteenth century. Yet every day for much of his life Gouberville noted the details of his own life and the events that touched the villagers around him. Numerous other nobles did the same, mingling in their *livres de raison* the details of their familial and financial lives and occasionally noting minor events in their neighborhoods.[57] That writing functioned to preserve glorious deeds was a still older assumption of chivalric culture, as well as of humanist historical theorists. Fourteenth- and fifteenth-century chivalric orders throughout western Europe proposed that their members recount any notable events that had befallen them each year, and these were recorded in books kept by the order. One order described

56. "Examen," in ibid., 28.
57. Madeleine Foisil, *Le sire de Gouberville: Un gentilhomme normand au XVIe siècle* (Paris, 1981).

its book as the "Livre et Romanz des Preux"; it was intended to include only veridical reports, but its title suggested the elements of invention and romance that its compilers expected it to include.[58]

Aristocratic dynasticism too might encourage writing, as a means of demonstrating the family's integrity and achievements from one generation to the next. Men and women wrote down their actions to instruct descendants, and with a strong awareness of the glorious models of antiquity. The prince de Tarente addressed his memoirs to his son: "I believe that I can give you no greater mark of the tenderness I feel for you and of the prayers that I address to God to bless your education and render you what I would wish [*conforme à mes souhaits*] than by leaving you a brief account of what has been most memorable in my life. . . . I know that the lives of many great men of antiquity and some from whom we descend . . . are examples that you should always have before your eyes. But the former are unrelated to you and the latter have neglected to leave to their posterity immortal marks of their paternal affection; so I am convinced that the care I am taking for your benefit should [yield] a very profitable study."[59] Tarente believed that his writing would help to discipline his lineage, molding his son to his wishes even in his absence. Writing, thus, could help the patriarchal family to function.

Arnauld d'Andilly likewise focused on his descendants in opening his memoirs: his son, he wrote, had insisted that he write "something that might serve my children, to lead them to virtue by domestic example and inspire in them scorn for those false goods" to which most people directed their lives.[60] Writing offered "immortal marks" and in this respect paralleled the immortality of the aristocratic lineage itself; it allowed individuals' virtues to influence the lineage from one generation to the next, an effort that came to seem more important as nobles became more sensitive to dynastic distinctions and to the force of bloodlines. Both Tarente and Arnauld presented themselves as shaping their children, dominating them through the mechanism of writing. Here there was no tension between writing and paternal morality. Even style might serve to glorify the lineage. Antoine Arnauld

58. D. J. A. Boulton, *The Knights of the Crown: The Monarchical Orders of Knighthood in Later Medieval Europe, 1325–1520* (New York, 1987), 314.

59. AN 1 AP 441, fol. 1r.

60. Robert Arnauld d'Andilly, *Mémoires*, in M. Petitot, ed., *Collection des mémoires relatifs à l'histoire de France*, 33–34 (Paris, 1824), 33: 301.

quoted his father's response to praise of another Arnauld's literary style: he said "that there was no reason to be surprised, and that he simply spoke the language of his *maison*."[61] Style could be seen as expressing the personality of the dynasty rather than of the individual; self-expression and self-depiction could be contained within dynastic ideology.

Writing had similar uses in the public realm, for the political atmosphere of the seventeenth century insistently demanded the use of writing to celebrate family and personal achievements. Politicians could see all around them the importance of public opinion, and they early recognized the usefulness of written propaganda in shaping it. Even the Crown in the 1630s began subsidizing a newspaper to present itself to the public; Théophraste Renaudot's *Gazette* presented a highly personal vision of the king and his associates, stressing, for instance, Louis's romantic attachment to his queen.[62] Nobles too sought to present themselves to the public in the best possible light, in furtherance of both specific political designs and more diffuse political standing. Henri II de Condé, the Grand Condé's father, went through his career leaving a trail of pamphlets celebrating even his most mediocre achievements: his "victory" at the château of Sully in 1621, his travels to Italy in 1624, his successes in the 1628 war with Rohan, his trip to Languedoc in 1629—all provided the occasion for written description by paid literary followers. His family's flight from court in 1609, to evade the king's efforts to seduce his beautiful bride, formed the subject of a lengthy Latin poem. Condé needed to woo the Crown's good opinion as well as the public's. As a result, following his failure at Fuentarabia he spent his time collecting and annotating documents to prove that responsibility lay elsewhere.[63]

Novels and dramas too could help court public opinion. Mademoiselle de Scudéry modeled her novel *Le grand Cyrus* directly on Condé's role in the Fronde, and she published as the events themselves unfolded, indeed before their outcome was clear. For the purpose Scudéry sought out contemporary documents and accounts from the

61. L'abbé Arnauld, *Mémoires*, 121.

62. Howard Solomon, *Public Welfare, Science, and Propaganda in Seventeenth-Century France: The Innovations of Théophraste Renaudot* (Princeton, 1972); Joseph Klaits, *Printed Propaganda Under Louis XIV* (Princeton, 1976).

63. M. le duc d'Aumale, *Histoire des princes de Condé pendant les XVIe et XVIIe siècles*, 6 vols. (Paris, 1885), 3: 154, n. 1; 170–71, n. 2; 217, n. 2; 313, n. 1; 2: 268, n. 1; 3: 401.

*Gazette,* and her rival La Calprenède did the same in *his* novel on
Condé.[64] Later Scudéry attached herself to Fouquet and used her
novel *Clélie* to praise him. She authoritatively described Fouquet's
house at Vaux, and stressed its moral value: "[H]e uses [his wealth] so
nobly that no one envies it."[65] Corneille offered equally transparent
recountings of contemporary events. The notice to the reader of his
*Nicomède* described the play as one in which "the grandeur of courage reigns alone. . . . It is attacked by *la politique,* and opposes to its
schemes only a generous prudence,"[66] obvious reference to the contemporary conflict between the *politique* Mazarin and the courageous
Condé. Writings such as these made the Fronde an event that received
artistic reflection and reformulation even as it took place.

Public fascination with such figures as Condé matched the propa-
gandists' efforts; their success in fact depended on a ready audience
for detailed accounts of the lives of the great. Hunger for news was of
course especially sharp among the political classes themselves. Between 1639 and 1642, Henri Arnauld (Robert's brother) wrote to an
exiled friend twice each week, describing all the minor events of court
life: that the dauphin was about to be weaned, how fashionable ladies
were to wear their collars, illnesses of leading figures, as well as the
more serious news about military and diplomatic events.[67] But such
interest extended much more deeply in society. During the Fronde, as
Tallemant remarked, "they published everything," so great was the
interest in political events.[68]

Such public interest and aristocratic readiness to address it remained lively in the political calm that followed 1660. News, it will be
remembered, was one of the goods that Pierre Nicole saw his society
as supplying to its ordinary members. A few years later the financier
Gourville described his habits in retirement, after a lifetime spent
among the great: "I have a great desire for the news; I'm among the

64. Georges Mongrédien, *Le Grand Condé: L'homme et son oeuvre* (Paris, 1959),
187–90.
65. Quoted in Micheline Cuénin and Chantal Morlet Chantalat, "Châteaux et romans au XVIIe siècle," *XVIIe Siècle* 118–19 (January–June 1978): 106.
66. Corneille, *Oeuvres complètes,* 519; discussed in Mongrédien, *Le Grand
Condé,* 203–4.
67. Claude Cochin, *Henri Arnauld évêque d'Angers (1597–1692)* (Paris, 1921),
36–42.
68. Tallemant des Réaux, *Historiettes,* 1: 514; for recent assessments of this
material, see Christian Jouhaud, *Mazarinades: La Fronde des mots* (Paris, 1985), and
Hubert Carrier, *La presse de la Fronde (1648–1653): Les mazarinades—la conquête
de l'opinion* (Geneva, 1989).

first to learn of everything that happens; I make reports for my provincial friends, which gives them great pleasure, and all my life I've wanted to do this." Gourville could draw his news from the band of *nouvelistes*, who offered their gleanings of scandal and politics in the Luxembourg gardens; one of his servants visited the gardens daily.[69] In the second half of the seventeenth century, news remained a widely distributed commodity. Nobles who hoped to play a role in politics needed this mechanism for securing support.

Practical reasons for turning to writing thus abounded. It served political ambitions and strengthened familial bonds; it aided in household management. But writing also touched desires that were deeper, less explicit—and less coherent. Mid-seventeenth-century nobles found writing fascinating partly for its capacity to establish distinctions, boundaries. Madame de La Meilleraye, it will be recalled, believed that without good writing "one is only a beast," and in this she expressed a view popular among humanist scholars of the sixteenth century.[70] Writing separated culture from nature. Closely related to this division was a second, that between social classes: writing and elegant language more generally, it was thought, established the boundary between polite society and the peasants, servants, and others beneath it. Tallemant recounted the story of Madame Pilon, the elderly confidante of several great Parisian ladies. Unable to dissuade them from sexual misconduct, she urged them at least to avoid the vulnerability that writing love letters would establish: " 'What!' they answered me," so she told Tallemant, " 'not write letters! That would be to make love like a chambermaid.' "[71] Letters established the difference between lady and maid precisely in the domain where difference seemed most tenuous, the domain of physical passion. Establishing the difference meant more than the increased risks of discovery and humiliation that love letters brought.

Charles Sorel's novel *Francion* made a comparable point about the capacity of language to establish between peasants and nobles the familiar barrier between a realm of nature and one of culture. To make

---

69. Jean Hérauld, sieur de Gourville, *Mémoires,* ed. Léon Lecestre, 2 vols. (Paris, 1894), 2: 151, 149; and, more generally, Erica Harth, *Ideology and Culture in Seventeenth-Century France* (Ithaca, 1983).

70. Donald Kelley, *The Beginning of Ideology: Consciousness and Society in the French Reformation* (Cambridge, 1981), 232.

71. Tallemant des Réaux, *Historiettes,* 1: 166.

the difference clear, Francion proposes renaming the sexual parts and acts. His friend objects: " '[D]on't we do it just like the peasants? why should we have other words than they?' 'You're wrong, Raymond,' replied Francion, 'we do it in quite a different manner, we use many more caresses than they, who have no other desire than to sate their brutal appetites, in no way different from that of the animals; they only do it bodily, while we do it with body and soul together.' "[72] Raymond is persuaded, and Francion proceeds to establish a list of more graceful names for the elements of sexuality. Like Madame Pilon's friends, he is intent on subjecting sexual impulse to language. Precisely where differences between classes might seem weakest—and where humanity of all classes might seem closest to the animals—refined language permits Francion to establish distinctions.

A marker of the differences between humanity and nature and between nobles and peasants, writing served also to distinguish past from present. The development of good writing offered the mid-seventeenth century more proof that society had advanced far beyond even its immediate past, part of the advance that contemporaries saw (so I argued in Chapter 4) in all domains of civilized behavior. Writing had a logical place in such visions of progress, given its capacity to delimit human behavior itself. Tallemant des Réaux, as we have seen, repeatedly stressed the contrast between the writing of his own age and that of even a generation earlier, referring, for instance, to some letters "written before the siege of La Rochelle, which was a time when people were not generally concerned to write well."[73] Guez de Balzac's first collection of letters in praise of the great created an impression that is scarcely to be understood today. "It is certain that we had seen nothing approaching this in France," wrote Tallemant, "and that all those who have written well in prose since then, and who will write well in the future in our language, will be obligated to him."[74] Even the irascible Malherbe was impressed: " 'This young man,' " he told his friends, " 'will go further in prose than anyone has ever been in France.' "[75] A generation later there were the letters of Voiture,

---

72. Charles Sorel, *Histoire comique de Francion*, ed. Yves Guiraud (Paris, 1979), 341. Cf. Roger Duchêne's discussion of this passage, in his *Ninon de L'Enclos: La courtisane du grand siècle* (Paris, 1984).
73. Tallemant des Réaux, *Historiettes*, 1: 458.
74. Ibid., 2: 42.
75. Quoted in ibid., 1: 124.

which again created an enormous impression and were seen as something genuinely new. To men and women of the mid-seventeenth century, nothing more clearly separated them from the crude world of the sixteenth and early seventeenth centuries than the contrast in written languages.

Most important to the seventeenth century, styles of writing created differences within the cultivated upper classes. Writing gave immediate visibility to the distinction between robe and sword, for literary style was thought to mirror differences between the pedantic world of the university-trained lawyers and the livelier, quicker world of the court. The contrast already impressed Etienne Pasquier in the sixteenth century: even this distinguished magistrate believed that the writing of judges and lawyers had a cumbersome quality, the product of excessive learning and attention to rules.[76] By the seventeenth century, this distinction was a literary commonplace. "I don't know whether you share my taste," wrote the first editor of La Rochefoucauld's *Maximes* in the 1660s, "but . . . I cannot help but say that I will always prefer the negligent writing style of a courtier with wit to the strained regularity of a professor [*docteur*] who has seen nothing but his books."[77] The courtier's lack of formal education offered no bar to excellent writing; on the contrary, it allowed wit and experience of life to emerge all the more readily.

Yet the association of the court nobility with an easy, direct style led also to paradoxical juxtapositions. For despite its power to reinforce some boundaries, writing tended to blur others. Gender in particular was obscured in print. Because learning had little importance in this realm, women could play an important role in the development of seventeenth-century writing despite their exclusion from so many educational institutions. Women wrote many of the leading seventeenth-century novels, and at least one male novelist presented himself in female guise.[78]

76. Quoted in Jonathan Dewald, *The Formation of a Provincial Nobility: The Magistrates of the Parlement of Rouen, 1499–1610* (Princeton, 1980), 40.

77. François de La Rochefoucauld, *Maximes et réflexions diverses*, ed. Jacques Truchet (Paris, 1977), 156; for Vaugelas's expression of similar ideas, see David Maland, *Culture and Society in Seventeenth-Century France* (New York, 1970), 57.

78. See Bernard Bray and Isabelle Landy-Houillon, eds., *Lettres portugaises* (Paris, 1983), 59ff., for a novel purporting to be by a woman but almost certainly written by a man; see also ibid., 19, for the seventeenth-century view that women were especially

Courtly writing could thus erase differences between men and women because it was to be transparent, natural. "You write extremely well; nobody writes better," wrote Madame de Sévigné to her daughter. "Never abandon what is natural: your turn of phrase is formed upon it, and it makes for perfect style."[79] Advice like this, of course, did not preclude efforts to purify language of vulgar words and phrases. But it did claim to detach writing from its collective setting. The good writer was to express an inner nature, without regard to external conventions. It was not unreasonable for Rousseau to link his own concerns with those of courtly culture, for seventeenth-century writing presented itself as a natural form of expression.

As the seventeenth century advanced, aristocratic writers widened the scope of this claim and sought to bring intimate directness to their writing. This meant, for instance, eliminating formality of address, which increasingly seemed an obstacle to the direct expression of real feelings. The courtly style, though based on pursuit of social distinction, thus led its practitioners in fact to ignore distinctions. Vincent Voiture, whose published letters addressed the great in lively, familiar terms, illustrated the social implications of the direct style and its spread through high society. His letters initially startled and even shocked some readers. By the 1660s, however, Voiture's style had prevailed. Charles Sorel observed that "this pleasant and intimate style is now in fashion for amusing oneself with one's friends; and thus we owe [Voiture] a great deal, for having saved our letters from those old-fashioned, flattering formulas and for having introduced a more beautiful and more fluent method of writing."[80] Under Voiture's influence, Sorel claimed, letter-writing had shed social formalities, replacing distinction with egalitarian intimacy.

Others made similar observations but saw more explicitly than Sorel the social significance of the new fashion. In about 1660 the duchesse de La Trémoille received a long, humorous letter from "Vostre fidelle & tresobligée servante La Lettre," apparently written by one of the writers whom the family patronized. "La Lettre" com-

able to write. Cf. Nancy K. Miller, *Subject to Change: Reading Feminist Writing* (New York, 1988), and Faith E. Beasley, *Revising Memory: Women's Fiction and Memoirs in Seventeenth-Century France* (New Brunswick, 1990), for arguments stressing divisions between men's and women's writing.

79. Madame de Sévigné, *Selected Letters*, 70.

80. Charles Sorel, *La bibliothèque françoise*, 2d ed. (Paris, 1667; repr. Geneva, 1970), 143.

plained "that my power is more limited . . . than it used to be; in many circles, the *billet* has taken over, has taken even my name, and reproaches me for being too formal and too difficult; it claims that there is nothing more easy and free than it; and . . . that I always needed Monsieur, Mademoiselle, or Madame for beginnings, and terms like 'your servant' to conclude. But I take these reproaches for praise, and will not apologize for being controlled, civil, and respectful, or for giving the well-born [*personnes de condition*] what is their due, or for staying within the rules of propriety and custom."[81] "La Lettre" interpreted divergent views of letter-writing with reference to social order. The *billet* offered immediacy, directness, freedom; it represented an effort to escape the formalities of titles and polite phrases and to replace them with expressions of feeling that were sincere, even if light-hearted. In contrast, the traditional letter represented the preservation of respect, tradition, and alertness to differences between ranks. It offered itself as a mechanism of deference, expressing formal respect rather than sincerity of content. Intimacy and directness opposed respect for the social order, and they were winning out: "La Lettre" complained that *billets* now called themselves letters, so that the genuine letter, with its formal structure, customary phrases, and respectful distance from its audience, was in danger of disappearing.[82]

Such tensions between directness and formality had emotional as well as social dimensions. The evolution of prose paralleled high society's growing preoccupation with intimate friendship, and epistolary style offered a means of expressing desire for intimacy. "Tell my brother," wrote the duchesse de Bouillon in 1595, "that he is not sufficiently open with me [*quil ne vit point assez librement avec moy*]. I complain of it, and that his letters are as restrained [*retenue*] as if he hardly knew me."[83] Enthusiasm for intimacy and directness permeates the duchesse's correspondence with her sister. "I speak freely with you; to whom else, if not to you whom I love as a second self [*un segond moy mesme*]?" she wrote to her sister in 1601;[84] of another relative she wrote in 1605, "[H]ow good is that princess! I live with her with the same liberty as with you. After supper I relax in my dressing

81. AN 1 AP 396, 245–46.
82. Cf. Orest Ranum, "The Refuges of Intimacy," in *A History of Private Life*, 3: 246, for the significance of letters.
83. AN 1 AP 333, 3, 22 August 1595.
84. Ibid., 22.

gown, and she does me the honor of visiting me in my room . . . that will tell you if we live by ceremony—certainly not!"[85] Of the same visit she wrote a week later, "[I]t was a group that could not be sufficiently esteemed and cherished; a better could not be found anywhere, nor one with whom one lives with less ceremony; every liberty and openness was approved of and desired."[86] In 1607, again of her correspondence with her sister, she wrote, "I have no trouble in writing to you, since it is without effort or seeking for effect, but in the simplicity that you've asked of me and to which the nature of my love obliges me."[87] A year later the same terms emerged as she described her husband's admiration for her sister: "[H]e is obliged to you for your liberty, which he approves as much as he detests ceremony between people who love one another without disguises."[88] Artlessness of written expression was to mirror a larger sincerity of relationship, a sincerity that precluded ceremony and distinction and required "liberty."

Letters were not the only genre to express this vision of the functions of writing. Aristocratic memorialists too stressed the connections among freedom of style, sincerity, and intimate friendship. Claims to artless prose were among the conventions of the memoir genre from the late sixteenth century on. Thus Blaise de Monluc: "I wished to draw up my [memoirs], crudely written [*mal polis*], coming as they do from the hand of a soldier, and indeed a Gascon, who has always sought rather to act than to speak well."[89] Early in the seventeenth century, François de Boyvin likewise stressed the simplicity of his language. Unlike the historians, he wrote, "I have not enriched my discourse with a single ancient example, or decorated it with language carefully selected from the rhetorical handbooks"; and he linked his directness of expression with his military experiences, for "in discussing arms and combats, it was better that my language smell of the cannon and the bearded, badly combed soldier than of the dandy."[90]

85. Ibid., 53.
86. Ibid., 54.
87. Ibid., 69.
88. Ibid., 104.
89. Blaise de Monluc, *Commentaires, 1521–1576*, ed. Paul Courteault (Paris, Pléiade, 1964), 22.
90. François de Boyvin, chevalier, baron du Villars . . . , *Mémoires*, in M. Petitot, ed., *Collection complète des mémoires relatifs à l'histoire de France*, vols. 28–30 (Paris, 1822), 28: 349–53.

By the reign of Louis XIV these claims had become fully conventional. At the end of his memoirs, the financier and adventurer Gourville stressed that he had not sought "to correct the style, believing that for a man as ignorant as I believe myself to be, it's enough that I make myself easily understood."[91] Unlike many others, Bussy-Rabutin was proud of his style, but he too stressed the simple openness of his account: "The reader may be astonished at my sincerity; and indeed there are no memoirs whose authors speak of themselves as they do of others." He alone, he claimed, fully presented his blemishes as well as his virtues.[92] At about the same time, Antoine Arnauld repeated these conventions about style and sincerity. "As for the style," he wrote at the outset of his memoirs, "I don't flatter myself that it is faultless; it is unstudied and artless, since I've never applied myself to the rules. I speak my natural language, as I learned it in the cradle." Like Madame de Sévigné, Arnauld claimed to be writing "naturally." Like Bussy-Rabutin, he grounded his claim to sincerity in an indifference to others' opinions; he wrote only for amusement, and even conceded that the events he remembered "are perhaps not those that ought to have stuck most tenaciously. But who can boast of commanding his thought? In the most serious occupations, in meditation and even in prayer, we are not its masters; it goes strolling as it pleases, without demanding permission, and often stops before trifles that have made the philosophers blush and the greatest saints cry out."[93]

Gourville, Bussy, and Arnauld thus attached writing to individualism. They claimed no absolute vision of events. Instead, they promised to record only such particulars as had come before them, without recourse to false artistry or efforts at a universal perspective. Such a focus on the self had come to the memoir genre only slowly. Sixteenth-century writers hesitated to use the first person at all. Monluc took this step but gave as justifications for writing about himself that his experiences would offer useful examples to other soldiers and that others had attacked his achievements; he stressed, in other words, the social nature of his undertaking, its relevance to national utility and public evaluations of honor. "Do not disdain," he urged his readers,

91. Gourville, *Mémoires*, 2: 175.
92. Bussy-Rabutin, *Mémoires*, 1: 16. Such language, of course, hints at Rousseau's claims to unique sincerity at the opening of the *Confessions*.
93. L'abbé Arnauld, *Mémoires*, 120–21.

"you who wish to follow the path of arms, instead of reading about Amadis and Lancelot, spending some time getting to know me in this book. You will learn to know yourselves and to form yourselves to be soldiers and captains."[94] His comment neatly bridged the gap between self-exploration and useful instruction. By exploring his own life he could encourage others to form themselves properly.

A century later, as we have seen, Antoine Arnauld had dismissed even the issue of public use. He noted the criticism that de Pontis's memoirs had evoked for their excessive devotion to the personal, but he proceeded to present himself as writing in isolation, indifferent to others' evaluation and possible use of his work. He had not even the excuse of descendants to write for, and he made no reference to other family members who might have urged him to take pen in hand; it was only the reading of de Pontis's memoirs that had stimulated him to undertake his own. His language was to be unstudied, "natural," an immediate expression of self rather than an application of "rules"—and in this it reflected, he claimed, his specific situation as a military nobleman. Unstudied in their language, his memoirs were also to range freely in content. For the mind, he emphasized, cannot be controlled by will or reason; it wanders according to its own inclinations, fastening on unimportant particulars. Arnauld made much of the absolute truthfulness of his account, but he also emphasized its personal quality. He had important events to recount, but they were of purely personal significance rather than essential components of national history. For Antoine, autobiography established a private selfhood. His writing, he claimed, directly translated the particulars of his life, without interference from the rules of composition or the expectations of an audience.

After long hesitation, thus, seventeenth-century writing had come to accord legitimacy to the personal, now seen as appropriate as both subject matter and authorial viewpoint. Whether in isolation like Arnauld or in intimate friendships like the duchesse de Bouillon, nobles sought to translate an authentic selfhood into written form. They contrasted the transparency with which writing could express selfhood with the distortions and concealments that collective life demanded;

94. Monluc, *Commentaires*, 833; on the reluctance to adopt the first-person voice, see André Bertière, *Le cardinal de Retz mémorialiste* (Paris, 1977), 25–26.

writing allowed sincerity because, unlike even the most intimate conversation, it could be carried on in isolation, with no regard for others' opinions.

Writing could serve this urge for individuation in other contexts, which might have little to do with intimate self-depiction. At several points in his memoirs, thus, Retz described turning to writing as a way of separating himself from others and allowing his thoughts free development. "As the discussion heated up," he noted of one debate among Frondeur leaders, "Monsieur de Bellièvre proposed writing down what was said on one side and the other." His advice was followed, and the conspirators promptly produced a series of incriminating statements. Retz himself made the same suggestion to Gaston d'Orléans on a later occasion: "As it is impossible to give form to a conversation whose subject is uncertainty itself . . . I begged [him] . . . to allow me to write out my sentiments on the state of affairs"; having done so in an alcove apart from his fellow plotters, Retz then read aloud his opinions.[95] These episodes contrasted the collective nature of oral communication with the isolation of writing. In conversation the terms of discussion continually shifted, allowing no one's thought full development. Writing freed the individual from this constraint; hence the readiness of Retz and his friends to turn to it even in dangerous situations. Like Madame de La Meilleraye and *her* friends, they wrote to each other within the confines of a single room, during moments when oral communication was entirely possible and less likely to produce dangerous documents.

Presentation of the self in written form in fact became something of a fashionable mania in seventeenth-century Paris. Even the highest nobles eagerly sought occasions to see themselves—and to allow others to see them—in print. Even the most extravagantly fantastic novels of the seventeenth century reflected this urge to convert lived experience into finished form. "That shepherdess," wrote Honoré d'Urfé about his novel *L'Astrée*, "really is nothing but the story of my youth."[96]

95. Retz, *Mémoires*, 255, 621; see, for a similar episode, 727.

96. Quoted in Jean-H. Mariéjol, *La vie de Marguerite de Valois, reine de Navarre et de France (1553–1615)* (Paris, 1928; repr. Geneva, 1970), 352. Seventeenth-century fashion accentuated this relationship between novel and experience by mocking sixteenth-century taste for the fantastic and by encouraging writers to produce short, realistic novellas, a genre based on contemporary newsletters—a change discussed in Harth, *Ideology and Culture*. "Few people like them today," wrote Sorel of the chivalric novels; he complained of their antiquated language, their lack of deeper meaning, and

Written portraits of aristocratic figures became a salon vogue in the 1650s and were quickly published under distinguished patronage; nobles described themselves in the one- or two-page format the genre called for, and they described others in the same format.[97] Mademoiselle de Scudéry brought such portraits to her novels, achieving enormous success among both her popular audience and the aristocratic subjects she described. "You wouldn't believe," wrote Tallemant des Réaux, "how happy ladies are to be in her novels, or, more accurately, that their portraits are there to be seen."[98] A few years later the king's sister-in-law Henrietta of England expressed comparable interest in being seen in written form. Madame de Lafayette described a conversation with her shortly before her death: " 'Don't you think,' she said to me, 'that if all that has happened to me and the related events were written down, they would make a fine story [*histoire*]? You write well,' she added; 'write, I'll furnish you with good material [*mémoires*].' "[99] The same impulses operated among the lesser nobility. In 1626, early in the genre's development, the pious novelist Jean-Pierre Camus complained that "the ease of printing and the passion for writing infinitely multiply these works; the least little secretary uses the romantic memories of his village lord to write a whole book under whatever name he wishes to give it."[100]

Together, the novel and the printing press transformed the particulars of aristocratic personality and experience into a public commodity—and nobles participated enthusiastically in the process. The transformation was already well along by the time of the Fronde and could be seen in the public's readiness to treat Frondeur leaders as, in effect, aesthetic objects. We have seen Condé transformed into the hero of novel and drama, in the works of Mademoiselle de Scudéry, La

the fact that "on y trouve des choses hors de raison" (*La bibliothèque françoise*, 175). What he called the *roman héroïque*, by contrast, appealed precisely because it accurately reflected the customs and mood of the present—despite its often being set in classical antiquity (ibid., 176). Cf. Georg Lukács, *The Historical Novel*, trans. Hannah Mitchell and Stanley Mitchell (Lincoln, Neb., 1983), 19: "The so-called historical novels of the seventeenth century ... are historical only as regards their purely external choice of theme and costume. Not only the psychology of the characters, but the manners depicted are entirely those of the writer's own day."

97. Maland, *Culture and Society*, 154–55.

98. Tallement des Réaux, *Historiettes*, 1: 36; 1: 90; 2: 689.

99. Madame de Lafayette, *Histoire de madame Henriette d'Angleterre, la princesse de Montpensier, la comtesse de Tende*, ed. Claudinne Hermann (Paris, 1979), 22–23.

100. Henri Coulet, *Le roman jusqu'à la Révolution*, 2 vols. (Paris, 1967–68), 2: 31.

Calprenède, and Corneille; and the public responded in kind. In 1649 Condé's prison at Vincennes became an immediate tourist attraction. The admiring Scudéry reported on the visits of "more than two hundred persons of standing, who were shown the places where he slept and ate, where he had planted some carnations that he watered every day, and a study where he sometimes daydreamed and often read."[101] Condé the political actor touched not only those directly involved in his struggles but also a larger public, which enthusiastically followed his tribulations and sought contact with the personal details of his experience. This public had less interest in Condé the political leader and distributor of patronage than in Condé the personality, reading, daydreaming, suffering injustice.

What did it mean that princes of the blood, petty squires, and even the king's sister-in-law sought to represent themselves for public consumption? We have seen the political advantages that Condé and others derived from publication, but the process also subjected nobles to the constraints that the seventeenth century saw in relations between art object and public. The public's critical evaluations dominated those relations, producing regular contrasts between the claims of aesthetic tradition and the public's insights. The rise of the theater, especially, had created a model of how a critical public might function, for it constituted an art form in which popular views were visible and important.[102] The aesthetic public was another domain in which seventeenth-century Parisians experienced a hesitant republicanism.

Thus Corneille used the public's opinions to justify innovation against the doubts of tradition-minded critics. He defended his criticism of the Aristotelian understanding of tragedy in terms of success with the public. "Success has justified numerous plays" in which Aristotle's rules are not followed, he argued; and he added that Aristotle's rules required changing "so as not to oblige us to condemn numerous poems that we have seen succeed in our theaters."[103] To challenge Aristotelian aesthetics on the ground of public "success" argues a striking confidence in the public's evaluations. Indeed, Corneille's language suggests a yet stronger view: that success and failure were to be defined only in terms of the public's responses. "Our first

101. Quoted in Mongrédien, *Le Grand Condé*, 92.
102. Erich Auerbach, " 'La Cour et la Ville,' " in Auerbach, *Scenes from the Drama of European Literature* (Minneapolis, 1984).
103. Corneille, "De la tragédie," in *Oeuvres complètes*, 832, 833.

objective should be to please the court and the people and to attract a large audience to their presentations," he wrote of his plays. "[A]bove all, we must win over public opinion [*la voix publique*]."[104] Racine made a comparable appeal to public opinion over the unease of learned critics, who disliked the imperfections in his heroes.[105] Obviously, neither playwright had a democratic public in mind, but neither did they envision one restricted by birth or traditional authority. Nobles who appeared before this public in printed novels, portraits, and memoirs placed themselves in an analogous situation, in which critical authority rested with audience rather than actor. It was partly to this reversal of powers that nobles' hesitation about publishing pointed.

When nobles wrote, then, they risked undercutting some of the bases of aristocratic society itself. They subjected both their ideas and, more dramatically, images of themselves to a broad public for consumption and criticism. They relinquished control of the circulation and interpretation of their words. They entered an area in which contemporaries explicitly rejected the claims of birth, and one in which Christian morality often seemed threatened. Money played a role in both challenges, opening up the circulation of words and encouraging the spread of dangerous images. Nobles sought to protect themselves from these consequences by restricting their writings to limited circles, but the uselessness of their efforts was demonstrated repeatedly. Seventeenth-century writing continually escaped the boundaries designed to contain it.

But for all its dangers, writing passionately attracted the nobles. Some of its attraction lay in the practical needs to which it responded, but, more important, it offered a series of overlapping pleasures. In writing, individuals could detach themselves from the surrounding world and function in complete liberty. In doing so, they experienced selfhood and a sense of control; as they wrote, they manipulated both the physical blank paper and the narrative of their lives. At both physical and mental levels, acts of writing, like those of civility, involved the mastery of small techniques and demanded careful training; like the development of elegant manners, writing represented an affirmation of self-control. Yet it also provided, in apparent opposition to

104. Preface to *La suivante*, in ibid., 127.
105. Racine, Preface to *Andromaque*, in *Oeuvres complètes*, 1: 242.

self-control, strong emotional experiences. Because it offered privileged access to an authentic inner self and freedom from the constraints of sociability, writing gave its practitioners feelings both of liberty and of connectedness with others. Writing offered mechanisms for the emotional closeness that seventeenth-century high society pursued so vigorously.

Selfhood, self-control, the claims of ability, the free circulation of objects unimpeded by social distinction: these are elements in what has conventionally been seen as capitalist liberalism.[106] Yet in this case they emerged from a highly aristocratic setting, among men and women who had no eagerness for a capitalist society or even serious doubts about distinctions of birth. Anxieties about the effects of writing were to some extent softened by its capacity to create new distinctions even as it challenged old ones. Like good manners, writing established new boundaries between some nobles and everyone else. Good writing separated humanity from beasts, nobles from peasants, courtiers from pedantic lawyers. Its practice could be ideologically comforting, suggesting that social differences ran so deep that they emerged even in this private activity.

Writing offered new bases for social hierarchy and shored up some old ones. Yet its main effects remained destructive of hierarchy. Seventeenth-century beliefs about writing tended to ground society in private selfhood rather than collective obligation, and they tended to stress the inner self's irresponsibility. As Antoine Arnauld asked, who could control the wanderings of thought? Writing offered the pleasures of capturing and consuming these wanderings without regard for others' controlling wishes. In writing as in other domains, nobles sought escape from collective constraints despite high ideological costs.

106. Cf. de Certeau's vision of the specifically bourgeois character of writing, cited above, n. 1.

# Conclusion

At a climactic moment in the novel, the prince de Clèves addresses his wife: "I have only violent and uncertain feelings, of which I am not the master . . . I adore you, I hate you; . . . I admire you, I feel shame at doing so. In the end there is no longer either calm or reason within me."[1] The prince's statement may stand for the elements in seventeenth-century culture that this study has explored. Seventeenth-century nobles, I have argued here, came to view the self as complex, unstable, yet ultimately more real than the groupings to which it belonged. The prince de Clèves needs others, yet is basically alone; to his emotion his wife can respond only with dutiful self-control. Containing the diverse impulses that the prince seeks to define, the self might develop in radically different directions, in response to both personal experience and wider cultural change. It had a history, which could not be predicted from its origins but required interpretation in the form of autobiography. Alongside this personal history, nobles saw a parallel historicity in the cultural expectations that surrounded the self. "All ages have their own characters," wrote Saint-Evremond. "[T]hey have their forms of politics, self-interest, business; they have their own moralities, in some sense, their own faults and virtues. It's always man, but nature varies within man."[2]

This vision of the self as subject to both personal and cultural change emerged during years when noble ideology purported to define identity with great certainty. The ethic of *race* fixed the self within a series of overlapping entities. Whatever her or his merits and achievements, the individual remained an expression of these larger entities, notably the lineage and order from which he or she emerged. The

1. Madame de Lafayette, *La princesse de Clèves*, in *Romans et nouvelles*, ed. Emile Magne (Paris, 1961), 362–63.

2. Charles de Marguetel, seigneur de Saint-Evremond, *Oeuvres mêlées*, ed. Charles Giraud, 3 vols. (Paris, 1867), 3: 179 (letter to Hortense Mancini, 1677).

individual might change, but the *race* was eternal, a chain of continuity to the distant past. French nobles believed these ideas and heard them often.

Yet they failed in much of their explanatory promise. Nobles in fact often chose not to employ the ideology of *race* as they described their lives, and they embraced ideas that contradicted the ideology. They interpreted their lives in terms of individual ambition and achievement; they stressed hostilities and barriers within the dynastic family; they used language that undercut the legitimacy of political and social hierarchy. Worse yet, daily practice often contradicted aristocratic ideology as well. Passionate friendships functioned as alternatives to the social world. Writing offered both retreat to a private selfhood and submersion in the anonymity of publication. Play with money erased social differences. Many of these practices blurred gender as well as social boundaries. Men and women mingled in friendships, at the gambling table, in the process of publication; contemporaries guessed wrong about the authorship of both the *Princesse de Clèves* and the *Lettres portugaises*. Strong emotions surrounded many of these practices. Contemporaries saw their fellows becoming passionately involved in poetry, gambling, love, and careers, and they stressed the moral dangers these involvements entailed. Their excitements conflicted with conventional religious as well as social beliefs.

This study has explored reasons, many of them highly specific, for such choices. The court encouraged a new elegance of manners and demanded new forms of political calculation. Long-standing educational assumptions encouraged the individual's departure from home and family; seventeenth-century political conditions often made this separation a confrontation with foreign cultures and religions. Changing patterns of warfare demonstrated the distance between current practice and traditional beliefs, and evolving theories of monarchy challenged old ideas about loyalty and political morality. Money became an increasingly common presence in ordinary life, and with the venality of offices it came to permeate public life as well. The rise of printing changed nobles' uses of writing, and the widening audience for both printed and staged words had similar effects.

All of these forces were important, but, I have argued here, they fail to explain the emotions with which nobles pursued new models of selfhood in these years. They fail to explain the excitement nobles felt about writing and new economic practices, the passion with which they entered friendships, or the intensity of their critique of dependency, whether on fathers, *les grands,* or the king himself. Such emotions, I believe, should be understood as responses to the increasing pressure that the ideology of hierarchy and lineage itself exerted on seventeenth-century men and women. Seventeenth-century ideology glorified dynasticism wherever it could be found, and in practical ways it strengthened the dynasty's hold over its members. Kings exercised tighter controls over courtiers, soldiers, and magistrates; fathers over sons; husbands over wives. Contemporaries came to define social status more purely in terms of ancestry, and their views received institutional form, with commoners excluded from a widening range of important positions. In the seventeenth century, vague social pressures in favor of ancestry and paternal authority acquired a newly systematic and effective character. Authority weighed more heavily on individual lives, and the weight was all the stronger because most seventeenth-century men and women accepted its moral legitimacy; they believed in the rights of ancestry and monarchy.

Yet they were not entirely comfortable with their beliefs and turned readily to alternatives. Some of these were explicit, as in the libertines' critique of religious tradition or the pursuit of friendship at the expense of family. Other alternatives were implicit and even unconscious: when tragedians presented royal fathers as rapacious and lawless, presumably the court audience could not have responded with explicit assent.

Few of these alternative visions were entirely new. Courtly elegance had a long history by the seventeenth century, and so did the social criticisms it generated. The ingratitude of the great was an old theme, and theatrical metaphors for the social world had circulated since the twelfth century.[3] The culture that seventeenth-century nobles inherited must be seen as a heterogeneous collection of images, ideas, expectations, and values, rather than a cohesive system of beliefs. Within this assemblage, contradiction was inevitable and not necessarily troubling. Different values applied in different contexts, and their contradictory implications rarely had to be faced.

3. Ernst Robert Curtius, *European Literature and the Latin Middle Ages*, trans. Willard R. Trask (New York, 1953), 138–40.

But seventeenth-century experiences, I argue, made cultural contradictions more visible and more painful.[4] On the one side, moral debate acquired a new centrality in seventeenth-century polite society. Religious-minded moral critics brought new scruples to the examination of conduct and spelled out its troubling implications; libertines proposed non-Christian alternatives; and both groups noted that widely accepted forms of behavior diverged from religious standards. On the other side, the growing coherence of official ideology allowed less room for the play of contradictory values. Seventeenth-century men and women were expected to display greater loyalty to the state and to the patriarchal ideas that it represented. Acknowledgment of contradiction could not so easily be avoided in these circumstances, and old practices acquired new colorings. Medieval literature had spoken of friendship, for instance, but in the seventeenth century friendship became a longed-for shelter from the society of orders. This study has tried to stress the number of comparable shelters seventeenth-century men and women sought to construct and the pleasure they took in them.

After 1715 and Louis XIV's death, the pressure that maintained this doubling of social practices diminished. The monarchy continued to police the values of the society of orders, jailing unruly sons and legislating advantages for high birth. But its efforts lacked the coherence of the seventeenth century and suffered from its own contradictory intentions. In response to this relative opening of practice, eighteenth-century nobles turned eagerly to a variety of liberal ideologies and to the visions of emotional life that accompanied them. Their enthusiasms have long been seen to prefigure and explain the Revolution; but eighteenth-century enthusiasms can also help us to understand the psychological pressures that seventeenth-century society had generated.

4. My understanding of how long-standing moral contradictions may move from implicit to conscious stature owes much to Roberto Mungabeira Unger, *Law in Modern Society: Toward a Criticism of Social Theory* (New York, 1976), passim.

# Appendix: Biographical Sketches

I offer here brief descriptions of the men and women who figure most prominently in this study. These range from Blaise de Monluc, who died in 1577, through Gourville, Saint-Evremond, and Racine, who died in the early eighteenth century. The large majority, however, are drawn from a single, long-lived generation, born in the years around 1610 and surviving into the 1680s or 1690s.

*The abbé Arnauld.*   Antoine Arnauld, son of Arnauld d'Andilly, 1616–1698. After eight years of military service, he retired in 1643 to the ecclesiastical career for which he had originally been educated. His brother the marquis de Pomponne became foreign minister in 1671 and was a close friend of Madame de Sévigné.

*Arnauld d'Andilly.*   Robert Arnauld d'Andilly, 1589–1674. Oldest son of a famous Parisian lawyer, he entered the royal court in the 1620s and subsequently held several important administrative positions. At about the time he entered the court he became closely attached to the abbé Saint-Cyran, one of the intellectual leaders of the Jansenist movement in France, and his younger brother became a leading theologian in the movement. In 1644 d'Andilly retired to the Jansenist stronghold at Port Royal des Champs, where two of his sons already resided. He retained during his retirement friendships with several leaders of Parisian high society, including La Rochefoucauld, Madame de Lafayette, and Madame de Sévigné, and he continued to use his influence to advance the career of his son the marquis de Pomponne, who in 1671 became foreign minister.

*Bussy-Rabutin.*   Roger de Rabutin, comte de Bussy, 1618–1693. A cousin and friend of Madame de Sévigné, Bussy was born to a substantial family of military nobility. He inherited a military command and enjoyed a successful career, but spent several months in the Bastille because his *Histoire amoureuse des Gaules* made fun of leading court figures and of the king himself; thereafter he was exiled to his estate in Burgundy, where he continued an extensive correspondence with leading figures in Parisian literature and society. His memoirs were published just after his death, in 1694.

*Campion.*   Henri de Campion, 1613–1663. A member of a relatively poor noble family of lower Normandy, Campion had a successful career as a military officer. He joined the comte de Soissons's conspiracies against

Richelieu, and during the Fronde he followed Longueville and Beaufort against the court, after which he returned to his career in the royal armies. Both his brothers shared his literary and philosophical interests and joined him in some of his political plotting. His memoirs remained unpublished until 1807.

*Condé.*    Henri II de Bourbon, prince de Condé, 1588–1646. Condé's father was Henri IV's first cousin and a leader of French Protestants during the later Wars of Religion; Condé himself was born after his father's death and was raised a Catholic at the royal court. During the minority of Louis XIII he led the princely opposition to the regency government, but after three years' imprisonment in the Bastille he emerged as a loyal and moderately successful military leader. His marriage to the beautiful Charlotte de Montmorency brought him control of one of the great French landed fortunes and ownership of the palace of Chantilly.

*Corneille.*    Pierre Corneille, 1606–1684. Born to a middle-class Rouennais family and educated at the city's Jesuit college, Corneille was trained as a lawyer and remained a lesser official until 1648; he continued to reside in Rouen all his life. His first comedy appeared in 1629; his tragedy *Le Cid* (1637) provoked a major literary controversy, briefly interrupted his career, but soon established him as a leading poet. In all he wrote thirty-five plays, remaining active, and much admired by aristocratic viewers such as Madame de Sévigné, through the 1670s.

*Gourville.*    Jean Hérauld, sieur de Gourville, 1625–1703. Born to humble parents in the town of La Rochefoucauld, Gourville rose through service to the La Rochefoucauld family. He aided La Rochefoucauld and the Condés during the Fronde but also assisted Mazarin in the negotiations that ended the conflict. Thereafter he worked with the finance minister Nicolas Fouquet, accumulating a large fortune but having to flee France when Fouquet was arrested. He spent seven years in exile but thereafter returned to royal favor, wealth, and close connections with Parisian high society. At some point he secretly married a daughter of the La Rochefoucauld family. His memoirs were published in 1724.

*The Grand Condé.*    Louis II de Bourbon, prince de Condé, 1621–1686, son of Henri II de Bourbon (above). In 1643 his success at the Battle of Rocroi, in which he led the French army to an unexpected victory over the Spanish, established him as one of the greatest generals of the age and as a popular hero. During the Fronde, courted by both sides, he turned from support of Mazarin to leadership of the princely opposition. After the defeat of the Fronde he fled to the Spanish and led their armies against France. He reentered France only after the peace treaty of 1659, but soon returned to military commands. In 1672 he led the French campaign against Holland. Condé was known as a literary patron and youthful freethinker; he became a fervent Catholic shortly before his death.

*Madame de Lafayette.*    Marie-Madeleine Pioche de La Vergne, comtesse de Lafayette, 1634–1693. Daughter of a military nobleman with a robe background, close connections to the court, but no great wealth, she married the much older comte de Lafayette; after 1661 she lived on her own in Paris, while he remained in the provinces. She moved in Parisian literary circles and wrote a series of short novels, the most important of them the *Princesse de Clèves.*

*La Rochefoucauld.*    François VI, prince de Marcillac and (from 1650) duc de La Rochefoucauld, 1613–1680. A member of a famous and very wealthy aristocratic family with a well-known military history, François fought in Italy, then played a leading role opposing the court during the Fronde. He was the lover of the duchesse de Longueville, the Grand Condé's sister, during the Fronde, and a close friend of Madame de Lafayette from the 1650s on. He published his *Mémoires* abroad in 1662 and his *Maximes* in Paris in 1665, with many subsequent printings; both were very widely read by contemporaries.

*La Trémoille.*    Henri, duc de La Trémoille, duc de Thouars, prince de Talmont, 1599–1674. Born to one of the greatest French aristocratic families, with an extensive landed base in Poitou and important interests in Brittany, Henri also enjoyed connections with leading families throughout Protestant Europe, as well as throughout France. His maternal grandfather was William of Orange, and his wife was the daughter of the duc de Bouillon, whose independent principality was an important Protestant refuge during the sixteenth and early seventeenth centuries; his aunt was the princesse de Condé, mother of the prince Henri II. Henri de La Trémoille abjured his Protestantism in 1628, following intense courtship from the Crown, but his wife remained Protestant. Wounded in military service, Henri spent most of his later life on his estates.

*Molière.*    Jean-Baptiste Poquelin, 1622–1673. From a Parisian mercantile family, Molière received an excellent education at aristocratic Parisian schools and there established connections with the prince de Conti, the Grand Condé's brother. Captivated by the theater, under Conti's patronage he began writing and producing plays, first in Paris, then in southern France. In 1658 he returned to Paris with a series of triumphantly successful comedies. These secured him the king's support, and Molière retained this standing despite controversy surrounding his plays; his mockery of the pious in *Tartuffe,* in particular, led to his excommunication.

*Monluc.*    Blaise de Lasseran-Massencombe, seigneur de Monluc, ca. 1502–1577. Born in Gascony of the high provincial nobility but in modest economic circumstances, Monluc began military service in his youth. He participated with great success in the French campaigns in Italy and became a favorite of the king Henri II; he played a leading role on the Catholic side during the Wars of Religion, acquiring a reputation for great ferocity and rising to the rank of maréchal de France. His *Commentaries,* written in retirement during the mid-1570s, were first published in 1592.

*Nicole.*    Pierre Nicole, 1625–1695. The son of a lawyer and minor official at Chartres, Nicole received an extensive education in Paris, then taught at the Jansenist convent at Port Royal, becoming one of the movement's leading writers. He established close friendships with the Arnauld family and enjoyed the protection of aristocratic Jansenists such as the duchesse de Longueville, sister of the Grand Condé. The Crown's prosecution of Jansenism led to a brief period of exile in 1678, but thereafter Nicole returned to reside in Paris.

*De Pontis.*    Louis de Pontis, 1583–1670. A member of a poor provincial family, he undertook a military career, fighting in the La Rochelle campaign against the French Protestants and in several campaigns of the Thirty Years' War and holding several high military offices. In 1650 he underwent a religious conversion and retired to Port Royal des Champs; his *Mémoires* were recorded there by a fellow Jansenist and were published in 1676, provoking enormous interest in contemporary high society.

*Racine.*    Jean Racine, 1639–1711. Born of a family of provincial fiscal officers, he was given an extensive education by pious relatives, including three years at the Jansenist school at Port Royal. Despite his relatives' plans for his legal career, he sought to make his way in Paris as a writer. In 1664 his first tragedy established him as a noted literary figure. After *Phèdre* (1676) he ceased writing secular drama and also renounced his youthful dissipations; he was already heavily subsidized by the court and soon after became one of Louis XIV's official historians.

*Retz.*    Paul de Gondi, cardinal de Retz, 1613–1679. His family were Florentine merchants who established themselves in Lyon in the early sixteenth century and received nobility and royal favor in the later sixteenth century. Self-consciously indifferent to religion, Retz was nonetheless directed to the priesthood by his family; in 1643 he became coadjutor of his uncle the archbishop of Paris, and in 1652 he was named cardinal. Retz played a complicated role during the Fronde, establishing himself as a leader of seditious Parisian popular opinion but also negotiating with the court in hopes of becoming a royal minister. The failure of the Fronde condemned him to several years of wandering exile. Eventually he returned to France, where he underwent a religious conversion. His *Mémoires* were first published in 1717. During his lifetime he had published several political pamphlets and a study of the *Conjuration de Fiesque.*

*Saint-Evremond.*    Charles de Marguetel de Saint-Denis, seigneur de Saint-Evremond, 1613–1703. A member of a substantial noble family of lower Normandy, the extensively educated Saint-Evremond enjoyed a successful military career under the patronage of the Grand Condé. During the Fronde he supported the court but soon after spent three months in the

Bastille for his critical comments about Mazarin. His military career resumed thereafter, but he underwent a second imprisonment in 1659 and was threatened with a third in 1661. At that point he fled to exile, first in Holland and then in England, where he lived comfortably and enjoyed close attachments with the English aristocracy and court. He continued to follow French literary developments while in England and was in close touch with English literary circles.

*Madame de Sévigné.*    Marie de Rabutin Chantal, 1626–1696. A cousin of Bussy-Rabutin, she was born in Paris to a substantial family of military nobles. Widowed with two children at age twenty-five, she lived most of the rest of her life in Paris, closely attached to contemporary literary figures: she was good friends with Madame de Lafayette and La Rochefoucauld, Mademoiselle de Scudéry, and Retz, as well as with the finance minister Fouquet.

*Tallemant des Réaux.*    Gédéon Tallemant des Réaux, 1619–1692. Tallemant was a member of a family of wealthy Protestant bankers, originally from La Rochelle but established in Paris during his childhood. He was extensively educated and closely connected with Madame de Rambouillet, who held the most noted salon of early-seventeenth-century Paris. In about 1659 he composed his *Historiettes,* biographical sketches of notable figures in French politics, society, and culture that were mixed with scandalous reports about their personal lives. These remained unpublished and almost entirely unknown until 1834.

*Tarente.*    Henri-Charles de La Trémoille, prince de Tarente, 1620–1672. Son of Henri de La Trémoille (above), the prince de Tarente fled to Holland as a young man to learn military skills. There he served his great-uncle the prince of Orange for several years. He returned to France just before the Fronde and joined Condé's princely opposition to the court. After the collapse of the Fronde he fled to exile in Holland. He returned to France in 1655, was exiled to his estates, then returned to Holland and service in the Dutch army from 1663 to 1670. At that point he abjured Protestantism and spent his last years in France.

# Bibliography

PRIMARY SOURCES

ARCHIVAL DOCUMENTS

All of the archival sources cited in this study come from two collections at the Archives Nationales, Paris: the series 1 AP (papers of the La Trémoille family) and 3 AP (papers of the Nicolay family). The materials cited here are:

1 AP 286:    correspondence between the Montmorencys and the La Trémoilles
1 AP 333:    letters of Elisabeth de Nassau, duchesse de Bouillon
1 AP 381:    letters of the comte de Laval
1 AP 382:    documents concerning the comte de Laval
1 AP 383:    documents concerning the comte de Laval
1 AP 393:    letters of Henri de La Trémoille, duc de Thouars, 1600–42
1 AP 394:    letters of Henri de La Trémoille, duc de Thouars, 1643–51
1 AP 395:    letters of Henri de La Trémoille, duc de Thouars, 1654–56
1 AP 396:    La Trémoille correspondence
1 AP 397:    La Trémoille correspondence
1 AP 398:    La Trémoille correspondence
1 AP 433:    "Lettres de consolation"
1 AP 435:    letters of the marquise de la Moussaye
1 AP 436:    letters of the marquis de la Moussaye
1 AP 441:    memoirs of the prince de Tarente
1 AP 443:    "Etat de dépense"
1 AP 444:    "Vie de la princesse de La Trémoille comtesse d'Aldenburg"
1 AP 642, 645, 648, 649, 651:    miscellaneous correspondence
3 AP 17:    Jehan II de Nicolay, correspondence
3 AP 20:    Louis and Aymard de Nicolay, correspondence and papers
3 AP 21:    Anthoine II de Nicolay, correspondence and papers
3 AP 26:    correspondence, seventeenth and eighteenth centuries
3 AP 59:    correspondence and memoirs
3 AP 256:    "Harangues de mon grandpère"

PRINTED SOURCES

Adam, Antoine, ed. *Les libertins au XVIIe siècle.* Paris, 1964.
Aristotle. *Ethics,* trans. J. A. K. Thomson. London, 1953.

———. *The Politics*, trans. T. A. Sinclair. London, 1962.

———. *On Rhetoric*, ed. George A. Kennedy. Oxford, 1991.

Arnauld, l'abbé. *Mémoires*. In M. Petitot, ed., *Collection des mémoires relatifs à l'histoire de France*, 34. Paris, 1824.

Arnauld d'Andilly, Robert. *Mémoires*. In M. Petitot, ed., *Collection des mémoires relatifs à l'histoire de France*, 33–34. Paris, 1824.

Aulotte, Robert, ed. *Plutarque en France au XVIe siècle: Trois opuscules moraux, traduits par Antoine du Saix, Pierre de Saint-Julien, et Jacques Amyot*. Paris, 1971.

Bassompierre, maréchal de. *Mémoires*. In Michaud and Poujolat, eds., *Nouvelle collection des mémoires relatifs à l'histoire de France . . .* , 20. Paris, 1854.

Boileau, Nicolas. *Oeuvres complètes*, ed. Françoise Escal. Paris, 1966.

Bouillon, Henri, duc de. *Mémoires*. In Michaud and Poujolat, eds., *Nouvelle collection des mémoires relatifs à l'histoire de France . . .* , 11. Paris, 1854.

Bray, Bernard, and Isabelle Landy-Houillon, eds. *Lettres portugaises*. Paris, 1983.

Bussy-Rabutin, Roger de. *Histoire amoureuse des Gaules*, ed. Paul Boiteau, 4 vols. Paris, 1866.

———. *Histoire amoureuse des Gaules*, ed. Charles-Augustin Sainte-Beuve, 2 vols. Paris, 1868.

———. *Mémoires*, ed. Ludovic Lalanne, 2 vols. Paris, 1857; repr. Westmead, 1972.

Campion, Henri de. *Mémoires*, ed. Marc Fumaroli. Paris, 1967.

Charnes, J.-A. de. *Conversations sur la critique de la princesse de Clèves*. Paris, 1679; repr. Tours, 1973.

Cicero. *De Senectute, De Amicitia, De Divinatione*, trans. William Armistead Falconer. Cambridge, Mass., Loeb Classical Library, 1964.

Cochrane, Eric, et al., eds. *Early Modern Europe: Crisis of Authority*. Chicago, 1987.

Conrart, Valentin. *Mémoires*, ed. J. N. Monmerqué. Paris, 1826; repr. Geneva, 1971.

Corneille, Pierre. *Oeuvres complètes*, ed. André Stegman. Paris, 1963.

Coulet, Henri. *Le roman jusqu'à la Révolution*, 2 vols. Paris, 1967–68.

Descartes, René. *Discourse on Method*, trans. F. E. Sutcliffe. London, 1968.

———. *The Philosophical Writings of René Descartes*, trans. John Cottingham, Robert Stoothoff, and Dugald Murdoch, 2 vols. Cambridge, 1985.

Faret, Nicolas. *L'honnête homme, ou l'art de plaire à la cour*, ed. Maurice Magendie. Paris, 1925; repr. Geneva, 1970.

Félice, M. de, ed. *Code de l'humanité ou la législation universelle, naturelle, civile et politique . . . composé par une société de gens de lettres . . .* , 13 vols. Yverdon, 1778.

Fénelon, François de Salignac de La Mothe-. *Oeuvres spirituelles*, ed. François Varillon, S.J. Paris, 1954.

Froissart, Jean. *Chronicles*, selected, ed., and trans. Geoffrey Brereton. London, 1968.

Furetière, Antoine. *Dictionnaire universel,* 3 vols. The Hague, 1690; repr. Geneva, 1970.

Gourville, Jean Hérauld, sieur de. *Mémoires,* ed. Léon Lecestre, 2 vols. Paris, 1894.

La Bruyère, Jean de. *Oeuvres complètes,* ed. Julien Benda. Paris, Pléiade, 1951.

La Châtre, comte de. *Mémoires.* In Michaud and Poujolat, eds., *Nouvelle collection des mémoires relatifs à l'histoire de France . . . ,* 27. Paris, 1854.

La Chesnaye-Desbois, François-Alexandre Aubert de. *Dictionnaire de la noblesse . . . ,* 15 vols. Paris, 1770–86.

Laclos, Choderlos de. *Les liaisons dangereuses.* In *Oeuvres complètes,* ed. Laurent Versini. Paris, Pléiade, 1979.

Lafayette, Madame de. *Histoire de madame Henriette d'Angleterre, la princesse de Montpensier, la comtesse de Tende,* ed. Claudinne Hermann. Paris, 1979.

———. *Romans et nouvelles,* ed. Emile Magne. Paris, 1961.

La Noue, François de. *Mémoires.* In Michaud and Poujolat, eds., *Nouvelle collection des mémoires relatifs à l'histoire de France . . . ,* 9. Paris, 1854.

La Roche Flavin, Bernard de. *Treze livres des Parlemens de France.* Bordeaux, 1617.

La Rochefoucauld, François de. *Maximes et réflexions diverses,* ed. Jacques Truchet. Paris, 1977.

———. *Oeuvres complètes,* ed. L. Martin-Chauffier. Paris, Pléiade, 1957.

Lefebvre d'Ormesson, Olivier. *Journal,* ed. M. Chéruel, 2 vols. Paris, 1860.

Lenet, Pierre. *Mémoires.* In M. Petitot and J. N. Monmerqué, eds., *Collection des mémoires relatifs à l'histoire de France,* 53. Paris, 1826.

Magne, Emile, ed. *Le Grand Condé et le duc d'Enghien: Lettres inédites à Marie-Louise de Gonzague, reine de Pologne, sur la cour de Louis XIV (1660–1667).* Paris, 1920.

Marguerite de Navarre. *The Heptameron,* trans. P. A. Chilton. London, 1984.

Marivaux, Pierre. *Le paysan parvenu.* Paris, 1965.

———. *Théâtre complet,* ed. Marcel Arland. Paris, Pléiade, 1949.

Mergey, Jean de. *Mémoires.* In Michaud and Poujolat, eds., *Nouvelle collection des mémoires relatifs à l'histoire de France . . . ,* 9. Paris, 1854.

Molière. *Oeuvres,* ed. Eugène Despois and Paul Mesnard. 13 vols. Paris, 1880.

Monluc, Blaise de. *Commentaires, 1521–1576,* ed. Paul Courteault. Paris, Pléiade, 1964.

Montaigne, Michel de. *The Complete Essays,* ed. Donald Frame. Stanford, 1958.

———. *Oeuvres complètes,* ed. Maurice Rat and Albert Thibaudet. Paris, Pléiade, 1962.

Montesquieu, Charles-Louis de Secondat, baron de. *Persian Letters,* trans. J. Robert Loy. Cleveland, 1961.

————. *The Spirit of the Laws,* ed. David Wallace Carrithers. Berkeley, 1977.

Montrésor, Claude de Bourdeille, comte de. *Mémoires.* In Michaud and Pou-jolat, eds., *Nouvelle collection des mémoires relatifs à l'histoire de France . . . ,* 27. Paris, 1854.

Nicole, Pierre. *Oeuvres philosophiques et morales,* ed. C. Jourdain. Paris, 1845; repr. Hildesheim, 1970.

Pascal, Blaise. *Pensées,* trans. A. J. Krailsheimer. London, 1966.

Perrault, Charles. *Contes,* ed. Jean-Pierre Collinet. Paris, 1981.

Pontis, Louis de. *Mémoires.* In M. Petitot, ed., *Collection des mémoires relatifs à l'histoire de France,* 31–32. Paris, 1824.

Racine, Jean. *Andromache, Britannicus, Berenice,* trans. John Cairncross. London, 1967.

————. *Oeuvres complètes.* Volume 1: *Théâtre-poésies,* ed. Raymond Picard. Paris, Pléiade, 1950.

Regnard, Jean-François. *Le Joueur,* ed. John Dunkley. Geneva, 1986.

Retz, Cardinal de. *Mémoires,* ed. Maurice Allem and Edith Thomas. Paris, Pléiade, 1956.

Richelieu, cardinal de. *Testament politique,* ed. Louis André. Paris, 1947.

Rohan, Henri de. *Le parfait capitaine ou abrégé des guerres des Commentaires de César.* New ed., expanded. N.p., 1757.

Rousseau, Jean-Jacques. *The Confessions,* trans. J. M. Cohen. London, 1953.

Saint-Evremond, Charles de Marguetel, seigneur de. *Oeuvres en prose,* ed. René Ternois, 3 vols. Paris, 1962–66.

————. *Oeuvres mêlées,* ed. Charles Giraud, 3 vols. Paris, 1867.

————. *Oeuvres mêlées,* ed. Luigi de Nardis. Rome, 1966.

Saint-Simon, Louis de Rouvroy, duc de. *Mémoires,* ed. Gonzague Truc, 8 vols. Paris, Pléiade, 1953–61.

Sévigné, Madame de. *Lettres,* ed. Roger Gailly, 3 vols. Paris, Pléiade, 1955.

————. *Selected Letters,* trans. Leonard Tancock. London, 1982.

Smith, Adam. *Wealth of Nations,* ed. Andrew Skinner. London, 1982.

Sorel, Charles. *La bibliothèque françoise,* 2d ed. Paris, 1667; repr. Geneva, 1970.

————. *Histoire comique de Francion,* ed. Yves Guiraud. Paris, 1979.

Souvigny, comte de. *Mémoires,* ed. Ludovic de Contenson, 3 vols. Paris, 1906–09.

Spanheim, Ezéchiel. *Relation de la cour de France en 1690,* ed. Charles Schefer. Paris, 1882.

Tallemant des Réaux, Gédéon. *Historiettes,* ed. Antoine Adam, 2 vols. Paris, Pléiade, 1960–61.

Urfé, Honoré d'. *L'Astrée,* abridged edition, ed. Jean Lafond. Paris, 1984.

Valois, Marguerite de. *Mémoires et lettres,* ed. F. Guessard. Paris, 1842.

Villars, François de Boyvin, chevalier, baron du. *Mémoires.* In M. Petitot, ed., *Collection complète des mémoires relatifs à l'histoire de France,* 28–30. Paris, 1822.

Villeroy, Monsieur de. *Mémoires d'Estat.* In M. Petitot, ed., *Collection des mémoires relatifs à l'histoire de France,* 44. Paris, 1824.

## SECONDARY WORKS

Adam, Antoine. *Du mysticisme à la révolte: Les jansénistes du XVIIe siècle.* Paris, 1968.

———. *La littérature française: L'âge classique,* 4 vols. Paris, 1968.

Adams, S. L. "Foreign Policy and the Parliaments of 1621 and 1624." In Kevin Sharpe, ed., *Faction and Parliament: Essays on Early Stuart History.* Oxford, 1978.

Agnew, Jean-Christophe. *Worlds Apart: The Market and the Theater in Anglo-American Thought, 1550–1750.* Cambridge, 1986.

Albanese, Ralph. "The Dynamics of Money in Post-Molièresque Comedy." *Stanford French Review* 7, 1 (Spring 1983).

Appleby, Joyce. *Economic Thought and Ideology in Seventeenth-Century England.* Princeton, 1978.

———. Review of Jean-Christophe Agnew, *Worlds Apart. Albion* 19, 1 (Spring 1987).

Ariès, Philippe. *Centuries of Childhood: The Social History of Family Life,* trans. Robert Baldick. London, 1962.

Aronson, Nicole. *Mademoiselle de Scudéry, ou le voyage au pays de Tendre.* Paris, 1986.

Arriaza, Armand. "Mousnier and Barber: The Theoretical Underpinning of the 'Society of Orders' in Early Modern Europe." *Past and Present* 89 (November 1980).

Auerbach, Erich. *Scenes from the Drama of European Literature.* Minneapolis, 1984.

Aumale, M. le duc d'. *Histoire des princes de Condé pendant les XVIe et XVIIe siècles,* 6 vols. Paris, 1885.

Barker, Nancy Nichols. *Brother to the Sun King: Philippe Duke of Orleans.* Baltimore, 1989.

Barthes, Roland. *On Racine,* trans. Richard Howard. New York, 1977.

Bayard, Françoise. *Le monde des financiers au XVIIe siècle.* Paris, 1988.

Beasley, Faith E. *Revising Memory: Women's Fiction and Memoirs in Seventeenth-Century France.* New Brunswick, 1990.

Bénichou, Paul. *Morales du grand siècle.* Paris, 1948.

Bergin, Joseph. *Cardinal Richelieu: Power and the Pursuit of Wealth.* New Haven, 1985.

Bertière, André. *Le cardinal de Retz mémorialiste.* Paris, 1977.

Billacois, François. *Le duel dans la société française des XVIe–XVIIe siècles: Essai de psychologie historique.* Paris, 1986.

Bluche, François. *Louis XIV.* Paris, 1986.

Bois, Guy. *Crise du féodalisme: Economie rurale et démographie en Normandie orientale.* Paris, 1976.

Boswell, John. *Christianity, Social Tolerance, and Homosexuality: Gay People in Western Europe from the Beginning of the Christian Era to the Fourteenth Century.* Chicago, 1980.

Boucher, Jacqueline. *La cour de Henri III.* Rennes, 1986.

Boulton, D. J. A. *The Knights of the Crown: The Monarchical Orders of Knighthood in Later Medieval Europe, 1325–1520.* New York, 1987.

Bourgeois, Emile, and Louis André. *Les sources de l'histoire de France, XVIIe siècle (1610–1715)*. Volume 2: *Mémoires et lettres*. Paris, 1913.

Bouwsma, William. *John Calvin: A Sixteenth-Century Portrait*. Oxford, 1988.

———. *A Usable Past: Essays in European Cultural History*. Berkeley, 1990.

Bray, Alan. "Homosexuality and the Signs of Male Friendship in Elizabethan England." *History Workshop* 29 (Spring 1990).

Brissaud, J. *Manuel d'histoire du droit français*. Paris, 1908.

Brown, Judith. *Immodest Acts: The Life of a Lesbian Nun in Renaissance Italy*. Oxford, 1986.

Buisseret, David. *Sully and the Growth of Centralized Government in France, 1598–1610*. London, 1968.

Burke, Peter. *The Italian Renaissance: Culture and Society in Italy*, 2d ed. Cambridge, 1987.

Carrier, Hubert. *La presse de la Fronde (1648–1653): Les mazarinades—la conquête de l'opinion*. Geneva, 1989.

Chartier, Roger, ed. *A History of Private Life*, vol. 3, trans. Arthur Goldhammer. Cambridge, Mass., 1989.

Church, William Farr. *Richelieu and Reason of State*. Princeton, 1972.

Cochin, Claude. *Henri Arnauld évêque d'Angers (1597–1692)*. Paris, 1921.

Collins, James. "Geographic and Social Mobility in Early Modern France." *Journal of Social History* 24, 3 (1989).

Constant, Jean-Marie. *Les conjurateurs: Le premier libéralisme sous Richelieu*. Paris, 1987.

———. "Nobles et paysans en Beauce aux XVIe et XVIIe siècles." Thèse d'Etat, University of Paris IV, 1978.

Contamine, Philippe. *Guerre, Etat et société à la fin du moyen âge*. Paris, 1972.

Corvisier, André. *Armies and Societies in Europe, 1494–1789*, trans. Abigail T. Siddall. Bloomington, Ill., 1979.

Crouzet, Denis. "Royalty, Nobility and Religion: Research on the Wars in Italy." *Proceedings of the Annual Meeting of the Western Society for French History* 18 (1991).

Cuénin, Micheline, and Chantal Morlet Chantalat. "Châteaux et romans au XVIIe siècle." *XVIIe Siècle* 118–19 (January–June 1978).

Curtius, Ernst Robert. *European Literature and the Latin Middle Ages*, trans. Willard R. Trask. New York, 1953.

Davis, Natalie Zemon. *Fiction in the Archives*. Stanford, 1987.

De Certeau, Michel. *L'invention du quotidien*. Volume 1: *Arts de faire*. Paris, 1980.

Descimon, Robert. *Qui étaient les Seize?* Paris, 1984.

Dessert, Daniel. *Argent, pouvoir et société au Grand Siècle*. Paris, 1984.

———. *Fouquet*. Paris, 1987.

Dewald, Jonathan. *The Formation of a Provincial Nobility: The Magistrates of the Parlement of Rouen, 1499–1610*. Princeton, 1980.

———. *Pont-St-Pierre, 1398–1789: Lordship, Community, and Capitalism in Early Modern France*. Berkeley, 1987.

Doyle, William. *The Old European Order, 1660–1800.* Oxford, 1978.

Duchêne, Roger. *Ninon de L'Enclos: La courtisane du grand siècle.* Paris, 1984.

Elias, Norbert. *The Court Society,* trans. Edmund Jephcott. New York, 1983.

Ellis, Harold A. *Boulainvilliers and the French Monarchy: Aristocratic Politics in Early Eighteenth-Century France.* Ithaca, 1988.

Erlanger, Philippe. *Richelieu and the Affair of Cinq-Mars,* trans. Gilles Cremonesi and Heather Cremonesi. London, 1971.

Flandrin, Jean-Louis. *Familles: Parenté, maison, sexualité dans l'ancienne France.* Paris, 1976.

Foisil, Madeleine. *Le sire de Gouberville: Un gentilhomme normand au XVIe siècle.* Paris, 1981.

Forster, Robert. "The Nobility During the French Revolution." *Past and Present* 37 (July 1967).

Foucault, Michel. *The History of Sexuality.* Volume 1: *An Introduction,* trans. Robert Hurley. New York, 1978.

Freedman, Estelle, and John D'Emilio. "Problems Encountered in Writing the History of Sexuality: Sources, Theory and Interpretation." *The Journal of Sex Research* 27, 4 (November 1990).

Fumaroli, Marc. *L'âge de l'éloquence: Rhétorique et "res literaria" de la Renaissance au seuil de l'époque classique.* Geneva, 1980.

———. "Le 'langage de cour' en France: Problèmes et points de repère." In August Buck et al., eds., *Europäische Hofkultur im 16. und 17. Jahrhundert,* vol. 2. Hamburg, 1981.

———. "Les mémoires du XVIIe siècle: Au carrefour des genres en prose." *XVIIe Siècle* 94–95 (1971).

Goldmann, Lucien. *Le dieu caché: Essai sur la vision tragique dans les* Pensées *de Pascal et dans le théâtre de Racine.* Paris, 1955.

Goldsmith, Elizabeth. *Exclusive Conversations: The Art of Interaction in Seventeenth-Century France.* Philadelphia, 1988.

Goldsmith, James Lowth. *Les Salers et les d'Escorailles: Seigneurs de Haute Auvergne, 1500–1789.* Clermont-Ferrand, 1984.

Greenblatt, Stephen. *Renaissance Self-Fashioning, from More to Shakespeare.* Chicago, 1980.

Griscelli, Paul. "Un aspect de la crise de la rhétorique à la fin du XVIIe siècle: Le problème des passions." *XVIIe Siècle* 143 (April–June 1984).

Hale, John. *War and Society in Renaissance Europe, 1450–1620.* Baltimore, 1985.

Hanley, Sarah. "Engendering the State: Family Formation and State Building in Early Modern France." *French Historical Studies* 16, 4 (Spring 1989).

Harding, Robert. *The Anatomy of a Power Elite: The Provincial Governors of Early Modern France.* New Haven, 1978.

Harth, Erica. *Ideology and Culture in Seventeenth-Century France.* Ithaca, 1983.

Huppert, George. *Les Bourgeois Gentilshommes: An Essay on the Definition of Elites in Renaissance France.* Chicago, 1977.

Jamati, Georges. *La querelle du Joueur: Regnard et Dufresny.* Paris, 1936.
Jordan, A. "L'esthétique de Malherbe." *XVIIe Siècle* 104 (1974).
Jouanna, Arlette. *Le devoir de révolte: La noblesse française et la gestation de l'Etat moderne, 1559–1661.* Paris, 1989.
———. *Ordre social: Mythes et hiérarchies dans la France du XVIe siècle.* Paris, 1977.
Jouhaud, Christian. *Mazarinades: La Fronde des mots.* Paris, 1985.
Keegan, John. *The Face of Battle.* London, 1976.
Kelley, Donald. *The Beginning of Ideology: Consciousness and Society in the French Reformation.* Cambridge, 1981.
Keohane, Nanerl O. *Philosophy and the State in France: The Renaissance to the Enlightenment.* Princeton, 1980.
Kettering, Sharon. *Patrons, Brokers, and Clients.* New York, 1986.
Klaits, Joseph. *Printed Propaganda Under Louis XIV.* Princeton, 1976.
Kleinman, Ruth. *Anne of Austria, Queen of France.* Columbus, Ohio, 1985.
Krailsheimer, A. J. *Studies in Self-Interest, from Descartes to La Bruyère.* Oxford, 1962.
Labatut, Jean-Pierre. *Les ducs et pairs de France au XVIIe siècle: Etude sociale.* Paris, 1972.
Langer, Suzanne. *Philosophy in a New Key: A Study in the Symbolism of Reason, Rite, and Art.* Cambridge, Mass., 1942.
Le Jeune, Philippe. *L'autobiographie en France.* Paris, 1973.
Le Roy Ladurie, Emmanuel. "Auprès du roi, la cour." *Annales ESC* 38, 1 (January–February 1983).
Le Roy Ladurie, Emmanuel, Hugues Neveux, and Jean Jacquart. *Histoire de la France rurale,* vol. 2. Paris, 1975.
Lever, Maurice. *Les bûchers de Sodome.* Paris, 1985.
Lougee, Carolyn. *Le Paradis des Femmes: Women, Salons, and Social Stratification in Seventeenth-Century France.* Princeton, 1976.
Luhman, Nicolas. *Love as Passion: The Codification of Intimacy,* trans. Jeremy Gaines and Doris L. Jones. Oxford, 1986.
Lukács, Georg. *The Historical Novel,* trans. Hannah Mitchell and Stanley Mitchell. Lincoln, Neb., 1983.
Macfarlane, Alan. *The Family Life of Ralph Josselin, a Seventeenth-Century Clergyman: An Essay in Historical Anthropology.* Cambridge, 1970.
Macfarlane, K. B. *The Nobility of Later Medieval England.* Oxford, 1973.
McGuire, Brian Patrick. *Friendship and Community: The Monastic Experience, 350–1250.* Kalamazoo, 1988.
Maland, David. *Culture and Society in Seventeenth-Century France.* New York, 1970.
Mariéjol, Jean-H. *La vie de Marguerite de Valois, reine de Navarre et de France (1553–1615).* Paris, 1928; repr. Geneva, 1970.
Martin, Henri-Jean. *Livre, pouvoirs, et société à Paris au XVIIe siècle,* 2 vols. Geneva, 1969.
Marvick, Elizabeth Wirth. *Louis XIII: The Making of a King.* New Haven, 1986.

————. *The Young Richelieu: A Psychoanalytic Approach to Leadership.* Chicago, 1983.

Miller, Nancy K. *Subject to Change: Reading Feminist Writing.* New York, 1988.

Misch, Georg. *Geschichte der Autobiographie,* 4 vols. Frankfurt am Main, 1969.

Mongrédien, Georges. *Le Grand Condé: L'homme et son oeuvre.* Paris, 1959.

Moote, A. Lloyd. *Louis XIII, the Just.* Berkeley, 1989.

Motley, Mark. *Becoming a French Aristocrat: The Education of the Court Nobility, 1580–1715.* Princeton, 1990.

Mousnier, Roland, et al. *Problèmes de stratification sociale: Deux cahiers de la noblesse pour les Etats généraux de 1649–1651.* Paris, 1965.

Nelson, Benjamin. *The Problem of Usury, from Tribal Brotherhood to Universal Otherhood.* Princeton, 1949.

Neuschel, Kristen. *Word of Honor.* Ithaca, 1989.

Nye, Robert A. "Honor, Impotence, and Male Sexuality in Nineteenth-Century French Medicine." *French Historical Studies* 16, 1 (Spring 1989).

Parker, Geoffrey. *Europe in Crisis, 1598–1648.* London, 1979.

————. *The Military Revolution: Military Innovation and the Rise of the West, 1500–1800.* Cambridge, 1988.

Paton, H. J. "Kant on Friendship." *Proceedings of the British Academy,* vol. 42. Dawes Hicks Lecture on Philosophy, 1956.

Pintard, René. *Le libertinage érudit dans la première moitié du XVIIe siècle,* 2 vols. Paris, 1943.

Plaisse, André. *La baronnie du Neubourg: Essai d'histoire agraire, économique, et sociale.* Paris, 1961.

Pocock, J. G. A. *The Machiavellian Moment: Florentine Political Thought and the Atlantic Republican Tradition.* Princeton, 1975.

Popkin, Richard. *The History of Skepticism from Erasmus to Descartes,* rev. ed. New York, 1968.

Ranum, Orest. *Artisans of Glory.* Chapel Hill, 1980.

————. "Courtesy, Absolutism, and the Rise of the French State." *Journal of Modern History* 52 (September 1980).

————. *Paris in the Age of Absolutism: An Essay.* New York, 1968.

Reddy, William. *The Rise of Market Culture: The Textile Trade and French Society, 1750–1900.* Cambridge, 1984.

Roche, Daniel. "Aperçus sur la fortune et les revenus des princes de Condé à l'aube du 18e siècle." *Revue d'Histoire Moderne et Contemporaine* 14 (July–September 1967).

Rouben, C. *Bussy-Rabutin épistolier.* Paris, 1974.

Sahlins, Marshall. *Culture and Practical Reason.* Chicago, 1976.

Saslow, James M. *Ganymede in the Renaissance: Homosexuality in Art and Society.* New Haven, 1986.

Schalk, Ellery. *From Valor to Pedigree: Ideas of Nobility in France in the Sixteenth and Seventeenth Centuries.* Princeton, 1986.

Scheffers, Henning. *Höfische Konvention und die Aufklärung: Wandlungen des honnête-homme-Ideals im 17. und 18. Jahrhundert.* Bonn, 1980.

Showalter, English. *The Evolution of the French Novel, 1641–1782.* Princeton, 1972.

Solnon, Jean-François. *La cour de France.* Paris, 1988.

Solomon, Howard. *Public Welfare, Science, and Propaganda in Seventeenth-Century France: The Innovations of Théophraste Renaudot.* Princeton, 1972.

Stone, Lawrence. *The Family, Sex, and Marriage in England, 1500–1800.* New York, 1977.

Stone, Lawrence, and Jeanne Fawtier Stone. *An Open Elite?* New York, 1987.

Tanner, Tony. *Adultery in the Novel: Contract and Transgression.* Baltimore, 1979.

Taylor, Charles. *Sources of the Self: The Making of Modern Identity.* Cambridge, Mass., 1989.

Taylor, George. "The Paris Bourse on the Eve of the Revolution." *American Historical Review* 67 (July 1962).

Thompson, E. P. *Whigs and Hunters: The Origins of the Black Act.* New York, 1975.

Tocqueville, Alexis de. *Democracy in America,* trans. George Lawrence, ed. J.-P. Mayer. New York, 1969.

Unger, Roberto Mungabeira. *Law in Modern Society: Toward a Criticism of Social Theory.* New York, 1976.

Vigarello, Georges. *Le propre et le sale.* Paris, 1985.

Watt, Ian. *The Rise of the Novel: Studies in Defoe, Richardson and Fielding.* Berkeley, 1962.

Wayne, Don E. *Penshurst: The Semiotics of Place and the Poetics of History.* Madison, Wis., 1984.

Weber, Max. *The Protestant Ethic and the Spirit of Capitalism,* trans. Talcott Parsons. New York, 1958.

Wood, James. *The Nobility of the Election of Bayeux, 1463–1666: Continuity Through Change.* Princeton, 1980.

———. "The Royal Army During the Early Wars of Religion, 1559–1576." In Mack P. Holt, ed., *Society and Institutions in Early Modern France.* Athens, Georgia, 1991.

# Index

| | |
|---:|:---|
| Compositor: | BookMasters, Inc. |
| Text: | 10/13 Sabon |
| Display: | Sabon |
| Printer: | Braun-Brumfield, Inc. |
| Binder: | Braun-Brumfield, Inc. |